No Better Friend,
NO WORSE ENEMY

No Better Friend,
NO WORSE ENEMY

THE LIFE OF
GENERAL
JAMES MATTIS

JIM PROSER

BROADSIDE BOOKS
An Imprint of HarperCollinsPublishers

HarperCollins books may be purchased for educational, business, or sales promotional use. For information, please email the Special Markets Department at SPsales@harpercollins.com.

FIRST EDITION

Library of Congress Cataloging-in-Publication Data

Names: Proser, Jim, author.
Title: No better friend, no worse enemy: the life of General James Mattis / Jim Proser.
Other titles: Life of General James Mattis
Description: First edition. | New York: Harper, [2018] | Includes bibliographical references and index. |
Identifiers: LCCN 2018010389 (print) | LCCN 2018012426 (ebook) | ISBN 9780062803931 (ebk) | ISBN 9780062803917 (hc: alk. paper) | ISBN 9780062864352 (pbk: alk. paper)
Subjects: LCSH: Mattis, James N., 1950– | Generals—United States—Biography. | United States. Marine Corps—Officers—Biography. | Cabinet officers—United States—Biography. | Iraq War, 2003–2011—Biography.
Classification: LCC E748.M414 (ebook) | LCC E748.M414 P76 2018 (print) | DDC 956.7044/345 [B] —dc23
LC record available at https://lccn.loc.gov/2018010389

18 19 20 21 22 LSC 10 9 8 7 6 5 4 3 2 1

CONTENTS

Introduction

JAMES N. MATTIS was the first Trump presidential cabinet nominee. His nomination received nearly unanimous bipartisan congressional support, with only one dissenting vote. He secured a rare waiver of the guidelines that exclude recently active military leaders from the position of secretary of defense.[1] What could create such unprecedented unity, even enthusiasm, in the hyperpartisan political rancor of 2017?

No doubt the urgency of accomplishing a quick, smooth transition of military leadership was in play, but what were the other reasons behind this easy consensus? Beyond Mattis's obvious military competence for the position on paper, what were the qualities of character, the much-reported personal magnetism, that created such universal confidence? These qualities are the primary focus of this book. With the awesome power of America's arsenal now under his command, we would be prudent to ask: Who is this man, underneath his general's stars?

We should ask how this humble and deeply thoughtful man has walked the path of mortal combat with the most barbaric evil of our time, Islamic terrorism. How is it possible that he has defeated the most bloodthirsty dictators and terrorists with insight, humor, fighting courage, and fierce compassion, not only for his fellow Marines but for the innocent victims of war? Fortunately many eyewitness accounts provide clues to these questions. We might look, for instance, to his lighthearted encouragement to his beloved Marines just before launching the Iraq invasion of Operation Iraqi Freedom, "Fight with a happy heart and strong spirit."[2] Or to his emotional warning to Sunni civilian tribal leaders during the Anbar Awakening in Iraq: "I come in peace. I didn't bring artillery. But I'm pleading with you, with tears in my eyes. Fuck with me and I'll kill you all."[3]

The martial and personal values examined here have earned Jim Mattis the trust of America's political leaders. But why should we, the people who must pay the price of freedom with our lives, trust this man? May you find the answer to that question here, in the words and deeds of a visionary warrior.

No Better Friend,
NO WORSE ENEMY

1

No Better Friend

General Krulak said, when he was commandant of the Marine Corps, every year starting about a week before Christmas he and his wife would bake hundreds and hundreds of Christmas cookies. They would package them in small bundles. Then on Christmas day, he would load his vehicle and drive to every Marine guard post in the Washington-Annapolis-Baltimore area to deliver a small package of Christmas cookies to Marines pulling guard duty that day.

One year, he had gone down to Quantico as one of his stops. He went to the command center and gave a package to the lance corporal on duty. He asked, "Who's the officer of the day?"

The lance corporal said, "Sir, it's Brigadier General Mattis."

And General Krulak said, "No, no, no. I know who General Mattis is. I mean, who's the officer of the day today, Christmas day?"

The lance corporal, feeling a little anxious, said, "Sir, it is Brigadier General Mattis."

General Krulak said that he spotted in the back room a cot, or a daybed. He said, "No, Lance Corporal. Who slept in that bed last night?"

The lance corporal said, "Sir, it was Brigadier General Mattis."

About that time, General Krulak said that General Mattis came in, in a duty uniform with a sword, and General Krulak said, "Jim, what are you doing here on Christmas day? Why do you have duty?"

General Mattis told him that the young officer who was scheduled to have duty had a family, and General Mattis decided it was better for the young officer to spend Christmas Day with his family, and so he chose to have duty on Christmas Day.

—Dr. Albert C. Pierce, the director of the Center for the
Study of Professional Military Ethics at the US Naval Academy,
introducing General Mattis at the academy

0800 Hours—23 April 2003—
Camp Commando, Kuwait

In a large, nondescript military tent, fifty-three-year-old Major General James Mattis, small and lean, with a reputation as a ferocious and brilliant warrior, briefs hundreds of his fellow US Marines. With him is Major General James Amos, who's in charge of the Third Marine Air Wing of Mattis's overall command, the First Marine Division. The division is geared up to invade Iraq, just thirty-five miles north, launching Operation Iraqi Freedom.

Mattis, a gentlemanly ladies' man but a lifelong bachelor, has dedicated his life completely to the success and safety of the warriors he commands. In return, he is deeply beloved by them. His constant study of history and philosophy has earned him the affectionate nickname the Warrior Monk and made being smart and well-read cool, elevating the sometimes anti-intellectual, tribal Marine culture. He ordered every Marine in the First Division to read Russell Braddon's *The Siege*, which follows the ill-fated British Expeditionary Force during World War I in what was then called Mesopotamia. Mattis wants every Marine to understand the inhospitable Iraqi terrain and the mistakes that cost the British twenty-five thousand men.

His voice is calm and loud, with a slight sibilance that softens some of his *s*'s. He speaks without notes, hands on hips or in "knife-hand" gestures, fixing his attention on individual Marines as he scans the rows of officers from the front to the back of the room. Marine commanders sit in rows before him now, Third Air Wing pilots up front in tan flight suits, pistols strapped across their chests, ground commanders behind them in desert camouflage. They are silent, intent on every word. Among the commanders is Lieutenant Colonel Stanton Coerr, who later reports on this meeting, "Gentlemen, this is going to be the most air-centric division in the history of warfare," Mattis says. "Don't you worry about the lack of shaping; if we need to kill something, it is going to get killed. I would storm the gates of Hell if Third Marine Air Wing was overhead."[1]

By shaping, he means shaping of the battlefield by air power and artillery. This is usually the preparation for battle meant to find and exploit the enemy's weakest spot. But instead of shaping, Mattis's new "maneuver warfare" relies on speed and mobility, as he then makes clear with typical good humor.

"There is one way to have a short but exciting conversation with me," he continues, "and that is to move too slow. Gentlemen, this is not a marathon, this is a sprint. In about a month, I am going to go forward of our Marines up to the border between Iraq and Kuwait. And when I get there, one of two things is going to happen. Either the commander of the Fifty-First Mechanized [Iraqi] Division is going to surrender his army in the field to me, or he and all his guys are going to die."[2]

Maps are flashed up, showing the initial battlespace coordination line, and the Marines are given their rules of engagement—they are permitted to kill anything beyond that line that appears to be a threat. But in the summer of 2002, when Mattis assumed command of the First Marine Division, he warned the division staff of several realities. According to one of his public affairs officers, Captain Joe

Plenzler, he said, "Iraq has a population of 33 million people, and we sure as hell don't want to fight all of them. We only want to fight the ones that are working to keep Saddam Hussein in power."[3] He goes on to insist that if the Iraqis they encountered wanted to help, or just to stand aside, they should find no better friend than a US Marine.

This phrase, "no better friend than a US Marine," came from Mattis's reading of Roman general Lucius Cornelius Sulla, who once remarked, "No friend ever served me, and no enemy ever wronged me, whom I have not repaid in full."[4] When he took command of the First Division in 2000, Mattis fashioned Sulla's quote into the division's now famous motto, "No better friend, no worse enemy."[5]

The second part of the briefing takes place in the open desert inside a bulldozed arena where the Marines and their coalition allies walk through the first five days of the coming battle on a scale replica of the battlefield representing the 345 miles of Iraqi terrain between the Kuwaiti border and Baghdad. Nearly the size of a football field, the sculpted topography includes every road, canal, village, and oil field that the fast-moving attack forces will encounter. Canals and rivers are filled with blue sand, and oil fields are marked with black pyramids representing oil derricks.

Mattis grabs a microphone and, again without notes, explains through a loudspeaker what each unit will do and in what sequence this will occur, emphasizing coordination but rejecting synchronization. No one is to wait, everyone is to advance. Constantly and quickly advance. Their mission is to capture Baghdad, not to get bogged down in firefights in every village.

Next to the gray-haired Mattis stands his surprising lead intelligence analyst, taking it all in. Twenty-year-old Lance Corporal Nathan Osowski is some kind of savant. He knows the Iraqi order of battle—the number and location of forces—better than anyone in the division. Osowski can recall the most intricate details, like the number and kinds of armor in different Iraqi units, on demand, and now he adds the battlefield details before him into his mental database. Mattis, who has always recognized and valued talent over rank, keeps Osowski in his inner circle of advisers, among the majors and generals.

Representatives of each unit wear football jerseys in specific colors, with unit-identifying numbers on their backs. As Mattis describes each advance, the representatives walk to their proper places on the terrain model. About three hundred officers stand and sit on the dune above the battlefield, watching Mattis's battle plan in action. This is a textbook demonstration of "maneuver warfare,"[6] which sliced through Iraq's defenses in one hundred hours during Operation Desert Storm twelve years earlier. Mattis specifies every objective for every unit at the end of every day for the first five days of the war, an impressive display of study and preparation.

At the end of this rehearsal of concept, questions are answered and Mattis dismisses the group. Mike Murdoch, one of the British company commanders, leans over to Lieutenant Colonel Coerr and asks, "Mate, are all your generals that good?"[7]

1900 Hours—20 March 2003—Camp Matilda on the Kuwait-Iraq Border

The seven-meter-high earthen berm marking the border between Kuwait and Iraq erupts from the high explosive charges placed by the combat engineers of the First Marine Expeditionary Force, often referred to as I MEF. Fine, chalky dust from the blast drifts down in the night breeze onto the growing traffic jam that will eventually grow to seventy-five thousand American and coalition invaders and their tens of thousands of trucks, amtracs (heavy trucks with tank treads instead of wheels), light armored vehicles (LAVs)—small, fast, tank-like vehicles—Jeep-sized Humvees, and gigantic M1A1 Abrams tanks.

Lieutenant Nathaniel "Nate" Fick, who served under General Mattis in Afghanistan two years earlier just after 9/11, assembles his platoon in the dusty, barren invasion staging area at Camp Matilda. He knows the vital importance Mattis places on every Marine understanding his commander's intent, and so he reads the general's "Message to All Hands" to his men:

For decades, Saddam Hussein has tortured, imprisoned, raped and murdered the Iraqi people; invaded neighboring countries without provocation; and threatened the world with weapons of mass destruction.

The time has come to end his reign of terror. On your young shoulders rest the hopes of mankind. When I give you the word, together we will cross the Line of Departure, close with those forces that choose to fight, and destroy them. Our fight is not with the Iraqi people, nor is it with members of the Iraqi army who choose to surrender. While we will move swiftly and aggressively against those who resist, we will treat all others with decency, demonstrating chivalry and soldierly compassion for people who have endured a lifetime under Saddam's oppression. Chemical attack, treachery, and use of the innocent as human shields can be expected, as can other unethical tactics.

Take it all in stride. Be the hunter, not the hunted: never allow your unit to be caught with its guard down. Use good judgment and act in the best interests of our nation. You are part of the world's most feared and trusted force. Engage your brain before you engage your weapon. Share your courage with each other as we enter the uncertain terrain north of the Line of Departure. Keep faith in your comrades on your left and right and Marine Air overhead. Fight with a happy heart and strong spirit.

For the mission's sake, our country's sake, and the sake of the men who carried the Division's colors in past battles—who fought for life and never lost their nerve—carry out your mission and keep your honor clean. Demonstrate to the world that there is "No Better Friend, No Worse Enemy" than a US Marine.[8]

In the futuristic-looking I MEF geodesic dome command post referred to as the Bug, crammed with computers, TV screens, communication radios, topographical models, and stacks of MRE boxes, Marine intelligence has hacked into the email account of the Iraqi general in command of forces near the border. Mattis emails the general, urging him to surrender, but the Iraqis continue to fire artillery intermittently and ineffectively toward I MEF positions. The Iraqi general doesn't reply to Mattis's emails. Earlier, Iraqi soldiers were observed by the border, laying more mines. Mattis has always hated mines, a fear that developed in his first days as a Marine over thirty-five years ago and has never left him. Their faceless, robotic nature may represent an unpredictable element to a student of human nature in warfare like Mattis. The new intel on the mines only adds to his growing disgust with the elusive and cowardly Iraqi commander. "I'm going to try one more time to save these fuckers' lives," he says.[9]

But he tries many times over the next two hours to appeal to his opposing general. He threatens him, begs him, appeals to him as an Iraqi patriot and family man, to save his own life and the lives of his men. The coalition invasion force is piling up and now stretches over eighteen miles back from the border, waiting for Mattis to give the order. But he tries and tries and tries again. If he doesn't give the invasion order soon, some of the last units through the berm will be transiting at dawn, putting them in danger from Iraqi artillery. Finally, after hours of receiving only inconclusive, delaying replies but no surrender, Mattis gives up on the general and launches the invasion.

The traffic at the border is now snarled as vehicles attempt to jockey toward their assigned breaches in the berm. In the American vehicles, four to five Marines, most around nineteen years old, are itching to "get some," to fire their weapons in combat, many for the first time. In the passenger seat of his overloaded Humvee, Lieutenant Fick waits in the dark with the four Marines of First Reconnaissance Battalion (First Recon), Bravo Company, Second Platoon. Mattis's battle plan designates the 347 Marines of First Recon, including Alpha, Bravo, and Charlie Companies, as one of the three spearheads of the invasion. Fick's second platoon will lead First Recon, at the very tip of the invasion's center spearhead.

First Recon's mission is to seize a remote bridge over the Euphrates at Nasariyah. Many may think this fairly routine mission might be their entire contribution to the war, but no one is sure what Saddam will throw at them on the way, now that the Marines were coming for him personally. Everyone expects chemical weapons attacks.

Evan Wright, a journalist embedded with Bravo Company, First Platoon, in the Humvee rolling directly in front of Fick, writes:

> The point of Mattis's plan to send First Recon ahead of his main battle forces is that this battalion will be among the fastest on the battlefield. As beat-up as First Recon's Humvees are, they are quicker than tanks and, due to their small numbers, they can outmaneuver large concentrations of enemy forces. According to the doctrine of maneuver warfare, their relative speed, not their meager firepower, is their primary weapon. True to his radio call sign, Chaos, Mattis will use First Recon as his main agent for causing disorder on the battlefield by sending the Recon Marines into places where no one is expecting them.[10]

Once First Recon clears the breach at the border, they are to race 120 miles north to the Euphrates bridge. Their biggest concern is that they will be operating alone, isolated from the US Army and other Marine units that include thousands of troops, armored vehicles, and heavy artillery. In Humvees with little or no armor and supply trucks, they will trek through open desert that, somewhere, holds fifty thousand Iraqi troops equipped with more than a thousand tanks and other heavy armor.

US Marines and British forces will be in a race to secure the oil facilities and ports around Rumaylah, Basra, and Umm Qasr, forty-four miles east of the border. Mattis knows Saddam will set these oil facilities on fire if given time, as he did in the Gulf War in 1991, creating an environmental disaster. Coalition forces are tasked to secure the oil fields within forty-eight hours of crossing the border.

Mattis signals his aide-de-camp, twenty-two-year-old Lieutenant Warren Cook, to approach him. He tells Cook to saddle up the jump, they're heading to Basra. Cook notifies the twenty-one members of the "jump platoon," Mattis's personal squad and mobile command post, to man their five lightly armored vehicles. Chaos, Mattis's personal call sign, a code name that identifies him in radio communications, is on the move.

The Marines of Bravo Company have been sitting in the invasion traffic jam in total darkness for three hours. Evan Wright reports from First Platoon's Humvee, "Unlike the Humvees used by elite Army units, which have armor and air-conditioning, most of First Recon's Humvees don't even have doors or roofs. Some teams modified them by welding in extra racks for ammo and removing windshields so they can fire their rifles through them. The Humvees are so stuffed full of weapons and supplies, the men hang their rucksacks filled with personal gear on the sides of the vehicles."[11]

For the next few hours, First Recon stops and starts, zigzagging back and forth just south of the border beneath the lightning flashes of streaking rockets and thunder of Saddam's artillery. Just as Mattis feared, oil facilities have been set on fire near Rumaylah, creating a glow on the eastern horizon.

In the command post, Mattis calmly suits up for battle. He puts on his flak jacket, which he prefers to wear backward, with its Velcro opening, two-star insignia, and name patch on his back. This may be a precaution against enemy snipers, who might pick out the two stars on his chest through a high-powered rifle scope. Since he is frequently inspecting the most forward positions and facing the enemy as he scans their positions through binoculars, it is certain that they are looking back. But no one really knows why he wears his "flak" backward, and no one seems to care. He checks his pistol, mission-oriented protective posture (MOPP) suit, and gas mask that will protect him from toxic chemicals as he continues to direct and advise his commanders through a mobile headset. He speaks evenly, calmly, with no hint of tension.

New information—from jet and helicopter pilots, satellite data, human intelligence (spies) in Baghdad, allied commanders, and policy guidance from Washington, DC—floods into the command post, to be acknowledged, prioritized, routed to the proper commanders, and relayed out to the troops in a constant flow of orders, advisories, and alerts. Mattis smiles and pats a few colleagues who will be staying behind on the back. He's completely relaxed among the commotion.

Osowski launches into rapid-fire chatter, advising Mattis on the likely disposition of enemy forces between them and their first destination, the oil and gas separation plant about twelve miles east of Basra. Mattis smiles and nods, giving his eager, brilliant, and slightly eccentric chief intelligence analyst his full attention. Osowski amuses the general, who marvels at the young man's nearly complete lack of conversational skill. Osowski might continue talking until everyone was asleep if Mattis didn't interrupt him with a gentle assurance, something like, "That's fine, Ski, that's fine, son. I got it. We'll be okay."[12]

Mattis sometimes listens to Osowski like a favorite news radio station as he eats his one or two meals a day from an MRE foil pouch. The general rarely bothers to heat or hydrate the freeze-dried meals inside. He drinks only water. Osowski will lay his battlefield map on the floor as the general eats, placing force indication icons on the map to make his points, rarely looking up to see if the general is listening.

For time by himself and to keep up his energy level, Mattis relies on push-ups and brief runs around the command post. Recently, the fifty-three-year-old commander completed a division-wide 5K run in just over twenty-one minutes, a blazing pace for any age. For his four hours of nightly rest, called "maintaining sleep discipline" in Marine-ese, he joins dozens of other Marines of all ranks, rolling out his sleeping bag on the plywood floor of a nearby tent. To settle and clear his mind, he reads passages from Roman emperor and general Marcus Aurelius's *Meditations*, which he keeps in a collection of books he takes on every deployment. For the past thirty-six years, he has contentedly lived this Spartan warrior's lifestyle, asking for no special treatment or comfort for himself that is unavailable to the lowest-ranking Marine.

Mattis has been on duty now with only latrine breaks for the past fourteen hours and will continue for the next twelve, at least, until his jump platoon and the last American and coalition units are through the berm and on their way toward their objectives. He straps on his Kevlar helmet. These are his last moments of close control over the largest allied invasion force since D-Day. He has let slip the dogs of war on Saddam's Iraq, with unpredictable consequences for both sides. With a wave to his fellow warfighters in the command post, he turns and walks out to his waiting jump platoon.

First Recon is redirected toward several different breach points at the border until 0400 hours, when commanders finally decide on which breach they should use. They have been in traffic now for eight hours. As they crawl toward the designated breach, the fog of war has begun to thicken around the men of Bravo Company when Fick's immediate superior, Bravo Company's commander, disrespectfully nicknamed "Encino Man"[13] clusterfucks the entire company by making a wrong turn in the dark. The commander's nickname refers to a movie character, a dimwitted caveman who thaws out and comes to life in Encino, California. Encino Man has an easygoing personality that makes him personally liked, but as a commander, particularly now that they are facing battle, the men of Bravo Company are concerned about his leadership. Their fears are again justified as they wait to get their bearings among the tens of thousands of other heavily armed vehicles moving toward the Iraqi desert.

The sky flashes and fades as artillery and aerial bombardment rain down on Iraqi positions near the border. Jet engines, attack helicopters, rockets, and artillery shells whistle, whomp, and whoosh overhead, the horizon flashing with each impact. The past ten hours of amped-up "Get some!" excitement eventually gives way to the mind-numbing boredom of being caught in traffic, lulling Corporal Trombley to sleep. He slumps over his squad automatic weapon, or SAW—a thousand-round-per-minute machine gun— snoring.

"Wake up, Trombley," Sergeant Colbert says. "You're missing the invasion."[14]

Bravo Company finally unfucks itself and crosses the border into enemy territory. After a few minutes heading north, they roll through a desolate border town, where smashed and abandoned vehicles sit alongside the road. As morning light begins to glare through the dust-caked windshield, black smoke from Rumaylah's oil fires lies atop the horizon like Saddam's greasy thumbprint. Colbert's first impression of Iraq is that it looks like "fucking Tijuana."[15] Colorful handmade signs mark the abandoned shops that line the empty central street. Steel shutters are padlocked in front, protecting the shops until the owners return. Wild, feral dogs nose around the alleys for scraps of garbage.

At 0600 hours, Mattis's rolling command post halts near the gas and oil separation plant outside Basra, a critical facility. Mattis and his platoon dismount the vehicles and greet Colonel Joe Dunford, the commander of the 5th Marines' Regimental Combat Team 5 (RCT-5). Dunford has secured the plant after encountering light resistance. On the way here, they have all seen piles of Iraqi uniforms and small arms cast off by the roadside, and dozens of military-age young men in civilian clothes walking away from them.

While Mattis and Dunford discuss the next objective after the gas plant, a call comes in from division command post. The Iraqi general that Mattis had been desperately emailing to surrender has complied, and is asking to be taken into custody at the border. The general's summary execution may have been ordered from Baghdad, and he no longer trusts his subordinate officers.

Mattis and Dunford plot Dunford's next objective, a bridge over the Euphrates River, fourteen miles north and west of Nasariyah. The wind kicks up dust and sand, making the commanders' conversation more difficult. They huddle closer together next to a Humvee. Osowski attempts to spread out his battlefield map and place his indicating icons on the hood of the Humvee as he starts his characteristic rapid-fire briefing on the opposing forces, terrain, and commanders Dunford will face on his advance north. The map flaps in the wind, scattering the icons. Osowski picks up his icons, drops a few, grabs them again, and attempts to hold the map and icons in place without stopping for a breath. Finally Mattis and Dunford stop talking and look at Osowski, who, deep into his analysis, is unaware that he is interrupting the commanders. Mattis and Dunford eventually look at each other, shrugging and shaking their heads as Osowski rattles on.

Finally, Mattis stops his young corporal. "Ski. Ski!"[16]

Osowski looks up from his map, startled. Mattis indicates a gaggle of embedded reporters with cameras who are gathered nearby, interviewing a junior officer. "Why don't you put on my flak and go over and talk to those reporters?"

Osowski looks over at the reporters and back at the general. "For real?"

Mattis shakes his head, and returns to his discussion with Dunford.

By late afternoon, First Recon has rolled north on unpaved trails in convoy with Regimental Combat Team 1 (RCT-1) and Marine Task Force Tarawa, which leads the way. Other Marine combat forces skirt the eastern border, leaving the convoy on its own as it heads north through open desert. Once Task Force Tarawa clears the first large town, Nasariyah, RCT-1 will race northwesterly to Baghdad on Highway 1 while First Recon continues due north on Highway 7 toward the city of Al Kut.

South of Nasariyah, the convoy travels north from Kuwait on Highway 8. This is the infamous "Highway of Death,"[17] where Operation Desert Storm mercilessly set fire to Saddam Hussein's retreating army. Now the occasional rusting tank or truck half buried in the sand along the road is the only reminder of the American "turkey shoot" that destroyed the heart of Iraq's fighting forces. The highway and the surrounding area is once again the province of advancing US and British heavy armor, again on their way to Baghdad, but this time with orders to finish the job.

Passing through scattered desert towns south of Nasariyah, Bravo Company's First and Second Platoons—call signs Hitman One and Hitman Two—keep up a constant chatter as each man scans his sector to the left, right, front, or rear, calling out everything he sees while trading information with the other Humvee teams over the radio, and receiving reports and advisories on enemy movement in the area.

They receive reports from battalion command of Iraqi tank units operating somewhere around them, but none appear. Instead, small groups of shepherds and women in black robes stand outside square mud huts, most staring but some waving to the "liberators" of Iraq, calling "Bush! Bush! Bush!"[18]

These Recon Marines, whom Mattis refers to affectionately as "cocky, obnoxious bastards,"[19] wave back while keeping their eyes glued to rifle scopes and binoculars to scan the locals for weapons, mindful of another Mattisism: "Be polite. Be professional. But have a plan to kill everyone you meet."[20]

There are only about a thousand Recon Marines in the entire Marine Corps at any one time. They are, first, supreme athletes. They can run twelve miles wearing 150-pound packs, then jump in the ocean, wearing boots and fatigues and carrying their weapons, and swim several more miles. They can deploy and fight on any terrain or body of water. They train in snowshoes, mountain boots, and scuba gear using parachutes, inflatable boats, and wheeled vehicles. They can rappel from hovering helicopters. Only 2 percent of all Marines are ever selected for Recon training, and half of those wash out. They are the best of the best, the toughest of the tough, and Mattis's personal tribe.

The convoy halts just south of Nasariya. The Marines dismount, stretch, and relax in the sand alongside Highway 8. They take off the tops of their MOPP suits, dripping with sweat, and feel the warm, gentle sun of the desert spring on their chests. They expect that soon they will roll into the shaded farmland and flowing canals of the Fertile Crescent, above Nasariyah, the land once called Mesopotamia.

They've seen pictures of an oasis. Towering palms heavy with sweet dates grow along canals carrying water from the Tigris River, forty-five miles to the east. Earthen berms ranging in height from two meters to several stories line the sides of dry and flowing canals. Berms are everywhere, facing all directions. They serve as walls to contain pastures, or protect crops as windbreaks, as well as potential military fortifications.

The berms can hide tank revetments, deep bulldozed pits intended to conceal tanks, artillery, or even ground troops that may be camouflaged from aerial surveillance by the canopy of palm and fruit trees. Along some berms are ten-foot-high conical towers capped with sandbags—potential machine-gun emplacements.

Evan Wright in his book *Generation Kill* reports:

> Saddam had viewed this route, with its almost impenetrable terrain of canals, villages, rickety bridges, hidden tar swamps and dense groves of palm trees, as his not-so-secret weapon in bogging down the Americans.
>
> When Saddam famously promised to sink the American invaders into a "quagmire," he was probably thinking of the road from Nasiriyah to Al Kut. It was the worst place in Iraq to send an invading army.[21]

Tactically, Mattis sees the Iraq invasion as the coup de grace, a quick spear thrust through the heart of Saddam's defenses, already weakened by decades of war. This would be followed by the movement of massed coalition forces into the occupation of Baghdad. Because of their defeat in Desert Storm, Mattis knew Saddam's surviving commanders would be cautious when facing US forces again. They would hide their heavy armor during the day to protect it from air attack, never permitting themselves to be caught out in the open desert as they had been on Highway 8. He also guessed they would be dug in and heavily camouflaged to avoid detection by American night vision capabilities. These restrictions to their mobility would leave them few options outside of ambush, and make them the perfect enemy for his type of maneuver warfare blitzkrieg.

At least that's the way it looked on paper. Mattis is well aware that control in battle is an illusion. That's why he values initiative and aggression over all other traits in his field commanders. They will ultimately be the ones to redeem the situation when his plan falls apart, as it is beginning to do now. He is on comms (secure radio communication) to Colonel Joe Dowdy, commander of Regimental Combat Team 1 (RCT-1), as the first reports of a halt and casualties come in from Nasariyah.

Mattis's plan calls for his shield, in the form of armored coalition battalions, to secure Iraq's southern oil facilities. That part seems to be working, except for the oil wells Saddam has already ignited in the oil fields. With his trident, a three-pronged spear, using First Recon in RCT-1 as the center prong, they will slice up the middle through the Fertile Crescent, flanked to the east and west by thirteen thousand more Marines in Regimental Combat Teams 5 and 7. Any one of the prongs might be stopped; RCT-1 is right now in Nasariyah, and has become entangled in the "quagmire" Saddam promised, but Mattis plans to impale Baghdad with at least one prong.

To get the plan back on track, Mattis focuses on pushing RCT-1 through Nasariyah. Casualties are mounting quickly; something has gone very wrong. Osowski sits next to Mattis in the close quarters of a light armored vehicle packed with communications equipment. The LAV has no air-conditioning, and the powerful equipment is adding heat on top of the heat from the midmorning desert sun. Mattis's frustration builds as he speaks several times with Dowdy, whose failure to clear the way through Nasariyah has stalled the advance.

With his tanks mired in Nasariyah's unpaved streets, which also serve as open sewers, Dowdy prepares but then changes his plan of attack several times. First, his six thousand Marines will execute a frontal assault through the center of the city. Then he decides to hold his position and divert part of his force toward other bridges to the east and west. Then he decides to divert some and attack with the rest. Dowdy's indecision is costing lives and pushing Mattis to the boiling point.

The central prong of Mattis's attack force is now a sitting duck, lined up on the highway south of the city in broad daylight. Saddam's artillery could break cover at any moment and rain shells of sarin and VX gas on the exposed convoy. Marine air scours the terrain north, east, and west of Nasariyah, looking for any sign of heavy weapons capable of the range to the convoy. But they are blind inside the dense neighborhoods of Nasariyah itself. Any number of warehouses or factories could be camouflaging enough artillery to cover the entire convoy in poison gas.

In the jump command post, Mattis has heard enough from Dowdy. He calls Lieutenant Cook in his lead vehicle. They are going north to Nasariyah now. The platoon pulls out and races north, passing stalled tanks, supply trucks, and Humvees, hatches open, Marines out of the vehicles. Mattis orders Sergeant Ryan Woolworth, his communications specialist, to get First Recon commander Colonel Stephen Ferrando on comms. Some changes are going to be made; the mission itself is now threatened by the delay at Nasariyah. And above all else, even above the cherished lives of Mattis's Marines, is the mission. Mattis's beloved First Recon, the best of the best, are about to take their positions at the tip of the spear earlier than he planned, in the very teeth of Saddam's army. They are the price he is now prepared to pay to take Nasariyah.

Eight months earlier, in August 2002, Mattis and Secretary of Defense Donald Rumsfeld, having worn down the objections of the Joint Chiefs of Staff, were cleared to execute their plan. It would be the first large-scale trial by fire of maneuver warfare. Mattis then set out to motivate his Marines to execute the nation's new shock and awe war strategy against Saddam's army.

Mattis briefed his First Division in the chapel of Camp Pendleton in Oceanside, California—an unusual spot for the briefing, but perhaps appropriate, since everyone knew that a desperate Saddam Hussein was likely to use chemical weapons. In that briefing was Lieutenant Nathaniel Fick, who had also served under Mattis in Afghanistan the year before.

Fick writes, "Good afternoon, Marines," Mattis said. "Thank you for your attention so late on a Friday. I know the women of Southern California are waiting for you, so I won't waste your time."[22]

He wasn't ready to discuss operational details at this time. Instead, he began his Marines' mental preparation for this new type of warfare. As he often said, "The most important territory on the battlefield is the six inches between your ears."[23] His first directive was "Be able to deploy without chaos on eight days' notice."[24]

Without chaos. Obsessed with detail and planning, Mattis demanded that all personal affairs be carefully considered and settled with time to spare. Deployment is always chaotic, with dozens of domestic details to arrange—vaccinations, houses to close up, cars to store, and farewell meals with friends and family. This was the first sharpening of the mindful, focused awareness Mattis knew his Marines would need for what was coming. From this point on, no one could afford the distraction of unsettled personal business.

Mattis continued, "Fight at every level as a combined-arms team."[25] Essentially, he meant, put the enemy in the dilemma of hiding from one weapon while being exposed to another. A rifleman and grenadier make up a combined-arms team, as do a mortar crew and a machine gunner, or a battalion and air cover. This was a fundamental dynamic of maneuver warfare—mobility and combined firepower.

"Aggressive NCO leadership is the key to victory" was Mattis's next directive.[26] Sergeants were generally the team leaders who got things done on the ground. Well trained and with long experience, they were a Recon grunt's lighthouse in the fog of war. Their aggression, or lack of it, would determine the success of Mattis's strategy. In the months to come, Colonel Dowdy would fail this standard of aggression at Nasariyah, with deadly consequences.

"Mistakes are forgivable," Mattis continued, "but a lack of self-discipline will be met with zero tolerance."[27] In the general's world, self-discipline included all the disciplines of men under arms: light discipline, noise discipline, sleep discipline, and fire discipline. A momentary lapse in any of these could prove fatal to men and mission. Again, the general was demanding and creating the mind-set of success on which his life and the lives of everyone in the theater of operations would depend.

"Build confidence in your NBC equipment."[28] NBC meant nuclear, biological, and chemical.[29] He paused for effect and added, "Expect to be slimed with chemicals." Everyone in the room had seen pictures of Saddam's mass murder of the Kurdish villagers of Halabja with sarin and VX gas. An extended moment of silence allowed the Marines time to process the fact that they were now committed to an unpredictable and extremely dangerous mission.

To emphasize the need for mental and physical preparation, the general pressed on: "Train to survive the first five days in combat."[30] He again called on his men's powers of visualization to anticipate biological warfare in 120-degree desert heat, encased in heavy, un-ventilated MOPP suits. They also knew to expect the full force of Saddam's attack immediately upon arrival in country. There would be no time for a learning curve.

"Finally, get your family ready to be without you."[31] The impli-cations—this could mean both tour of duty separation and possi-ble death—were clear. It meant putting personal affairs in order and emotionally steeling one's self and family for the worst. Part of why the general was so revered among his Marines was his di-rect and plain language. If Marines were thinking it, they could count on Mattis saying it—even if it got him into trouble with his bosses, as it frequently did. He was telling them, clearly, to pay their life insurance premiums and write their final letters to loved ones now.

Finally, he told them that when it came to the privileges of rank, there would be none. No general would be allowed any more personal gear than the lowest infantry lance corporal, and that the comforts of home were banned. No cots, coffee makers, or electronic distractions like hand-held video games, CD players, or even satellite telephones were allowed. They were traveling light. In this battle, they would live and fight like the Spartan warriors of ancient Greece.

Once the full operational details of the new maneuver warfare were worked out and briefed to unit commanders, even experienced Marines like First Recon commander Ferrando were more than a little unsettled. "Major General Mattis's plan went against all our training and doctrine," Ferrando said, "but I can't tell a general I don't do windows."[32]

As Mattis knew from his reading of Braddon's *The Siege*, Iraq's defenders would tie themselves to key water and land approaches to Baghdad. US intelligence confirmed that this was where the Iraqi IV Corps was dug in. Mattis planned to flank the IV Corps to the east and west by advancing along the Kurdish border to the east and up Highway 1 to the west. By quickly outmaneuvering IV Corps in this way, he would cut them off at Al Kut on the Tigris and prevent them from reinforcing Baghdad. At least, that was the plan.

On Highway 8, twelve miles south of Nasariyah, the convoy has been stalled for hours. Sergeant Colbert, whom the men call Iceman for his cool head under fire, listens glumly to the BBC news on his smuggled shortwave radio. It seems Dowdy's Task Force Tarawa, leading the convoy, has found Saddam's army directly in front of them, inside Nasariyah. The BBC reports heavy fighting, with Americans being captured and significant casualties among the Marines. His platoon gathers around Colbert as he sits in the Humvee, silently taking in the news.

Three hours pass with no further news and no movement. Finally, Lieutentant Fick receives orders from Colonel Ferrando. Fick calls in the leaders of Alpha, Bravo, and Charlie for a briefing at his Humvee: "In approximately one hour, we are going to bust north to the bridge at the Euphrates. Change in the ROE [rules of engagement]—anyone with a weapon is declared hostile. If it's a woman walking away from you with a weapon on her back, shoot her. If there is an armed Iraqi out there, shoot him. I don't care if you hit him with a forty-millimeter grenade in the chest."[33]

Apparently, aggressive NCO leadership, one of Mattis's essential directives for success, is in short supply at Nasariyah. Eighteen Marines are dead; four Marines and US Army personnel—including, as widely reported, Army private Jessica Lynch—are missing; and seventy Marines are wounded, some pinned down inside the city. Confidence in Mattis's maneuver warfare plan is shaken. The risk-averse "Clinton Generals" are on comms from Washington to his jump command post, now parked just a mile south of Nasariyah. They want answers.

Mattis has driven—in and out of traffic, overland and on the highway—three hours from Basra. He has now been on duty thirty-six hours, receiving intel, advising commanders, and issuing orders, catching the occasional catnap in his seat in the hot LAV as it rolls north from Basra. The general is wide awake now, and at the end of his patience with the situation in Nasariyah. Osowski hears him lose it with Dowdy: "If you're taking fire from a building, you level the fucking building!"

From their position, the jump platoon can see shell impacts in the city and hear small-arms fire. Mattis makes his decision. He gets on comms back to Brigadier General John Kelly at division command post. Colonel John Toolan should get prepared to take over command of Task Force Tarawa.

Fick and First Recon are rolling toward the firefight inside Nasariyah. Fick is receiving intel on how to get into the city, but no one can tell him how to get out again, carrying wounded Marines. The only thing he knows for sure—tonight's objective is Ambush Alley.

Mattis pulls out, leaving the battle for Nasariyah to First Recon and RCT-1. His rolling command post skirts Nasariyah to the west and then heads north toward a new front line. Dunford has charged ahead after securing the gas and oil separation plant near Basra in the south, and his 5th Marines are now engaged in heavy fighting and taking casualties just north of the ancient city of Ur, below a critical Euphrates River bridge. Mattis's platoon rolls toward the fight through the dark, empty desert. Occasionally a SCUD missile flashes through the night sky, seeking the Marines at the front lines ahead of them.

Inside the LAV it's quiet, just the humming of tires on pavement. Even Osowski has stopped talking. The young man slumps in his seat, asleep and off duty for the moment. Mattis lets him sleep. The general's mind is elsewhere, inside Nasariyah, where First Recon, his "cocky, obnoxious bastards," young men like Fick who have lived and fought beside him for years, are about to get "lit up." On his orders, they will be driving straight into a kill zone prepared for them by Saddam Hussein. They will be taking direct fire as they fight to rescue wounded fellow Marines. They are his tribe, and some of them are nearly family. On his orders, a few more of their names are about to be added to the butcher's bill.

2

No Worse Enemy

Be polite, be professional, but have a plan to kill everybody
you meet.

   *—Lieutenant General Jim Mattis to his Marines, Operation
Iraqi Freedom*

0100 Hours—22 March 2003—Near Ur, Iraq

The five vehicles of General Mattis's jump command post pull
off the blacktop of Highway 7 into the desert sand. They are close
enough to the fighting to hear the small-arms fire and Saddam's
SCUD missiles exploding near Joe Dunford's Fifth Marines, less
than a half mile ahead. Mattis and his personal company of twenty-
one men are now close to 40 hours without sleep, except for occasional catnaps inside the rolling command post. Mattis calls a halt
and orders a rest break for his crew, enforcing the sleep discipline
that is proving to be crucial in the campaign. They park their vehicles diagonally to the pavement, a few feet apart, "herringboned" to
provide protection from incoming fire for the men, who will sleep
between and under the vehicles, and quick access to the road when
they move out.

   Mattis is on secure radio to Dunford, who reports taking heavy
fire up ahead as the general's men pile out of the vehicles and stretch.
They listen to the battle raging just down the road for a moment

while Sergeant Major Juan Duff assesses the wisdom of parking this close to the fight. SCUD missiles are notoriously inaccurate, and his men are well within range. Weighing the risk of bombardment against the advantage of more reliable radio communications this close to the front, and knowing Mattis's disdain for timid Marines, Duff shows his decision by grabbing his sleeping bag, which is lashed to the top of the LAV. The others follow their sergeant.

They pull their sleeping gear, a box of MREs (Meals Ready to Eat), and their field toilet off the various vehicles. Field toilets are not issued by the Marine Corps. When they exist at all, they are improvised out of grenade boxes or other packing crates. But this particular field toilet, the improvised excretive device used by everyone in Mattis's jump platoon, is a small triumph of Marine Corps engineering and adaptation: a flimsy plastic outdoor garden chair with a hole punched in the seat and a toilet seat stolen from a Kuwaiti portable construction site toilet duct-taped around the hole. To use it, you dig a hole in the ground and line up the hole in the chair with the hole in the ground. It is a point of pride in the unit and a combat luxury fit for their commanding general.

Two Marines are assigned to take the first watch. They are tasked with scanning 360 degrees of their perimeter for hostile activity while monitoring communications over the radios. The others dig their shallow sleeping holes, called ranger graves, between or under the vehicles. Long after the others have turned in for the night, Mattis climbs out, gets his sleeping bag, finds a spot among his men within earshot of the radios, and digs his own ranger grave. Constant chatter from the stack of radios in the LAV mixes with gunfire, jet engines overhead, the whoosh and earth-shaking boom of SCUDs, and the whopping of Cobra attack helicopters. Mattis loosens his bootlaces, gets into his bag. On this particular night, perhaps he reads his copy of *Meditations* by red-lensed penlight under the cover of his bag.

Marcus Aurelius, a Roman general, emperor, and the author of *Meditations*, may have spoken down through the ages to his modern counterpart lying quietly under the stars in the Iraqi desert through passages like this: "Let these be the objects of your ordinary meditation: to consider what manner of men both in soul and body we ought to be, whenever death shall surprise us: the shortness of this our mortal life: the immense vastness of the time that has been before, and will be after us: the frailty of every worldly material object: all these things to consider, and see clearly in themselves, all disguise being removed and taken away. Again, consider the causes of all things: the proper ends and references of all actions: what pain is in itself; what pleasure, what death: what fame or honour . . ."[1]

Soon the general is asleep, in spite of the Marine artillery that has begun to "fire for effect"—the military term for zeroed-in, concentrated bombardment. It slaughters hundreds of Iraqi soldiers just down the road, trembling the ground underneath the general's untroubled, sleeping head.

Before dawn, the Marines have circled their vehicles in a perimeter around the I MEF forward command post, a few collapsible tables loaded with radios and laptop computers. The platoon is putting up a nylon canopy over the tables. Mattis works alongside the other men, draping the sides of the canopy to protect the equipment from the fine desert dust. Osowski offers to take over the menial task from the general, to which he receives a quick "Nah."

At 0900 hours, the word comes down: Dowdy is still stuck in Nasariyah. Casualties are now over eighty killed and wounded, with captured US Army private Jessica Lynch and seven other Army truck drivers still missing. Every television news program in the world is broadcasting the story of Lynch, Saddam's star prisoner of war, the petite blond small-town girl from rural West Virginia. It is a public relations dream for Saddam[2] that cuts through the heartland of America, and a public relations nightmare for Mattis. Calls from the Pentagon flood into the central command base, the Bug, which has been moved up from Kuwait to the Jalibah airfield, eighty miles inside Iraq and 40 miles south of the problem at Nasariyah. Mattis calls his assistant division commander, John Kelly, and tells him to fly to Nasariyah now and get the attack moving again.

Kelly already spoke to Dowdy the night before, while Mattis was traveling north toward Joe Dunford's lines. Thomas Ricks reports on the exchange in his book *The Generals: American Military Command from World War II to Today*:

"Are you attacking?" he asked.

"Yes," Dowdy said, "but we're still shaping"—meaning he was using artillery and maneuvering to find the Iraqi weak spots before attacking. Apparently, Mattis's directive that shaping was to take a distant back seat to lightning-fast advance was not being followed.

"Why don't you drive through to Al Kut?" Kelly questioned.

Dowdy said he had reports of Iraqi minefields along that route and didn't want to run another gauntlet like Nasariyah. He was the commander in place, he insisted, and best equipped to decide how and when to attack.

Kelly called Dowdy again at two o'clock in the morning, just after Mattis had checked in with Kelly about the situation. Kelly lit into Dowdy: "What's wrong with you?"

"There's nothing wrong," Dowdy replied.

"I don't want to hear any excuses."

"They're not excuses. I'm the commander on the ground."[3]

Kelly told Dowdy that he was tired of the First Regiment "sitting on its ass," and he was going to recommend that Dowdy be relieved of his command. "Maybe General Mattis won't do it," he said. "Maybe he'll decide he can get along with a regiment that isn't worth a shit. But that's what I'm going to recommend."[4]

The following day, Kelly does just that. He hangs up with Mattis, grabs his flak jacket and helmet, exits the Bug, and sees his helicopter pilot across the airfield. He turns his index finger in a circular "go" signal above his head. Turbines whine as the chopper's rotors spin up to speed.

In thirty minutes, Kelly has landed at Dowdy's position. They hop in Dowdy's Humvee and drive up to the current front line—the causeway of the eastern bridge over the Euphrates. AK-47 rounds zip overhead from across the river, telling them they are close enough. They get out of the Humvee and move behind it for cover. Lieutenant General James T. Conway, I MEF commander for the entire Middle East, Mattis's boss, and the highest-ranking officer in the region, rolls up to them in an armored vehicle. Conway's appearance tells them that the situation across the river is now critical. Soon Brigadier General Richard Natonski, commanding Task Force Tarawa, and Colonel Ronald Bailey, commanding the Second Marine Regiment, a component of Task Force Tarawa, are all there to see the situation for themselves.

Retired Marine captain Bing West traveling in the Marine column in an unarmored Nissan Pathfinder sport utility vehicle with retired Marine major general Ray L. Smith, reports on the action in their book *The March Up: Taking Baghdad with the United States Marines*:

> What they saw was the fire from the 155mm artillery batteries pounding the city with volley after volley. Cobra gunships were raking the tree lines on the far bank. Two Marines had just been wounded on the southern embankment. The 2nd Marines had taken heavy casualties at the northern bridge and in the middle of the route through the city.[5]

Bullets whiz past and rattle the palm tree fronds overhead. The bullets spit dust where they hit the tree trunks. Two Marines get hit near the commanders. Over two hundred Marines lying on and near the riverbank around them return fire. The commanders have to shout over the noise.

The commanders know that Alpha Company of Colonel Bailey's Second Marine Regiment is pinned down inside the city and taking heavy fire. Saddam's quagmire claims its first tactical victims by bogging down Alpha's vehicles in the tar and mud. Bravo and Charlie Companies have made it through and according to last radio reports hold the bridge over the Saddam Canal on the north side of the city. Charlie Company reports are being lost in the sporadic radio communication.

Conway, without knowing exactly how many or what kind of forces are waiting for them inside the city, takes just moments to assess the situation and set the strategy—get control of the main route and forget about using the eastern and western avenues through the city. Secure the center of the city, the main thoroughfare and the buildings on either side. Once secured, this will protect the column's flanks. No more delays.

Mattis, on the radio with Kelly, confirms with Dowdy that he will execute a picket line. Dismounted Marines, using tanks and armored vehicles for cover, will walk down the main street of the city, looking for gunfights. And they are going to do it tonight.

Mattis is hunkered down in his LAV, sweating into the radio handset. His men have broken camp and moved the communications equipment back into the general's vehicle to protect it from the fierce sandstorm that now rages outside. Effectively blind in the storm, he is trapped inside the overheated vehicle.

Dowdy drives back from the meeting to a garbage dump, the only available large flat space near the city, where his officers are parked on the shoulder. He orders the attack at midnight. Third Battalion, First Regiment (3/1), will lead the way, setting the picket line. Ferrando's First Recon will act as a quick-reaction force to rush in and take out wounded as the picket line advances, while 3/1 lines Ambush Alley with their forty-two amtracs and a dozen tanks, then walk down the street with night vision goggles on, locked and loaded, leading the thirty-mile-long line of Marine vehicles toward Baghdad. Every Marine has been briefed on Mattis's new rules of engagement: anyone with a weapon is going to be shot, and in this war, a cell phone is also a weapon.

Just after 0200 the picket line has fought through sporadic gun-fights and is at the north end of Ambush Alley. Bing West describes the scene:

> As the vehicles drove through the northern end of town, the Marines saw three wrecked Amtracs on the median strip. One trac had been hit and disabled but was largely intact. The other two had been ripped apart, the force of the explosions having torn off the tops and peeled back the sides. The ground was littered with bloody battle dress-ings, pieces of uniforms, and torn-up individual fighting gear. Several dead Marines were still inside the Amtrac. Lt. Harry Thompson of Lima Company, 3/1, had placed a white cloth over the burned body of a fallen comrade. Each Marine in RCT-1 passing by viewed this gruesome scene, and remembered it.[6]

By 0400 the Marines of 3/1 have secured Ambush Alley and stand guard while the rest of Regimental Combat Team 1 moves through the city. At the head of the column, now six miles north of the city, First Battalion, Fourth Regiment (1/4), is ambushed by Saddam's regular fedayeen forces, which have retreated from the city to prepositioned defenses after stopping Dowdy's initial advance. They now surround 1/4 and pour fire into the column from several buildings four hundred yards to the east.

Inside Nasariyah, the entire column once again comes to a dead halt, but now its packed-up artillery battalion with its unarmored ammunition trucks is stopped exactly in the middle of the city—a massive, vulnerable cluster bomb. Even though it's the middle of the night, dozens of Iraqis have gathered on street corners to watch the Marines pass through. Guns up, the Marines scan the people for any hostile movement, even someone using a cell phone. A forward ob-server for a mortar team could phone in one mortar round onto one Marine ammunition truck that would ignite the others, destroying the Marine artillery, killing hundreds of Marines and civilians, and halting the advance for days.

This is the perfect public relations opportunity for Saddam. Support for the unpopular invasion would very likely weaken dramatically at the news of a second and larger defeat in the same city within a week. And if he can also send a few hundred Americans home in body bags, even better. Support could evaporate completely.

At the head of the column, hundreds of Iraqi fighters attack from positions to the east and northeast. The raging sandstorm now mixes with rain, cutting the Marines' visibility to almost zero, eliminating the advantage of their night vision. From concealed positions, the Iraqis fire into the prepared kill zone without exposing themselves. On the highway, an Iraqi rocket-propelled grenade blows through a Humvee door, severing a Marine captain's hand. Other Marines are hit and go down.

With his headquarters platoon farther back in the column, Dowdy can't get a clear picture of the situation up ahead; the weather is scrambling even satellite communications. Word comes that one or possibly more gravely wounded Marines are lying in the middle of Highway 7, waiting for a medevac, holding up the entire column. Dowdy, beloved by his men because he values their lives over the mission, does not order the wounded Marines moved. Kelly observes and doesn't countermand Dowdy's decision. Dowdy has now gone over forty-eight hours without sleep, all the time under severe and constant pressure.

The minutes tick by in Mattis's command vehicle as he monitors the broken radio communications between Dowdy and the 1/4 at the head of Dowdy's column. In a few hours the sun will come up, exposing the vulnerable part of the column still inside Nasariyah to even more danger. Even with the hellacious sandstorm raging, fifty miles northwest of his position enough aircraft are still flying to report the movement of three Iraqi divisions southwest from Baghdad. Osowski informs Mattis that these are commanded by Saddam's son Qusay and rattles off their composition, which includes long-range artillery. Mattis now knows that Saddam has taken the bait—Dunford's advance up Highway 1 to the west is just a feint, intended to draw Saddam's best forces away from Baghdad. The real attack will come from Dowdy's RCT-1, coming up Highway 7 to the east. That is, if Dowdy can get it moving again in time.

Mattis also knows that while he has drawn Saddam toward his trap, Saddam has already sprung his own. With his artillery confined and "combat-ineffective" inside Nasariyah, Mattis's entire central invasion force is now trapped in the Mesopotamian mud. Nothing—no sacrifice of men or equipment—is too costly to get the column moving again. That is why Mattis placed First Recon, his most aggressive and mobile warfighters, with Dowdy's RCT-1. Everything now depends on Dowdy's aggression in continuing to fight his way through and beyond Nasariyah.

On Highway 7, between the dust and rainstorm, it's now effectively raining mud. It blows sideways in bursts of icy wind as the ambushed Marines return fire against their attackers. The Marines deploy a company to attack the cement buildings and farmhouses to the east, where most of the Iraqi fire seems to be coming from. Aircraft are overhead again as the storm loses strength. As the sun comes up, it reveals a coat of mud that covers everything. The Marines begin to evacuate their wounded by helicopter as Kelly, who has been keeping his distance from Dowdy, back in the column, drives up to Dowdy's headquarters Humvee to see what the delay is now. Dowdy is surrounded by his puzzled officers, slouched forward, head down, in the front passenger seat of his vehicle. He has finally, after almost three days without a rest break, fallen asleep.

The radios near Mattis slowly come to life again, but with bad news. RCT-1 is still not moving.

"Fucking . . ." The general doesn't finish the sentence. He orders his platoon to move out in spite of still nearly zero visibility and the exhaustion of his own men, who have spent the last six hours trying to sleep in the seats of their vehicles. Their destination: northeast toward al-Gharaff on Highway 7, where the general will intercept

Dowdy's column. If he has read his history correctly, Saddam will have prepared more defenses there, like those in Nasariyah, or worse, to harass and delay the column's advance north. Mattis again races ahead into the teeth of Saddam's best defenses to make sure Dowdy pushes his men forward, at all costs.

A helicopter is waiting for Dowdy when he arrives in Numaniyah. In the week since Nasariyah, his RCT-1 has kicked ass in a hundred-mile running gunfight through the swamps, canals, tar pits, and fortified ambushes of Iraq's central farmland. They have secured the critical bridges over the Tigris at Al Kut and turned west to assist in crushing what was left of Iraq's elite Republican Guard forces outside Baghdad. Now, Mattis wants to see him.

Dowdy and his top aide, Sergeant Major Oscar Leal, are flown to the general's camp, about thirty miles northwest.

When they arrive, Mattis welcomes them and takes Leal aside. "How's your boss doing?"

"He's doing fine, sir."

"You're not engaged enough," Mattis responds. "You've got four battalions, and you're not pressing the attack."

"Tell me what we need to do, and we'll do it," Leal replies. The word is out that Dowdy's job is on the line. Loyal Sergeant Leal pleads with Mattis, "Don't fire him."[7]

Mattis doesn't respond. He turns away and crosses to the forward command post.

As Dowdy walks across an open field toward the CP, a dog leaps out and attacks him, "which you know kind of seemed symbolic," he will later say. Outside the CP he meets Kelly, who tells him he's lost the trust of his superiors.[8] Dowdy, still deeply tired after two weeks of ambush and counterattack against Iraqi irregulars and fedayeen fighters along a hundred miles of Highway 7, reels at this.

It's a body blow and his morale plummets. Like a condemned man climbing the last few steps to the gallows, he walks the last few feet to the CP.

Thomas Ricks describes the meeting:

> He walked inside the command post and saw the division chief of staff. "You're doing great," the officer said. "I think I'm being relieved," Dowdy responded. "Nah, that's bull-shit," the officer said.
>
> Dowdy went in to see Gen. Mattis, a quiet but intense officer with a reputation for favoring fiercely aggressive tactics. They were so near the front that artillery shells were passing overhead and tanks were rolling by the tent, creating what Dowdy heard as a whirlwind of noise. Mattis began asking questions that indicated to Dowdy that he would be removed on the grounds of fatigue. Dowdy had not slept for two days and felt that Kelly had just crushed his spirit. "I didn't give a very good account of myself," he told the Marine historian when he recounted his relief. "What's wrong?" Mattis gently and repeatedly asked him. "Why aren't you pressing in the cities more?" Dowdy, fatigued and confused, said that he was attacking but that "I love my Marines, and I don't want to waste their lives." By his own account, he then babbled a bit about his "lack of self-esteem" when he was younger. Even he recognized that such talk was a fatal misstep. At that point, he said, "I knew I was screwed."

In a report by Chris Cooper in the *Wall Street Journal*, Dowdy is quoted as responding "I've been fighting my way up this m-f-ing road for the past two weeks."[9]

Either way, Mattis is apparently unmoved by Dowdy's response. Mattis may have recalled the bulldozer incident at the Hantush air-field. A week earlier, when Mattis caught up with Dowdy and RCT-1 at Hantush, the general drove directly to the main runway. The air-field was critical for the resupply of the column, which had outrun its supply lines. With typical attention to detail, Mattis wanted to see the condition of the runway firsthand. As he feared, the main runway was pockmarked with shell craters. But even worse, a Marine captain, instead of repairing the craters, was sitting on his bulldozer, reading a paperback book. Mattis went ballistic, and Dowdy's only response was to suggest that perhaps he should have given the cap-tain a written order.

In the CP, Mattis moves past the Hantush episode. "You worry too much about enemy resistance and that may be your lack of battle experience,"[10] he says. Mattis speaks from his own expe-rience as a battalion commander in Operation Desert Storm. He knows very well about the horrible decision faced by every com-bat commander—whether to risk your men's lives or risk the suc-cess of the mission.

After babbling about his lack of esteem, Dowdy recovers his composure. "We'll do better," he appeals to Mattis. But it's too little and far too late.

"No, no, no," Mattis says, and gets up. He walks out of the CP to think things over.

Outside, artillery rounds zip overhead and explode down-range. Tanks and trucks rumble past on their way north toward Baghdad. Mattis walks in no particular direction as he weighs his decision. If he relieves Dowdy of command, it will be a blow to troop morale, and to public confidence in the operation. It will be a shitstorm of bad publicity, certain to get underwear in the White House in a twist: the first Marine commander relieved of command during combat in over forty years. It will be a blow to the prestige of the entire Marine Corps. It will crush Dowdy, a good Marine, but with a soft heart.

But under the extreme pressure, fatigue, and confusion of the coming street fighting in Baghdad, Dowdy might choose the safety of his men over the success of the mission again. Mattis can't take that chance.

When Mattis reenters the CP, Dowdy knows he is sunk. Mattis tells him that he is being relieved. John Toolan will be taking command of RCT-1.

"Think of my family, my unit," Dowdy pleads.

Mattis has thought of them, but it's over. Dowdy accepts the judgment and asks if he can work as a watch officer on the division staff, but Mattis tells him, "We're going to get you some rest. You need to go away." Dowdy's career as a combat commander is over.

Dowdy leaves the CP heartsick with failure. He and Sergeant Major Leal helicopter south back to the Hantush airfield. Dowdy says goodbye to his loyal friend and aide and climbs out of the helicopter. He boards a Marine C-130 aircraft that flies him back to Camp Commando, the rear base in Kuwait. He takes a shower and calls his wife, Priscilla. She already knows. She just saw the news on CNN.

June 1968—The Town of Richland, Washington State, USA

Jim Mattis, the shy, skinny captain of Columbia High School's varsity basketball team, accepts his high school diploma with typical reserve—a slight smile and nod. He's a good but unremarkable student known for his quiet style and pleasant personality. He enjoys his classmates and the rambunctious energy of his youth, apparently without any need to distinguish himself. He's just happy to be one of the team, one of the group. Even as captain of the basketball team and, previously, the junior varsity team manager, his position and title just doesn't seem to matter.

At home, his parents encourage Jim and his two brothers toward a life of the mind by providing only a large library for entertainment.

They have never owned a TV, a choice that young Jim will carry with him into adulthood. Jim will also adopt the practice of keeping a personal library; as an adult, he will own over seven thousand books. In his parents' library, Jim is drawn to books on geology and tales of the rugged, moral characters of the American West—the sheriffs and heroes who tamed savagery with courage and righted wrongs with true grit. A book that captivates the three Mattis brothers for months is MacKinlay Kantor's *Follow Me, Boys,* the tale of a Boy Scout scoutmaster who molds his troop of troubled boys into strong, self-reliant, and fearless young men. The Mattis boys emulate the heroic scoutmaster and practice Boy Scout survival skills while hiking, camping, and hunting in the high desert and conifer forest wilderness around Richland.

The Mattis home in Richland is a quiet, orderly place. Jim's father, John Mattis, is a power-plant operator at the nearby top-secret Hanford Nuclear Facility, and his mother, Lucille, is a homemaker. John and Lucille have both traveled the world, John as a merchant marine during World War II and Lucille as a US Army intelligence officer based in South Africa. In a 2014 interview Jim will recall, "They introduced us to a world of great ideas—not a fearful place—but a place to enjoy."[11]

At that time, nearly everyone in Richland had come to the area from somewhere else. "Nobody had extended families, so the families that you relied on were neighbors,"[12] recalled Jim Albaugh, a classmate and childhood friend of young Jim Mattis. Richland became a tight-knit community united by national pride and a common purpose in their important work for America's military at Hanford, which manufactured the plutonium for Fat Man, the atomic bomb that incinerated seventy thousand Japanese civilians in Nagasaki. The plant was a vital element of America's nuclear arsenal and a deterrent against Soviet Russia's well-publicized aggression.

By the time of Jim's high school graduation in 1968, at the height of America's counterculture influence and Vietnam War protests, Hanford was still the lifeblood of the community. Hippies and antiwar protests never took hold in Richland. Jim's basketball team was called the Bombers, and their emblem was—and remains—a mushroom cloud.

The military draft was in effect. On their sixteenth birthdays, the young men of Richland dutifully registered for the armed forces. Even though Jim was not in the top 10 percent of his high school class academically, he was still eligible for a college deferment to continue his education. The Reserve Officer Training Corps (ROTC) seemed the best option once Jim got to his intended college, Central Washington University. Although both parents had served, young Jim had no thoughts of making a career in the military. More likely, because of his great love of books, he might become a teacher or academic.

Instead of protesting the Vietnam War, the young men of Richland hung around the Spudnut Shop, which served freshly made potato-flour doughnuts, the Uptown movie theater, and Columbia High School. Of his classmate, Jim Albaugh later said, "I don't think anyone would have singled him out for greatness." And although Mattis would never marry, Albaugh said that his friend enjoyed high school social life and "was no straight arrow."[13]

Other classmates, like Lloyd Campbell, recalled a self-assured young man ready to stand up to bullies: "I was bullied a lot, but this was one of the guys who respected me for who I was and what my character was."[14] Jim Mattis was already living the model of his Western heroes, the sheriffs in white cowboy hats who stood up for truth, protected the weak, and never backed down from a fight. His small size and slender build didn't seem to matter.

"I owe this town a great deal, because it gave me the values that allowed me to be where I'm at today," Mattis told the Richland Rotary Club when he returned to Richland in 2011, after being on the front lines of battle with his men in distant parts of the world. "It was this town that formed me."[15]

Years later, employed by a man who many said had bullied and lied his way into the presidency of the United States, Jim Mattis again stood up for truth and protected the weak, in this case America's prisoners of war. On the subject of waterboarding, on which President-elect Trump had deferred to the wisdom of military commanders, Mattis instructed his new boss, "It doesn't work as well as offering a detainee cigarettes and a beer."[16]

Throughout his life and career, Jim Mattis has continued to speak his mind, often bluntly. At times that trait, among others he learned in Richland, puts him at odds with his bosses in the military, up to and including the president of the United States. His position and their title just never seems to matter.

1300 Hours—1 April 2003— Southeast of Baghdad

In the forward command post, on one of a dozen or so TV screens, CNN scrolls news of Colonel Joseph Dowdy's firing horizontally across the bottom of the screen. General Mattis stands in front of a printout of the battlefield between himself and Baghdad, with blue icons representing his RCT-1, RCT-5, and RCT-7 positions and red icons representing the positions of Saddam's Al Nida Division fifty miles southeast of Baghdad, on Highway 6 in the city of Aziziyah, and the Baghdad Division another fifty-three miles farther southeast, on Highway 6 in Al Kut.

Between Aziziyah and Al Kut, a small secondary road, Route 27, intersects Highway 6. Route 27 connects Highway 1 to the west with Highway 6 to the east. It is the hinge in the trapdoor that Mattis is nearly ready to spring.

Mattis is on an encrypted radio line to Dunford, who is paused on Highway 1: "Be prepared to take the bridge across the Saddam Canal 20 kilometers east on Route 27 at first light on 3 April and continue the attack to the Tigris from there."[17]

The pace in the last hours has picked up since Mattis was "cleared hot" to attack into the "red zone" surrounding Baghdad, a circle drawn around the city where it is expected that Saddam keeps his most experienced and well-equipped fighters. This is where, if the coalition is slimed with chemical weapons, it will happen. For the past hours, a pause in the advance has been in effect from Central Command to allow for the resupply and re-fueling of the US Army's V Corps, advancing on Baghdad not up paved highways like the Marines but across the hard desert directly from the west.

Mattis is chafing at the pause. He developed his "log lite" (light-ened logistics) as an essential part of his maneuver warfare plans specifically so his forces could move fast and far without relying on traditional supply lines. His units carry only as much food, water, and fuel as it takes to get them to the next airfield of any kind. In this case, airfields are often created out of Iraqi highways that have the median strips bulldozed out of the way. His reliable Third Marine Air Wing pilots are experts at landing their giant C-130s on four-lane blacktop. Inside the planes are six-thousand-gallon rubber fuel bladders, crates of ammunition, full water tanks, and everything else a rolling attack force needs.

Mattis calls Dunford back, moving the attack date up a full twenty-four hours:

"Take the Canal on 2 April."[18]

Every moment his men are paused, waiting in camp or in the field, exposes them to more danger. He doesn't much care that everybody thinks the rear areas are secure. It was this kind of happy horse-shit thinking that got twenty-five thousand British soldiers killed in this same location. Every moment they are paused, Saddam is repositioning and resupplying his forces too, even though they are generally commanded by his two inexperienced sons and their cowardly fedayeen fighters. Mattis has seen these fedayeen scurry-ing between positions disguised in civilian clothing, using women and children as human shields. His disgust is overwhelming. They are the type of dishonorable cowards he despises, "the most unworthy opponents we have ever faced."

He calls Dunford back a third time, asking how soon RCT-5 can attack.

"In four hours," Dunford says.

"Do it," Mattis replies.[19]

Fuck the pause—they'll pause after he rolls his tanks through Saddam's bedroom. He turns to aide-de-camp Captain Warren Cook and tells him to get the jump ready. They're rolling out for Numaniyah. Mattis wants to be there when Dunford's Fifth Marines spring his trap on the Baghdad Division in Al Kut.

On Mattis's chessboard, he is trapping four Iraqi divisions with Dunford's single Marine regiment. Because Qusay Hussein's Baghdad Division is expecting Dunford's attack from the south, he draws three divisions out of Baghdad to defend against it. But Dunford leaves a shadow force behind, pinning Qusay's forces in place, while he outflanks him, rolling his main force east to Numaniyah and then north, cutting off Qusay's northern route back to Baghdad and trapping him in Al Kut.

Bing West reports on traveling across Route 27 toward Numaniyah:

> The contrast between Route 27 and the highways we had so far taken during the campaign was striking. No berms or bunkers dotted the road, and no bulldozers had plowed long lines of trenches. Even the ubiquitous white sandbags, seen in every tiny village at some tiny intersection, were absent.
>
> No Iraqi military planner—not even Saddam's son Uday and his fedayeen—had expected the coalition forces to leave Route 1 and turn east onto this secondary road. Civilians were going about their evening business at a steady pace. Most waved if they made eye contact, but none seemed awed or frightened by the hundreds of armed vehicles rolling by. Boys out in a schoolyard playing soccer did not interrupt their game to watch the amtracs clatter past. The friendly and normal atmosphere made it obvious that the fedayeen were not lurking on this route.[20]

Mattis and his jump crew reach the Numaniyah airfield south of the city just after Dunford's Marines complete their move across Route 27 and begin their attack on the airfield, just before dawn. Heavy return fire from the Iraqis crackles and thuds. The airfield is critical for supplying the final push into Baghdad, just over 80 miles north. Saddam has prepared his defenses here for Mattis's attack.

Mattis leans forward in his LAV's commander's seat, scrutinizing the telltale sounds of the pitched battle just a thousand yards away. Sergeant Ryan Woolworth turns up the speakers on the PRC-119 radio that monitors the various company, battalion, and regimental networks in the area. Mattis listens to the direction and intensity of fire outside with the trained ear of a combat commander, distinguishing between enemy and Marine weapons, gauging distance and position. Over the radio, he hears Dunford calmly commanding the attack at the airport while receiving sitreps (situation reports) on his tanks attacking two miles east, down the main street of Numaniyah toward the bridge over the Tigris. Dunford's front-line company commanders at the airport call in air and artillery support on Iraqi positions. The end game at Numaniyah begins.

At 6:30, dawn is breaking over the green marshes of Mesopotamia as the latest of dozens of invading armies over the centuries asserts its will. A brief situation report comes over the nets from Dunford's command post to all battalions: "Iron Horse [call sign for Second Tank Battalion] has seized the Tigris bridge at Numaniyah intact and are crossing it now. Have taken some RPG [rocket-propelled grenade] hits, but all tanks still in the fight at this time."[21]

Once across the bridge, Second Tank Battalion's orders are to turn south again, back to Al Kut, attacking it from the north in a pincer move, with RCT-1 attacking up Highway 7 from the south.

The Numaniyah airfield is quiet except for the distant rumble of a C-130 supply plane approaching from the south. Mattis's driver, Sergeant Yaniv Newman, herringbones and parks the general's LAV just off the airfield, and the others in the jump platoon follow it into formation. Objectives secured, and Dunford headed north to Aziziyah, Mattis calls for a few hours of rest for his men. As the others climb out of their vehicles, the general reviews his laptop computer screen one more time. It shows the new positions of his forces on the battlefield. But what has he forgotten? What have his commanders overlooked? Who needs advance orders? What is Saddam's next move?

Even though the intensity of close combat is over for the moment, Mattis's predator reflexes are still engaged, and the chatter in his head won't stop. To quiet his mind, he may have again summoned his therapist and closest adviser, General Marcus Aurelius. Writing his meditations from the distant past, Aurelius advises the general frequently about what is outside of his control, even as a general: "What is the present state of my understanding? For here lies all indeed. As for all other things, they are outside the compass of my own will; and if outside the compass of my will, then they are as dead things to me, and as it were, mere smoke."

Aziziyah, at first look from the south, appears like a fortified city, with stout concrete buildings standing shoulder to shoulder above a narrow canal that seems to be almost a medieval moat. The city lies just fifty miles south of Baghdad, and through the centuries has been the capital city's last line of defense against invaders from the south. At one o'clock on the afternoon of April 3, 2003, everything President Saddam Hussein has left in his arsenal is firing directly at Dunford's Marine invaders, just across the canal.

As Iraqi AK-47 bullets whiz by like angry hornets and 155-millimeter coalition artillery shells zip overhead in the opposite direction, detonating on Iraqi Republican Guard positions in Aziziyah with concussive *whumps* like car doors being slammed, Dunford and Lieutenant Colonel Sam Mundy, the commander of Dunford's go-to Marine battalion, the 3/5, discuss attack routes into the city. They hunker down in front of a battle map of the city that leans against the rear tire of Dunford's command vehicle. Their faces only an inch apart, they yell over the deafening clatter of shouting Marines firing M-16s and machine guns back at the Iraqis.

Yards away, behind his own vehicle, Mattis stands upright, seemingly unaware of the fierce firefight around him. He contemplates his own battle map of the territory between Aziziyah and Baghdad with a dozen red and blue sticky notes pasted to it, red indicating the positions of Saddam's forces, blue indicating his coalition positions. He yells into a satellite phone over the roar of battle as Marines trot past him toward the front lines, hunched over, keeping their heads down as they press the attack forward. It's eighty degrees. The dust, diesel fumes from a thousand engines of war, and smoke from burning oil fires nearby make it tough on the grunts, who each carry around eighty pounds on their backs.

Bing West writes:

> He [Mattis] could see that the Marines, although tired, were continuing to press forward, while the enemy had retreated into the town. He could see with his own eyes that his troops had the initiative. And Mattis always had a sense for the troops. As he was studying the map, a Marine stumbled by him breathing hoarsely in the dust. "Want some water?" Mattis said, gesturing at the gypsy rack that every Humvee carried with five-gallon water jugs. The Marine refilled his canteens, took a deep gulp, and patted Mattis on the shoulder. "Thanks, man," he said, trotting off, apparently unaware that he was talking to his division commander.[22]

Mattis, equally unimpressed, continues his phone conversation with his assistant division commander, General John Kelly, sixty miles back at the Bug. Mattis can likely sense from the attitude of the Marines trotting forward past his position and the tempo of artillery fire into Saddam's elite Al Nida Division across the canal that Saddam's final defense perimeter is beginning to give way. If he can break through now, he might be able to thrust his spearhead, Dunford's 3/5, into the heart of Baghdad and end the killing.[23]

But these good Marines have been running and gunning without a break for the past forty-eight hours. They have led the way and won every gunfight since seizing the gas and oil separation plant outside Basra two weeks ago. He can tell from their body language and the grime they haven't had time to wash off their faces that they need rest. He has to bring up reinforcements.

"Tell Steve to come up here right away to his friend Joe's location," he tells Kelly. "Make sure he knows I want him to bring all his friends with him." Mattis speaks in this type of familiar, personal code because he doesn't trust the technology that is supposed to be encrypting his communications. It's the same reason he relies on old-fashioned maps with sticky notes instead of computer images of the battlefield. The Steve he mentions is Colonel Steven Hummer, who is ordered to break off the assault on Al Kut to the south and hustle his one thousand vehicles and six thousand men up Route 6 to the front at Aziziyah.[24]

In Baghdad, Iraqi deputy prime minister Tariq Aziz holds a news conference assuring reporters that Saddam Hussein is "in full control of the army and the country." Information Minister Mohammed Saeed al-Sahhaf adds to Aziz's assurances, saying reports of US advances on Baghdad are "illusions."[25]

3

Liberation

MARGARET WARNER: We want to talk about your experience running the occupation for these months. The most remarkable statistics, in the months running the huge area of Iraq while the army was taking all kinds of casualties up around north of Baghdad you lost not one Marine to hostile attack. How do you explain that?

MAJ. GEN. JAMES MATTIS: Well, we didn't lose one killed. We had about 40 men wounded, but we sat out there to carry out the commander in chief's intent, and that was that we were going to liberate these people. We were going to try to avoid adversarial relationships and we were going to try to remain friendly one week longer, one day longer, one hour longer than perhaps some of the people who distrusted us coming in might have expected. And that's worked out pretty well.

MARGARET WARNER: How did you go about it? I read that you said one of your principles was do no harm. Describe that for us.

MAJ. GEN. JAMES MATTIS: We went into the attack with the motto that said no better friend, no worse enemy. So if you want to be our friend, we'll be the best friends you ever had. If you want to fight us, you're going to regret it. When we were up there in the stability operations, we added to it, first do no harm. In other words, if the enemy tried to provoke us into a fight and that fight would cause innocent people to die, then we would forgo the fight. We would try to find a way to get them another day.

But we were out to win the trust of the Iraqi people. We knew we were an American foreign force, largely Christian force, and we occupied, for example, two of the holy cities of the Shia. What we did not want to do was find ourselves in a position of creating a conflict. So I sent about 15,000 of my 23,000 men home [in June]. I got rid of all my tanks and armored personnel carriers. Marines went on dismounted patrols. We had wave tactics, waving to the people, assuming we were there as friends. Eventually that expectation paid off.

MARGARET WARNER: I gather—I read somewhere that you gave your troops instructions about things like eye contact.

MAJ. GEN. JAMES MATTIS: Yes, when soldiers walk into a city, and they're foreign soldiers, the first thing people are going to look at is all that gear and the weapons hanging off them. Generally the second place people look is into people's eyes, to see if they can trust them. So Marines removed their sunglasses and we tried to build the trust one act at a time. They learned quickly to trust us; they would even protest against us at times. On the suggestion of my Catholic chaplain, the Marines would take chilled drinking water in bottles and walk out amongst the protestors and hand it out. It is just hard to throw a rock at somebody who has given you a cold drink of water and it's 120 degrees outside.

— *General James Mattis, September 26, 2003, interviewed on PBS during the occupation of Baghdad and southern Iraq*

1100 Hours—4 April 2003—Route 6, Advancing Toward Baghdad

General Mattis's four jump platoon vehicles roll north, well back in the column and indistinguishable from the 150 other vehicles of the Second Tank Battalion. Humvees and LAVs are in the left lane, and thirty-five M1A1 Abrams tanks in the right. Behind them, extending for 6 miles, is the rest of Regimental Combat Team 5—now the tip of Mattis's spearhead, aimed at the beating heart of Baghdad.

The countryside looks like some poorer parts of rural Mexico, semi-arid, flat and featureless dirt dotted with bush scrub. Scattered adobe homes and industrial sites slide by on the right side as the column rolls past a line of trenches belching black smoke that partially obscures the industrial sites. Bing West reports:

> The double column, which extended in length for 14 kilometers, had just straightened out and hit a cruising speed of about 25 kilometers per hour when the battle began. . . . The Iraqis let the Marines' lead tank company go by, and then as Alpha Company was passing, there was a loud woosh, as if a jet had passed only a few meters overhead, and an explosive blast to the right that seemed as big as a 155mm shell, only with more flame and red sparks. There was another woosh and another boom and another red fireball to the right of our SUV. The company net came alive as the tankers tried to identify the weapon.
>
> "SAM! SA-7 malfunctioning! He's aiming for the Cobras."
>
> "Negative. Those are Saggers. Repeat, Saggers."[1]

The tankers are trying to determine the weapon they are facing when Second Tank Battalion commander Captain Todd Sudmeyer breaks in, "This is Alpha Six. Pick up the pace. Pick it up. Open some space between us and those palm trees."[2]

The lead tanks put the pedal to the metal while opening fire toward the industrial park with 7.62-millimeter machine guns. On their right, Humvees with turret-mounted .50-caliber machine guns fire into the palm grove in that direction, expecting an ambush from there as well. Tank commanders drop inside their tanks and close their hatches. The TOW (tube-launched, optically tracked, wire-guided) antitank missile and .50-caliber gunners on the Humvee top turrets can't drop inside a hatch behind heavy armor. The only armor they have are the ceramic plates in their flak vests.[3]

The tankers scan the park with thermal imaging to pick up heat signatures of rocket positions and day optics to pick out visual targets. The TOW-mounted Humvees on the right spot a line of Russian T-72 tanks and small armored vehicles called BMPs racing north toward Baghdad through the palm grove about 1,500 meters away. All along the road, impacting bullets from Marine .50-caliber guns throw up sprays of dirt along the six-foot berm.

Seemingly all at once the tanks of 3/5 lock in targets, and dozens of main guns fire into the industrial park, vaporizing sections of the high cement wall that surrounds it and collapsing structures behind it. The howling thunderstorm of cannon fire drowns out even the 155-millimeter Marine artillery and Cobra helicopter rockets as they begin to rain down on the park and cracks the windshield of Bing West's Nissan SUV traveling in the midst of the tanks. At the head of the column, Second Battalion tanks take on a Russian T-72 tank and several BMPs that try to block the column, stopping it in the ambush kill zone.

Over the net the news comes that Tank Charlie Six, commanded by Captain Jeffrey Houston, is a mobility kill, meaning that the tank is immobilized by enemy fire but the tankers are not injured. Second Tank Battalion charges forward around Charlie Six and begins littering Highway 6 with burning Iraqi tanks and trucks in its wake.

In Mattis's LAV, concussion waves from tank cannon fire rock the vehicle as the smell of burning oil smoke seeps into the interior. They roll past dozens of burning vehicles, adding to the smoke from the trenches of oil along the road. The tanks cut through thick black curtains of smoke, spiraling it behind them and into Mattis's ventilation ducts. Adding to the deafening cannon fire and noxious smoke, a burning Iraqi truck by the side of the road explodes in a tremendous roar as the ammunition inside cooks off. The company radio can barely be heard above the noise. Mattis puts his finger in one ear to block some of the pandemonium around him as he yells into the radio about his next objective, crossing the Diyala River outside Baghdad.

The Marines of RCT-5 fought for ten hours the day before, advancing through Aziziyah, and they looked tired when they started out this morning. Now, Mattis realizes, they will have to dismount and sweep forward on foot at least four or five kilometers to clear any secondary ambushes. That means fighting, sprinting, and flopping, for probably another five hours. It is going to be a long day for them and will delay the crossing of the Diyala River. The column slows down as enemy and return fire dwindles. Damage reports file in from the column. Three Marines are dead and almost a dozen wounded. First Lieutenant Brian McPhillips, twenty-five years old, of Pembroke, Massachusetts, a machine gunner exposed to enemy fire in his Humvee turret, is dead.[4]

Mattis hears the news. By now he knows many of the hard-charging grunts of 3/5 by sight, and some by first name. He tells his communications technician, Sergeant Ryan Woolworth, to get Lieutenant Colonel Duffy White, commander of the First Light Armored Reconnaissance (LAR), on the radio. He wants to know White's progress in finding fording spots over the Diyala River for the attack into Baghdad.

The column halts for the night at a small intersection surrounded on all four sides by groups of small, shabby car repair garages and stores. Second Battalion tanks pull in, blocking two corners of the intersection as Dunford's jump platoon claims a third corner as the regiment's forward command post. Hundreds of war-making vehicles spread out across the hardpan desert around the intersection; the sky flashes red and orange with fireworks from burning Iraqi ammunition trucks. Flaming shrapnel sprays across the sunset sky as Mattis's jump platoon joins Dunford's corner command post.

Night and fatigue fall like heavy blankets, silencing the roar and clang of battle. Marines fall fast asleep on the filthy, oil-smelling pavement around the machine shops or in shallow ranger graves next to their vehicles in the hard-packed dirt. Mattis's platoon shoulders into their sleeping holes, trying to find a soft spot in the earth just off the intersection. Silence finally comes, except for occasional radio chatter buzzing across the net from hundreds of vehicles.

Somewhere out in the dark a pack of dogs fights over a kill, drawing the attention of the exhausted Marines standing the first watch. Somewhere beyond the dogs, an Iraqi rocket team moves quietly to remove the camouflage over their Russian-made BM 21 rocket launchers.

About 2200, the first Iraqi rocket hits at the crossroads with a sharp bang. Then a second rocket hits. The net in Mattis's LAV blurts coordinates and weapon configurations. Marines on the ground roll under vehicles or just turn their faces into the ground and pray. If tonight is the night their number comes up, there's nothing they can do about it now. Might as well try to get some sleep. A third rocket hits a shop near the intersection as rockets begin to rain down out of a pitch-black sky all around the Marines.

Nearby, the first watch commander of the Eleventh Marines artillery battalion scans his radar and sees it has picked up the flight paths of the rockets. The radar feeds this rocket flight data into a computer that calculates the flight paths backward to the location of the rocket launchers. The computer sends the launcher coordinates over to a waiting battery of six 155-millimeter cannons. Within seconds, the rocket launchers and Iraqi soldiers manning them explode into fragments under the barrage of Marine artillery.

The rockets stop. In a moment the net hisses with confirmation of the effective fire mission. Mattis and the Marines at the intersection roll over and fall back asleep.

The Diyala River bordering Baghdad on the southeast is fifty feet wide. Mattis peeks around broken bricks of what used to be the front wall of a burned-out one-room house on the southern bank of the river. Lieutenant Colonel White has assured him it is too deep to wade across, and there are no natural fording spots within twenty miles in either direction that can be used by the tanks and heavy equipment of the Marines. Where the river skirts the city, thirty- to forty-foot sandstone cliffs on both sides of the river stand as natural fortress walls against invaders, as they have for centuries, starting with the first Persian kings.

Mattis's bombed-out observation post is on top of the southern cliff, directly across the river from the slums of Saddam City in southeast Baghdad. On the far cliff, 155-millimeter Marine artillery shells explode, putting him and the men with him within a "danger close" radius of shrapnel spraying out from each shell impact. He scans past the far, city-side cliff through binoculars, peering down the crooked streets and alleys of Saddam City, the ghetto home of Iraq's Shia minority. With him Colonel Steve Hummer and Lieutenant Colonel Brian P. "Base Plate" McCoy also take cover as they scan across the river toward the last objective of their three-hundred-mile march up from Kuwait. Base Plate McCoy got his nickname both from his initials and from his reputation for volunteering to shoulder his mortar team's heavy metal base plate as an infantryman. Now, as commander of the 3/4 Marines, he is one of Mattis and Dunford's most reliably aggressive front-line commanders, the perfect choice for the age-old infantry ground assault now being readied.

An old-fashioned iron pedestrian bridge sits just fifteen feet to the right of the general's shattered observation post. Just beyond that, the modern four-lane concrete Baghdad Bridge spans the sandstone palisades into the city. The pedestrian bridge has a six-foot-wide hole blown into its center, but the Baghdad Bridge sits invitingly undamaged and apparently ready for American tanks to take advantage of it. It's an obvious trap that Mattis is not going to fall into. A few kilometers north, a blown concrete bridge is being repaired while Marine engineers, under small-arms and RPG fire, construct their own pontoon bridges nearby in case the repaired bridge is retargeted and blown again.

Mattis's orders are to encircle this southeastern part of the city and join up with the US Army's Third Infantry Division, which has already taken Baghdad International Airport to the southwest. Once the encirclement is complete, Army and Marine battalions will make raids into the city to seize key objectives such as Saddam's Fedayeen Training Center, the Rasheed Military Complex, the Atomic Energy Commission, and Adhamiyah Palace.[5] They are not going to seize and hold entire neighborhoods or large areas of the city, as they did with the smaller cities on the route north. Command-level intelligence indicates that Saddam's defenses are already collapsing inside the city, and large-scale defections from the defenders are expected.

Mattis and Hummer decide to send the amtracs and LAVs that can "swim" directly across the Diyala to take up positions outside Saddam City. Tanks, trucks, and Humvees will divert to bridges to the north and south, circle back, and rejoin their units on the other side. Mattis knows he has outrun his supply line and is low on food rations and artillery shells. To conserve artillery, he orders the Third Marine Air Wing to take over most of the preparatory fire missions for the coming assault. The invasion of Baghdad must happen today.

Resting in the house behind the commanders, the men of Kilo Company, some of the "friends" that "Steve" was ordered to bring up two days ago, sit behind the partially collapsed back wall of the house inside a small courtyard. With them are Mattis's jump platoon, including Lance Corporal Osowski. This close to Baghdad, intelligence estimates that the chance of a chemical attack is minimal, so the men have shed their bulky, hot MOPP suits and enjoy the relative coolness for the first time in weeks.

Among the Marines, M-16 rifles, AT-4 rocket launchers, machine guns, and 60-millimeter mortars are thick wooden planks, metal piping, and a large metal gate Kilo managed to scrounge from somewhere. They are going to use these materials to cover the hole in the pedestrian bridge as they assault Baghdad on foot. A few of Mattis's dwindling number of artillery shells are directed toward the palm grove that lies on the edge of the city just north of the two bridges—a possible ambush position against Kilo as they cross the pedestrian bridge.

Mattis, Hummer, and Base Plate turn from their observations and walk back to say a few words to the men of Kilo before they begin the assault on Baghdad. Mattis assures Base Plate that his men will have all the cover fire they need to get across the pedestrian bridge. Hummer offers Base Plate his own encouragement, "McCoy, don't fuck up."[6] Mattis leaves the house satisfied that the assault is well thought out and in good hands.

Across the river, unseen eyes observe the Marines moving inside and around the house. Deafening explosions of Marine artillery begin to splinter the palm grove on the Baghdad side, as something large flies from inside the city and splashes into the river near the house. Radios along the American front line spit out an urgent warning. It seems that Saddam has finally launched his defense of Baghdad. Third Air Wing hunts the Iraqi artillery but not before the first volley finds the Marines.

In the house, Marines start diving for cover, yelling "Incoming! Incoming!"

The next shell lands so close it shakes the earth under the Marines' feet with a sharp crack so loud that they freeze, expecting to hear screams of pain or see worse. The Marines don't know whether being inside or outside the courtyard is safer, or if it is friendly or enemy shells they are dodging. Some want to run for different cover, some want to stay. They all start yelling. Bing West reports,

> [Sergeant Major] Howell rushed into the courtyard. "Shut up!" he screamed.
>
> "Only the chain of command talks! Sit down along the walls. No one stands up!"
>
> Behind the courtyard an Amtrac was smoking, its turret peeled back like the top of an open can of soup. The back

hatch was flung open, and Marines were pulling out the bodies. The radio net was crackling with raised voices.

"Turn it off! Turn it off!" Kilo Six was shouting loudly into his radio.

"Enemy incoming! Enemy incoming! Continue to fire!" someone countermanded him over the radio.

"You continue to fire, and I'm going to shove this handset up your ass. That fire gets turned off now. Do you read me? Now!"[7]

A Marine artillery commander comes on the net and confirms that it is not friendly fire—Kilo is taking enemy fire. The Iraqi general is picked up by the intercept team, yelling at his terrified taxi driver not to stop driving, or they will be targeted by the Americans. He is also yelling over his cell phone for his artillery to continue firing on the Marines' position, but no one responds.

Across the river, Kilo Company picks themselves up off the floor and listens for more incoming shells and net reports. They hear Eleventh Marines artillery and Third Air Wing pilots calling in co-ordinates as they attack a location inside the city.

If the Iraqi general had been able to direct his fire a few feet north and a few moments earlier, inside the house, it would prob-ably have killed most of Kilo, several division commanders, and Mattis. Instead, the blackened bodies of Corporal Martin Medellin and Lance Corporal Andrew Aviles are pulled out of the shattered amtrac behind the house. They are covered, and carried away on stretchers. The Iraqi general achieved a direct hit on the two young Marines. Aviles, only eighteen years old, is the youngest Marine to die in Iraq.

Sergeant Major Howell divides Kilo Company into two assault teams. They pick up their primitive bridging materials and run head-long toward Saddam's last line of defense beyond the pedestrian bridge. A dead Iraqi lies face up, naked, his bloated belly extended toward the sun at the entrance to the bridge. Weapons up, the assault teams run around the dead body onto the bridge. A gaggle of international photographers, cameramen, and reporters run along with Kilo, televising the latest invasion of Baghdad.

The planning for Phase IV, the occupation of Baghdad, had not yet started in the fall of 2001. The undersecretary for policy at the Pentagon, Douglas Feith, was sent a report created by seventy national security experts and Middle East scholars called "Iraq: Looking Beyond Saddam's Role." The report concluded that occupying Iraq "will be the most daunting and complex task the US and the international community will have undertaken since the end of World War II." It strongly recommended against dissolving the Iraqi military, saying, "There should be a phased downsizing to avoid dumping 1.4 million men into a shattered economy."[8]

In December 2001, the subject of postwar Iraq was carefully considered by a second group of about a dozen Middle East experts including diplomats, State Department officials, and military intelligence officers meeting at the Army War College. After several days of intense discussions the group produced recommendations for the eventual planners, senior military commanders and civilian administrators who would be responsible for the country after Saddam was defeated. They offered exactly the same advice as the first study group. Their report warned, "To tear apart the army in the war's aftermath could lead to the destruction of one of the only forces for unity within the society," as would wholesale "de-Ba'athification," the destruction of the majority political party of Saddam Hussein.[9]

Because neither study was widely distributed among the Pentagon's war planners, there was never a detailed Phase IV or occupation phase developed for coalition commanders. The eventual plan, entitled Eclipse II, told field commanders what not to do, but very little about what they should do. Marine commander Mattis, like his British coalition counterpart, Major General Robin Brims, recognized the lack of detail in the Pentagon's occupation plan and prepared himself and his troops in spite of this lack of guidance. Brims, who had invaded and occupied Northern Ireland for years, knew full well the civilian dimensions involved. Mattis, who commanded a rifle company during the invasion and occupation of Kuwait and then commanded the first task force to invade and briefly occupy Afghanistan after 9/11, had also seen the civilian side of occupation firsthand.

Seven months after the second study group met, postwar planning for Iraq began in earnest. It was rammed through an overworked staff group within Central Command that laid an incomplete foundation virtually guaranteeing the disaster Iraq was to become. Colonel John Agoglia of Central Command's planning staff said, "End of July [2002], we've just finished the second plan [for Iraq], and we get an order from Joint Staff saying, 'You're in charge of the postwar plan.' We said, 'Oh, shit,' did a mission analysis, and focused on humanitarian issues, such as minimizing the displacement of people, stockpiling food to stave off famine, and protecting the infrastructure of the oil fields."[10]

This rushed strategy by the Pentagon planners lacked deep thinking about the needs of the Iraqi people beyond their basic survival and provided few details on what Iraq's tribes, communities, and cities would need after their country was invaded and their government overtaken. Mattis's lifelong devotion to the study of philosophy and experience in occupied territories gave him a much keener sense of human needs, particularly in times of war. He could no more overlook the humanity of the Iraqis he would become responsible for under the rules of war than he could that of his own troops. In Mattis's educated view, Iraqis and his occupying troops would have to form a community with specific physical, emotional, and spiritual needs.

The human aspect of warfare is apparently always first in Mattis's thinking. After working closely with Secretary of Defense Rumsfeld developing maneuver warfare, he then dismissed his superior's idea of "net-centric" warfare. Rumsfeld had taken warfare into the abstract, insisting that fighting wars had to do primarily with the movement of data. Rumsfeld felt that computers and the internet would now control the rhythm of battle.

In what has become his trademark style, Mattis contradicted his distant boss Rumsfeld in comments to a reporter. "Computers by their nature are isolating," he said. "They build walls. The nature of war is immutable: You need trust and connection. It is a Marxian view—it ignores the spiritual."[11]

In his elevated contradiction of Rumsfeld, it seems Mattis has learned to moderate his comments to the press. Part of his formal press education as a battlefield commander came when he accepted command of the First Marine Expeditionary Brigade at Camp Pendleton in July of 2001. After the ceremony, he encountered his new communications watchdog, Captain Joe Plenzler, a former infantry officer. Plenzler introduced himself as Mattis's new public affairs officer to which Mattis replied, "What are you going to do? Follow me around and make sure I don't say fuck?" Plenzler just smiled and said, "Well, if it smoothes your hackles, general, I was an infantryman in your old regiment. I'll do whatever you need. Just treat me like another gun-hand around the ranch."

Mattis smiled and accepted his press muzzle in good humor. "It looks like you and me are going to get along just fine."[12]

1030 Hours—9 April 2003—
Saddam City, Baghdad

Mattis stands outside his LAV, consulting his low-tech paper map of the city, held in place by spring clips on a piece of poster board. Osowski and Cook write battalion objectives on Post-it notes with markers and paste them on the general's map. The three regimental sectors of East Baghdad, the areas the RCTs are responsible for, are outlined by colored marker lines.

RCT-7's sector is outlined in bright blue and stretches all the way from the southeast to the northwest of the city. In that sector are eighteen numbered squares, each marking an objective, with six objectives assigned to each of RCT-7's three battalions—the 1/7, 3/7, and 3/4.

Colonel Conlin's 1/7 has already captured the Atomic Energy Commission, only half a mile away, and the other battalions, instead of meeting Republican Guard or fedayeen fighters, are rolling on their objectives past crowds of jubilant Iraqis eight or nine deep, waving and shouting, "Good! Good! Mister!" Captain Brian Smalley said later, "It was like driving through Paris in 1944."[13]

In the Bug, now moved up to Numaniyah, I MEF commander General James Conway watches CNN's live feed of the happy conquest of Saddam City. Mattis is on the satellite phone with Conway, requesting to scrap the plan and push his advance until they run into somebody who wants to fight. Conway is cautious; he can't be sure the same happy reception is happening all over the city. The plan is to seize critical locations of power in a coordinated degradation of Saddam's control. He's going to check in with the Army.[14]

Mattis hangs up and doesn't bother to inform his field commanders of the boss's hesitancy. He lets them continue to operate under Mattis's well-known intent—advance, attack, and advance. Base Plate McCoy's 3/4 Marines roll into Firdos Square in downtown Baghdad. The square is dominated by a six-meter-high statue of Saddam Hussein lifting his right arm in a gesture of benevolent greeting. The nearby Palestine Hotel empties dozens of foreign journalists into the square, who join the crowds of cheering, liberated Iraqis.

The psyops (psychological operations) team attached to Base Plate's unit announces over loudspeaker in Arabic that the Marines have decided the statue of Saddam should come down. A cheer goes up from the crowd, and Iraqis begin to clap in unison.

As Mattis studiously notates his map with a marker in the hot sun while fending off the aggressive ghetto-bred flies of Saddam

City, all of his bosses—including Generals James Conway, David McKiernan, and Tommy Franks; President George Bush, standing next to General Colin Powell in the Oval Office; the Joint Chiefs of Staff; and the US Congress—watch in air-conditioned awe as CNN broadcasts twenty-year-old Marine corporal Edward Chin climbing out on the derrick arm of his M-88 tank retriever and laying an American flag over the face of Saddam's statue. The Iraqi crowd shouts, "No, we want an Iraqi flag." Chin hears the crowd, waves, and climbs down. He gets an Iraqi flag and climbs back up the derrick with the new flag and a length of stout rope prepared with a hangman's noose. He replaces the American flag with the Iraqi flag and loops the noose around Saddam's neck. His tank retriever pulls, and Saddam keels over slowly, breaks at the ankles, and slips off his pedestal. The crowd cheers and rushes forward, swarming over the statue. They begin cutting off Saddam's head.[15]

By radio, Mattis gets the news that Adhamiyah Palace is now captured. According to the reports, the palace is lavishly decorated, furnished with a king-size waterbed and well stocked with liquor. A CNN reporter asks Mattis if he thinks Saddam is still giving orders. Mattis replies, "When you take over his country and drink his liquor, it doesn't much matter."[16]

Phase IV, the occupation of Iraq, begins immediately. Lieutenant Colonel Conlin, while patrolling in his sector near Firdos Square, is presented with a dying man injured in a car accident. The normal Iraqi civil procedure of taking the man to a hospital or calling the police is apparently forgotten. It is now the Americans' problem. Soon after, frantic Iraqis run to the Marines explaining their phone service is out and the hospital is being looted. The water is off, and what about trash collection? Is it okay to use their cell phones?

As the day wears on, the transition from urban warfighting into civil administration begins to overwhelm his battalion commanders and trickles up to Mattis's attention. There are tribal chiefs asking to meet "His Excellency, the General," and wanting to swear their allegiance to President George Bush. Mattis repeats his commander's intent for his field commanders. He wants to win over the Iraqis, not conquer them. He doesn't want to leave ". . . a heavy boot print or the sense of oppression . . . if everywhere you looked you saw a Marine. . . . If we need more people, I want to enlist the Iraqis [for] . . . our common cause."[17]

Mattis is counting on the Iraqi police and army to gradually take over security and deliver services, but he has prepared his combat battalions to govern seven specific regions of the country in the interim by reinforcing the battalions with teams trained to deal with occupation issues. These teams might include a governate support team, a psyops team, a human intelligence exploitation team, civil affairs elements, and perhaps engineers or Seabee units. Combat battalions of five to seven hundred Marines will each be responsible for one of seven governates of southern Iraq over an area three times the size of the state of Virginia. Because of their limited manpower, battalion commanders will have to rely heavily on nongovernment organizations and local tribes to maintain security and provide essential services.

In the southern city of Basra, British general Brims, a single, career military man with the same vast experience in the realities of occupation that Mattis has, is finding a similar situation as he moves his troops through the city. He encounters Iraqis in the Old Town quarter who clearly demonstrate the expectations of Iraq's Shia minority. British paratroopers dismount from their tanks and armored personnel carriers and patrol briefly through the Old Town, guns up, helmets strapped tight. Encountering only welcoming Shia citizens, they retreat to their vehicles and begin to withdraw. The Shia crowds who had just welcomed them start throwing rocks and cursing. One of the battle group commanders, a veteran of Northern Ireland, immediately recognizes what is happening. He orders a halt. He orders his men to get out of their vehicles, stow their weapons, replace their helmets with berets, and mingle with the angry crowd. Instantly the rock throwing ends, and the Shia smile and clap their hands for the troops. They happily welcome their new governors, but they are not going to accept being abandoned.

In Baghdad, the first wave of looters, hundreds of men, women, and children, rushes into government buildings near Marine positions, swiping whatever they can carry—metal desks, plastic chairs, computer keyboards, lamp fixtures, wastebaskets, and empty picture frames. As soon as they are back out on the street, they happily approach the Marines, offering their loot for sale. It is one big swap meet and block party, celebrating the end of decades of torment.

In Saddam City, Mattis moves his forward command base into an abandoned medical clinic as night falls on the mostly triumphant first day of occupation. The clinic has an office and a few patient beds. First watch is set, and the general's platoon open their MREs as chatter over the net gradually dies down, with situation reports trickling in of several casualties from sporadic fighting in different parts of the city.

In the command post, Mattis enjoys a moment of relief with his "battle family," Osowski, Duff, and Cook. The men trade stories they've heard over comms of looting and dancing in the streets, and ask why they are bunking in a run-down clinic while other units are enjoying Saddam's palaces—one lucky grunt is even reportedly sleeping on Saddam's king-size waterbed. The general seems to relax a bit over their little victory dinner of freeze-dried meat and vegetables, but the relief is short-lived. The burden of responsibility for thirty million Iraqi citizens descends almost immediately.

Under the Geneva Convention, Mattis is now directly responsible, with his superiors, for the lives and well-being of all Iraqi citizens. In particular, Mattis will answer for the treatment of the nine million Shia who live in the south, which he has just rampaged through. Pentagon planners estimated that it would take him fifty-five days to reach Baghdad after launching from Kuwait, a task Mattis completed in seventeen. The Pentagon planners have also neglected to tell him exactly how to deal with the mess they've helped him create.

4

Beyond Baghdad

Q: What do you see as the skill set and temperament that are really
   important for a Marine?
MATTIS: Under its rather Prussian exterior, we expect people who
   are very curious. They have got to have a curiosity about life that
   will carry them beyond any kind of institutional learning.

   The Marines enjoy having people who are somewhat mavericks,
   frankly. They protect them and they find many times that that
   sort of independent thinking is a big help to our Corps and its
   mission . . .

   . . . And in that regard, there is nothing new, really, under the
   sun. You can always find a history book somewhere that can
   guide you. So there is a strong bent toward intellectual rigor and a
   historical appreciation of where we're at today.

   Obviously physical fitness. Marines are expected to be at the top
   of their game.

   And then there's another aspect, whether you call it spiritual or
   emotional or psychological, where you actually see your attitude
   as a weapon when you go into tough times that transmits down
   through your ranks. So it's a combination of the mental, the
   physical and the spiritual or as Confucius would put it, body, mind
   and spirit.

   —*"Conversations with History," interview by Harry
   Kreisler, moderator, University of California TV, June 5, 2014*

5 May 2003—Operation Iraqi Freedom 1— Ba'quba, Iraq

Now, in Baghdad, Mattis sees that his northern flank is exposed. Osowski reminds him that the Forty-First Armored Brigade of the Al Nida Division is less than an hour north of the city. Al Nida losses on the Route 6 ambush have not been enough to seriously degrade them. They are still in force and still have senior command guidance. Mattis's order to attack goes out over the net: "At fourteen hundred Zulu, First Recon Battalion will attack north to Ba'quba, locating and identifying enemy forces in order to help the division develop its situation. Be prepared to engage targets of opportunity. We'll link up with LAR at the zero-zero northing and then continue up to the three-zero northing."[1]

It may seem to Mattis that Pentagon war planners who expect to turn over control of Baghdad to Iraqis in June, just sixty days away, are dreaming. Reporters from every newspaper and network in the world now buzz around Mattis thicker than the flies from Saddam City. "War is a human endeavor," he tells *Defense News.* "It's a social problem and we have to have rather modest expectations . . . no war is over until the enemy says it is. We may think it's over, we may declare it over but in fact the enemy gets a vote."[2]

The vote is definitely out, since no Iraqi senior commanders are in custody. Like Baghdad Bob, the broadcaster who once assured listeners that coalition forces were being destroyed in every battle but is now silent, Iraqi leaders are also now silent but still somewhere close by, unless they have been smuggled across a border. US commanders issue a deck of playing cards with the pictures, names, and titles of fifty-two Iraqi leaders on them. In addition to the search for Saddam's inexplicably missing WMDs (weapons of mass destruction), coalition forces are now engaged in nationwide manhunts, as well as civil administration.

Combat troops are being transitioned to playing the role of traffic cops and small-town detectives among people who can't speak

English and are sometimes engaged in generations-long vendettas against their neighbors. This is the first sustained test of the troops actually implementing Mattis's commander's intent. It will also reveal whether or not the troops can execute the tactics learned from Los Angeles police detectives in Iraq.

Directly counter to Mattis's commander's intent among his Marines, US Army units to the west and north of Baghdad have been rounding up whole villages to look for the faces on the playing cards. To make matters worse, they don't even have a system to process the thousands of people they detain. At first, prisoners are held in barbed wire holding pens or soccer stadiums. Soon they will be shipped to the infamous Abu Ghraib prison, lighting the fuse of the insurgency.

In Ad Diwaniyah, ninety-five miles south of Baghdad, Lieutenant Colonel Sam Mundy, commander of Mattis's 3/5 Marine battalion, meets Brigadier General Fuad Hani Faris, a wounded Iraqi veteran. As Faris disclosed in a survey done by Marine civil teams, he moved to Ad Diwaniyah so his wife could be among her large family. Mundy greets Faris with the respect due a general, a husband, and a grandfather. In return, General Faris happily welcomes Mundy and his Marines, who replace the combat-oriented Seventy-Fifth Army Rangers. The Rangers have been patrolling the city in armored vehicles, behind machine guns and mirrored sunglasses, before disappearing back into their secure encampment. Together Faris and Mundy begin to help transition the people of Ad Diwaniyah from war to peace and from dictatorship to the beginnings of liberty.

Because Marines love to rename places to honor their history, the 3/5 headquarters company moves into the administration building of Ad Qadisiyah University and calls it Camp Edson, in honor of the legendary Edson's Raiders of World War II. The 3/5, also known as the Postal Marines, deliver mail to the First Marine Division as part of their regular duty. While they are administrating and rebuilding Ad Diwaniyah, the Postal Marines will also handle about five- to eight thousand cubic feet of mail per day manually.

Mundy and Faris form one of the first civil-military operations in postinvasion Iraq, while fighting continues in the northern part of the country, around Baghdad. Because Mattis stressed to his commanders the importance of tending to the postwar needs of Iraqi children first, Mundy assigns Naval Mobile Construction Battalion 7 to begin work with local contractors rebuilding 18 schools in the city. Further orders from Mattis direct all Marines to grow their mustaches to look more like the locals, to remove their sunglasses, and to wave and make eye contact as they patrol on foot, not in armored vehicles. Because Ad Diwaniyah's children are taken care of first, the Marines begin to receive wide support in the city as they go on to rebuild the courthouse, a jail, and a police station.

The 3/5 continues to provide security, including arresting looters and rebuilding infrastructure, as General Faris organizes a new Ad Diwaniyah police force, relieving Mundy and his Marines of some of that difficult civil responsibility. By July 4, Mundy and Faris will be celebrating America's Independence Day together by grilling hot dogs on the campus of the reopened Ad Qadisiyah University.

10 April 2003—The White House, Washington, DC

National Security Advisor Condoleezza Rice and Secretary of State Colin Powell are concerned about the whereabouts of Saddam Hussein. Still convinced that he may have access to undiscovered stockpiles of poison gas and possibly radioactive dirty bombs, they access back channels to push for the seizure and search of his hometown of Tikrit. With a population of just 30,000, Tikrit is also the tribal base of Saddam's Ba'ath Party, and so is a primarily political rather than military target. Also, it seems the Kurds have crossed the border when they heard that Baghdad collapsed and are holding Iraqi territory near Tikrit, a second political reason to seize the city. The US Army's Fourth Infantry Division, operating north of Baghdad, has plans to take the city in about ten days, but apparently Washington can't wait that long. I MEF commander Conway gets an "unofficial" call from Washington, asking whether they can take care of this problem. Conway assures his bosses the Marines will get it done. He hangs up and calls Mattis.

0100 Hours—April 12, 2003—First Marine Division Forward Command Post—Baghdad

Although Tikrit is 93 miles north of the Marines' area of operation, it is now on Mattis's growing task list. Mattis and his second-in-command, Brigadier General John Kelly, review intelligence reports that indicate about two thousand paramilitaries and elements of the Republican Guards' Adnan Division are in the city. The two commanders watch video from unmanned aerial vehicles that show abandoned military equipment in the city. Mattis turns to Kelly, says a few words, and Tikrit is suddenly at the top of Kelly's task list.

Kelly saddles up with a task force of three thousand Marines and six hundred vehicles from the First, Second, and Third LAR Battalions, Golf Company from battalion 2/23, artillery battalion 5/11, SEAL team 3, engineers, and a combat support element. They have four days' worth of supplies. He's not taking any Abrams tanks; they take too much fuel and would have limited use in the small streets of the city. The Third Marine Air Wing will be his tanks in the sky for heavy fire support. They call the group Task Force Tripoli.

The objective is to seize Tikrit, prevent the escape of any organized military units, and find the ace of spades—Saddam Hussein. Reporters are all over Kelly as the task force moves out. They want to know what the operation is, where he's headed, and why.

Kelly says only, "We want all jihad fighters to come here. That way we can kill them all before they get bus tickets to New York City."[3]

Mattis travels with his jump platoon to the hours-long daily meeting with Baghdad's city leaders and Pentagon planners in the Palestine Hotel. General Jay Garner of the Pentagon's Office for Reconstruction and Humanitarian Assistance (ORHA) generally leads the discussions for the coalition, so Mattis is reduced from battlefield commander to a silent clerk taking notes. Every day more leaders show up with more complaints, requests, and inquiries, some of which go onto Mattis's now endless task list.

Doubtless he envies the uncomplicated assignment of Kelly, riding into battle in the footsteps of Alexander the Great in 331 BC toward the epic Battle of Arbela near Tikrit. There, Alexander defeated the much larger army of Darius, the king of Persia, a victory that crushed the Persian Empire and began the enduring dominance of the West over the Middle East and Asia. Kelly is also making history as he extends the Marine expedition to nearly 450 miles, from the Persian Gulf to Tikrit. It is the longest sustained march in Marine history.

Meanwhile, the endless droning and paperwork of the daily civil administration meeting is testing the patience of Mattis and his staff. Making matters worse, it soon becomes obvious that Garner and the ORHA don't have the knowledge, money, or manpower to get their job done. The years of infighting between Secretary of Defense Rumsfeld and the commander in chief of Central Command, General Tommy Franks, has left a gaping hole where the postwar plan and resources should be.

The ORHA doesn't have a well-trained, coherent team of professionals, but rather an odd collection of young Republican campaign workers and other novices. It doesn't even appear to have enough of those. As the incompetence of the ORHA becomes obvious, their replacement, the Coalition Provisional Authority (CPA), headed by Ambassador Paul Bremer, is being readied in Washington. It will be a case of partial incompetence being replaced by complete disaster.

In Washington, DC, Rumsfeld is being interviewed on *Meet the Press*, revealing the lack of critical thinking and planning that is about to engulf America in its most costly guerrilla insurgency since Vietnam.[4]

Q: General Garner will have an interim government in place in a few weeks—would you think that's a pretty good timetable?

RUMSFELD: At the present time the war is still going on, and it's a little premature to be setting timetables and dates. I just don't know. The first task is to win the war . . . , and then to get the Iraqi people to think through exactly what kind of a model they want to select for their own government.

Q: . . . What's going to happen the first time we hold an election in Iraq, and it turns out the radicals win?

In Baghdad, Mattis watches as the situation quickly overwhelms the ORHA. He immediately recognizes the repeat of history. In *The Insurrection in Mesopotamia, 1920*, British lieutenant general Aylmer Haldane writes, "We were hampered by having a 'scratch and somewhat incongruous team' of administrators, with the majority possessing 'little exact knowledge of the people they were called upon to govern.'"[5] Mattis, who has read Haldane, no doubt understands the disaster that is unfolding; he anticipated it, knowing Rumsfeld and the Pentagon as he does, and has been preparing his Marines to shoulder the burden of occupation, on their own, for over a year. He knows his battalions, reinforced with civil (C-5) teams, are keeping the lights on, the water running, and the bad guys dead, so he doesn't complain to his superiors or interfere in what some Marines might call the "rolling clusterfuck" in front of him. Instead, he sits quietly in the meetings alert and on duty in spite of the numbing drudgery, adding fumbled item after fumbled item to his own task list.

★ ★ ★ ★

Mattis executes his radical plan for occupation by sending home 15,000 of the 23,000 Marines he's brought with him. For them, Operation Iraqi Freedom is over. He sends home all of his tanks, artillery, amtracs, and armored personnel carriers. He keeps only his light armored vehicles and the Third Marine Air Wing. It is a bold move, and directly counter to the "heavy footprint" policy of the US Army and the lack of policy of Ambassador Bremer and the CPA.

"Most of us were flabbergasted to be told to leave Baghdad at the end of April," Colonel John Toolan says. "I turned over my sector, which was east Baghdad, to 2nd ACR [Armored Cavalry Regiment], which had about one-fifth the capability of my regiment."[6]

Before Toolan ships out, Mattis takes him aside and tells him the situation is bad and getting worse, and the Marines will be back soon. "Don't lose sight of what you've learned, because you're going to need to get your guys ready to come back."[7]

The general picks a date in the future out of the air, November 10—the Marine Corps' birthday. This, he predicts, will be the target date for his troops to be "recocked" and ready to fight again. He misses the date by two days; the redeployment order will arrive November 7.

Even more unexpectedly, Mattis writes that the configuration of the US Army is wrong for an occupation force. They need more infantry, while the Marines need less. He says, "The lack of Army dismounts [regular infantry] is creating a void in personal contact and public perception of our civil-military ops."

In place of the First Division, the entire Polish contingent of two hundred soldiers take over command of the remaining coalition forces in the south. General James Conway, commander of I MEF, sums up the situation and he and Mattis's humanitarian approach after attending the transfer ceremony in Baghdad with Mattis:

As we rolled south out of Baghdad for these provinces, we did so with a certain amount of trepidation. Marines don't traditionally do nation-building or security operations. We have no doctrine for it. We weren't sure where the resources would come from. And we weren't sure how we would be received by the people of southern Iraq, who had seen American troops attack up through their governates . . . [But] in some regards, a negative can become a positive. A lack of doctrine allowed us to pass some very simple rules to our Marines and soldiers. They were; treat others as you would like to be treated. Deal with the people with fairness and firmness and dignity. Among other things, we empha-sized the children. They are the future of this country. It's hard to be angry with someone when he's doing good things for your children.[8]

In addition to preparing for civil affairs, Mattis spends months before the invasion working on legal affairs with I MEF's legal of-fice. Much of the time he works on the rules of engagement so all Marines will stay out of legal jeopardy in all situations. He twice issues detailed guidance on the law of war to his Marines and continuously uses and explains the division's motto, "No Better Friend, No Worse Enemy," to drive home his commander's intent. Simplifying the intent to four words, the motto of the division, en-sures that every grunt will have a clear moral compass for bringing peaceful order to civilians but deadly chaos to the enemy.

Mattis lets everyone under his command know that "discipline will be severely tested by an unscrupulously led enemy who is likely to commit Law of War violations."[9] Leaving nothing to chance, he orders his staff judge advocate, Lieutenant Colonel John R. Ewers, and deputy, Major Joseph Lore, to teach classes on the rules of engagement and law of war before and throughout the invasion. The two men create a team that travels the battlefield, responding to legal issues even before the dust settles. This level of planning and preparation for occupation of the country was not even imagined in the Pentagon's Phase IV occupation war plans.

Even now, as the division is winding down operations, Mattis posts messages nearly every day on the division website, communicating constantly with his Marines, particularly those he hasn't met personally at and around the front lines. In this sense, Rumsfeld is correct: battle is now also about the flow of data. Posting to the website revolutionizes the chain of command, replacing the traditional top-down "command and control" structure with the horizontal and democratic "command and feedback." Now front-line commanders are free to make quick decisions and seize opportunities without asking permission.

While First Division is washing down, packing up, and shipping equipment back to Pendleton, Mattis tours the seven governates administered by his civil-reinforced battalions for a final inspection. He pays particular deference to tribal elders and civic leaders who are unhappy for one reason or another. He sits with them to speak of the future of Iraq—privately, man to man.

Near Nasariyah, site of some of the most bitter fighting in the campaign, he calls together a gathering of local restive leaders— men hardened by years of war and dictatorship. Men with deep scars they didn't get from being mechanics, farmers, and shopkeepers. Men whose grandfathers taught them to smile at the powerful but never trust them, to keep their knives sharpened and guns oiled. Some harbor generations-long grudges against each other, some say they hate Saddam, and some say "George Bush! Good!" They are disarmed at the meeting, their weapons held by Mattis's security platoon. They sit in a classroom in a school the Marines are rebuilding. Water is served, introductions are made. Hard eyes scrutinize the slim, physically unimposing man in front of them. Mattis gauges the hard looks and concealed mistrust around the room. His first thoughts, as always, go to the safety of his Marines. He addresses them in the coarse, direct language of men used to war.

He is sincere and deadly calm. He says some version of his now well-known quote:

"I'm going to plead with you, do not cross us. Because if you do, the survivors will write about what we do here for the next 10,000 years."[10]

5

A Girl Named Alice

A friend of Mattis's said, "A few years after enlisting he met a girl named Alice who said that she would marry him only if he left the Corps." Mattis began the resignation process, but his fellow Marines stopped him.

The friend continued, "Basically, a lot of the officers got together and tried to talk Alice into withdrawing her demand. They told her that his future was too bright."

Alice agreed, and a wedding date was set.

—*from Dexter Filkins, "James Mattis: A Warrior in Washington,"* The New Yorker, *May 29, 2017*

July 1968—Columbia River, Central Washington State

For 419 million years, as North America split and drifted apart from the rest of Pangaea, volcanic eruptions poured a thick layer of molten basalt across the northwestern edge of the new continent. Rainwater pouring off the volcanoes and new mountain ranges cut a deep V channel, 1,900 miles long, through the hard, volcanic basalt toward the Pacific Ocean.

Seventeen-year-old Jim Mattis, amateur geologist and historian, sits on a sun-warmed basalt boulder watching the deep, black Columbia River roll away west to the Pacific. He ponders the sweep of a million years, then ten million years, then a hundred million, then four hundred million.

In less than two months, on his birthday, he'll have to register for the military draft. They'll take him, put a rifle in his hands, and send him to the front of the line, walking point, looking for a gunfight on the jungle paths of Vietnam. It's all over the news. Ten thousand Americans just got killed in the Tet Offensive in January. They'll take him all right and put him right up front.

All new guys walk point, at the front of the patrol, because the old guys with only a short time left on their tours figure they have used up all their luck. New guys haven't used up their luck yet, so they walk point, up front. So is he lucky enough, brave enough, to walk point? He has swum the half-mile breadth of the river, but that's a different kind of bravery.

The Yakama and Nez Perce people who have lived on the river for five thousand years have their own tests of bravery, the rites of passage for a young man. What will be his test? His head is still full of a boy's questions about the world and his place in it. "I had a natural curiosity about life," he said of himself in later years. "Eventually, that became very helpful as a military officer charged with taking people off to war."[1]

By challenging himself physically, he has developed a strong core of confidence and self-control, but he still has a wild streak that continues to push him to take chances and test his luck. He reflected on his rambunctious youth along the Columbia, "I nearly missed graduation because I was drunk," and he spent a lot of time "swimming in the Columbia River, drinking surreptitiously, and chasing the ladies."[2]

This maverick trait is also vital to a warrior, according to his own estimation in later years. "Take the mavericks in your service, the ones that wear rumpled uniforms and look like a bag of mud but whose ideas are so offsetting that they actually upset the people in the bureaucracy. One of your primary jobs is to take the risk and protect these people, because if they are not nurtured in your service, the enemy will bring their contrary ideas to you."[3]

10 September 1968

Jim Mattis walks onto the Central Washington College campus just days after his eighteenth birthday, having just registered for the military draft. The tree-shaded campus occupies most of the farming village of Ellensburg, an isolated river valley on the Yakima bordered by the denuded, channeled scablands a hundred miles east of the Columbia River. As a first step away from home, it barely qualifies as going away to college, since a two-hour drive puts him back on the quiet street where he grew up.

In class, he pursues his interests in history, geology, and native North American tribes but is frequently distracted by a growing dilemma: Is his patriotic duty to protest the Vietnam War or help fight it by following his older brother, Tom, into the Marine Corps? If his problem fades for a moment, there is always someone burning their draft card in a TV news report or yelling through a loudspeaker about it on campus. Away from the political isolation of Richland and its defense industry citizens, the "Free Love," "Ban the Bomb" counterculture is loud and getting louder as the body counts escalate. For the moment, as a full-time student, he is safe to ponder his decision. But the question of honor begins to weigh more heavily.

If, as the protestors scream, the war is immoral, then Mattis is honor-bound to oppose it. If, as his older brother, Tom, believes, the Marine Corps is the patriotic course, then he must support it. There is no help for the decision from his family upbringing. Military service, while a clear duty for his parents and their generation, has never been valued over other career paths in their home. He might be happiest just being a history professor and fishing in the Yakima and Columbia. Why should he risk getting shot in a war on the other side of the world?

If he refuses to make a decision, the Selective Service Bureau, commonly known as the draft board, is waiting to make it for him. In fact, they already have. Out of the 365 days in his birth year, his birth date of September 8 is selected as seventh in line to be inducted. They are taking everyone up to number 165 of that year, so it seems the draft board has already put him at the front of the line. The day his studies end, he will be ordered to report to the nearest induction center. There, he will be assigned a number and sent wherever the military needs him most. Unless he enlists. Then he will have a choice of service branch and possibly an area of specialty.

Then there is the nagging question of his luck. Is he lucky? If he is going to be a warrior and not a professor, he will need to be lucky. As he would know from his wide-ranging reading of history and native peoples, the warriors of the local Nez Perce, Sioux, and Crow tribes covered themselves and their horses with lucky talismans before going to war. Napoleon's most important question about possible new commanders was "Is he known to be lucky?"[4] In Vietnam, Tom's buddies carry the ace of spades playing card in their helmet or a pocket-size Bible over their heart for luck. Unfortunately, going by his first encounter with the military, in which he is one of the first in line for induction, it seems that he is not lucky.

And his luck will definitely not improve with the ladies if he joins up. Short hair and a possible reputation as a "baby killer" after the recent news reports of civilian massacres are not going to help him or his fellow soldiers with the long-haired, free-love hippie chicks who occupy a significant portion of his brain space. Walking point in a steaming, booby-trapped jungle may be about even with being rejected by young women on his list of downsides of military service.

Months fly by in a happy blur of intense study, skirt-chasing, and drinking contests. When the thought does occasionally push its way to the front of his mind, it still seems there is no upside to military service. It is a fun-wrecking, dangerous, maybe even fatal decision to join the United States military in 1969, particularly for those who are unlucky. Even so, the idea of being a tough Marine has always appealed to him.

He writes letters to his brother, Tom, who has been in the Marines for two years and is now in Vietnam. It's true that now more than ever, military service, especially in the Marines, is the ultimate test of courage. And he has never and would never shrink from a test of courage. It is a point of personal honor and pride.[5]

Finally, in his sophomore year, he makes his decision. Luck or no luck, ladies or no ladies, Jim Mattis walks into a Marine Corps recruitment office and signs up for the Marine's Platoon Leaders Course (PLC). He says to an interviewer years later about this decision, "I don't think I had the intention of making it a career at that point. I wasn't closed-minded about it. . . . In those days we had the draft, so there was little choice."[6]

But the decision is not as casual as he will later imply. In Vietnam, the Tet Offensive has just killed ten thousand American soldiers and Marines, so the American military is aggressively seeking new blood to refill the ranks. Does he really want to be walking point in a jungle, looking for a gunfight?

Reinforcing his possible unluckiness, just weeks after he enlists, President Richard Nixon launches his "madman theory" by sending bombers armed with nuclear weapons jetting toward the Soviet border for three days in a row. As Nixon tells his chief of staff, H. R. Haldeman, "I call it the Madman Theory, Bob. I want the North Vietnamese to believe I've reached the point where I might do anything to stop the war. We'll just slip the word to them that, 'for God's sake, you know Nixon is obsessed about communism. We can't restrain him when he's angry—and he has his hand on the nuclear button' and Ho Chi Minh himself will be in Paris in two days begging for peace."[7]

Apparently Nixon's bluff works. The military term for this maneuver is a feint; "an offensive action involving contact with the adversary conducted for the purpose of deceiving the adversary as to the location and/or time of the actual main offensive action." In this case, the main offensive action is taking place at the negotiating table.

The fact that war and politics often use the same terms, as Mattis and his future platoon leader classmates are learning, is because they are actually parts of the same phenomenon. Among their fundamental classroom textbooks is *On War* by German general Carl von Clausewitz. The general clarifies the eternal truth of the dance between war and politics: "War is simply the continuation of state policy by other means."

Along with other diplomatic efforts by Secretary of State Henry Kissinger, Nixon's nuclear-armed feint causes peace talks to begin again and continue for the next three years. In this time, Mattis finds himself becoming more comfortable with the prospect of military life. It appeals to his need for clear direction. It tests his strength and intelligence, and demands that he face the big questions still lurking in his young mind about morality, duty, and the killing of other human beings for a government. Mattis graduates from the PLC as a second lieutenant in the Marine Corps, skilled as a rifleman and fledgling leader of Marines, about the time a major breakthrough in the peace talks occurs.

On May 8, 1972, under intense domestic pressure to end the war, President Nixon accepts a cease-fire. He will withdraw from South Vietnam, but will do so without North Vietnam reciprocating. For any student of war, and probably for Mattis by this time, this is obviously a tactical blunder. Nixon seems to believe that America's mighty military has reached its practical limit. He also seems to believe that political negotiation alone can conclude the war. Within ten days Kissinger returns from Paris and holds a press conference in Washington. He naively announces, in a statement reminiscent of British Prime Minister Neville Chamberlain after concluding a similar agreement with Adolf Hitler, that "peace is at hand."[8]

This cease-fire agreement is simply a political counterfeint by Nixon's adversaries, Ho Chi Minh, the Communist leader of North Vietnam, and his commanding general Nguyen Giap, both ardent followers of another master of politics and warfare, Chinese general Sun Tzu. In this counterfeint, the true offensive action will take place on the ground in Vietnam. When America has withdrawn nearly all of its forces and is at its weakest militarily, the North Vietnamese launch the 1975 Spring Offensive. America is driven out of Vietnam in a humiliating rout, just as the French were twenty years before them. It is a hammer blow that destroys America's confidence and powerful military legacy. In defeat and disgrace, America retreats from the world stage, buries its fifty thousand war dead, and turns against its own military.

It is a disheartening time to be seen in the uniforms of the United States military, but Mattis is now committed to pursue his higher education through the Marine Corps. He wears the cloth and Prussian "high and tight" haircut that marks him as a Marine. In many parts of America, military uniforms are drawing insults and hard stares. Soldiers and Marines returning from war through San Francisco airport are met by violent crowds, spit on, and called "baby killers" to their face.

In spite of this reflected disgrace and open disrespect, Mattis's commitment to the Marine Corps extends through his achievement of a master's degree in history from the Marine Corps Command and Staff College. Particularly useful for a career in the Marine Corps is his study of the recently translated Chinese general Sun Tzu. Perhaps like the rest of the country, which is seeking inner peace through the new imports of Eastern philosophies, he absorbs lessons from Sun Tzu that were well applied by the victorious Nguyen Giap. Sun Tzu says, in his *Art of War*, on the skills a general should possess: "The four desires are: desire for the extraordinary and unexpected in strategy, desire for thoroughness in security, desire for calm among the masses, and desire for unity of hearts and minds."[9] The phrase "hearts and minds" has entered the English language too late to help America in Vietnam, but it comes in time to help prepare Mattis and his warrior classmates for wars to come in the East.

The Eastern philosophy of Taoism is fundamental to the understanding of Sun Tzu. In Taoism, the concept of yin and yang—of duality, derived from the observation of the ebb and flow of the natural world—is essential. The roots of Taoism go back at least to the fourth century BC, where it began in the philosophical School of Naturalists, also called the School of Yin-yang, derived from one of the oldest texts of Chinese culture, the *Yijing*, which offers a philosophy to regulate human behavior based on the alternating cycles of nature. Taoist strategies are often "peaceful and passive, favoring silence over speech." This form of communication avoids confrontation and accents the spiritual, and thus the political solution to the human invention of war. No doubt deeply appealing to Mattis as a student of history and the natural world, the duality of Taoism seems to have informed his approach to warfare profoundly.

Mattis seems completely comfortable with the opposing yin and yang of compassion and violence in his later statements to his men—"Be polite. Be professional. But have a plan to kill everyone you meet"[10]—and to his enemies—"I'm going to plead with you, do not cross us. Because if you do, the survivors will write about what we do here for 10,000 years."[11] This philosophy also seems to be at the heart of the motto he later popularizes for Marines of the First Marine Division: "No better friend, no worse enemy."

Along with Mattis, America's top corporate leaders are soon quoting Sun Tzu. His pithier quotes are being shouted in the locker rooms of leading sports teams and exhorted in the speeches of politicians. As Mattis's graduate studies of warfare advance through the US Marine Corps Amphibious Warfare School, the pragmatic politics of Thucydides of ancient Greece, the amoral strategies of Niccolo Machiavelli, and the endless debates about Vietnam, Mattis seems to have absorbed the natural interplay, the yin and yang, of warfare and politics.

20 July 1978

Captain James Mattis takes command of Kilo Company of the Third Marine Battalion of the Third Marine Division (3/3) under the command of Colonel Ken Jordan, a Vietnam veteran.[12] His life is now out of classrooms and onto the rolling decks of warships. In September he deploys as part of the Thirty-First Marine Amphibious Unit (MAU) on a deployment or "float" to the Philippines, Hong Kong, Taiwan, Japan, Okinawa, and Korea. On this float the Marines find boat people, war refugees fleeing the genocides and political purges of the killing fields of Vietnam, Cambodia, and Laos in overloaded, open fishing boats, often floating aimlessly and out of fuel in the open sea. In emotional rescues, the Marines are literal lifesavers, and veterans of Vietnam like Jordan are revered by the refugees as faithful brothers in arms.

The human aftermath of US political defeat in Vietnam and the ensuing political instability crowds every available inch of deck space around Mattis. They fill the sweaty hold of the ship, clutching their children and meager possessions, often shaking with fear and trauma. This is Mattis's first real-world experience of war as a Marine. As soldiers of the navy, the first in and often the last out of smaller, third-world conflicts, Marines frequently end up with the responsibility for evacuation of war victims. Compassion is a necessary part of an officer's training and here it is put to the test as Mattis shares overheated sleeping spaces, food, and a few toilets, often for days on end, with successive swarms of desperate, frequently ill people who don't speak English.

The 3/3 returns to base at Kaneohe, Hawaii, for additional combat exercises and training. Jordan and his command-level colleagues are tasked with standing up several battalion landing teams (BLTs). They use the Kilauea training area in the mouth of an ancient volcano to simulate helicopter assaults and to launch "seize and defend," "seize and hold," and "attack and continue" missions against "aggressor forces" of other Marines, who attempt to confuse and defeat them. Mattis transfers field command of Kilo Company and joins the battalion command center as an S-3 or staff officer. Under the supervision of Jordan, he learns the intricacies of intelligence, operations, and logistics. He evaluates situation reports from the field, issues fragmentary (partial) orders, and masters the logistics of supplying combat companies on the move in battle.

As if on cue, in November 1979, theocratic Iranians overthrow the ruling shah of Iran,[13] and students overrun the US Embassy in Tehran, taking fifty-two American hostages. For a month, President Jimmy Carter's State Department attempts to negotiate with the young revolutionaries. As any student of Thucydides such as Mattis would know, this is a modern repetition of the Melian Dialogue, and destined for failure.

The Melian Dialogue was between the nearly defenseless Greek island people of Melos and the overwhelmingly powerful military emissaries of Athens who tried to appeal to the Melians' pragmatism. Instead of fighting a costly war they were certain to lose, they suggested that the Melians should simply surrender under reasonable terms and agree to pay tribute to Athens. The Melians appealed to the Athenians' sense of decency: they had done nothing to Athens, asked nothing of Athens, and so felt the gods were on their side. Neither side was able to sway the other, and the negotiations failed. Today the Melian Dialogue and its inevitable result is often called political realism. It demonstrates the foolishness of using decency or fairness as a concept in a political negotiation, and that selfish, pragmatic concerns drive wars. Knowing that if they did not attack, they would be seen as weak and invite an attack on themselves from rival Sparta, the Athenians attacked Melos. They killed every man on the island and took every woman into slavery. The Melian culture disappeared from the world.

President Carter, unlike the warrior Athenians, dickers endlessly with the fanatic Muslim students of Tehran. The students insist on the decency and fairness of reparations for America's support of the deposed shah of Iran. And so negotiations predictably break down.

Yet Carter cannot face the prospect of an annihilating attack on the Iranians, and so, again predictably, invites an attack from America's rival, the Soviet Union. Seeing Carter's fecklessness with his overwhelming American military in the face of a few lightly armed students, the Soviet Union, as Sparta in this replay of history, invades Afghanistan on December 24.

Finally, in response to this Soviet aggression and continuing Iranian intransigence, President Carter acts. He orders a show of force by the Thirty-First MAU, including Mattis and the Third Marine Division, in early February 1980. Not exactly an Athenian annihilation, this display is intended to show the Soviets that America can deploy ground troops to the region if necessary.

When this bluster fails, Carter orders a helicopter assault on the Tehran embassy—a rescue mission. Mattis and other Marines of the 3/3 are flown from the USS *Coral Sea* to the USS *Nimitz* to plan Operation Eagle Claw and prepare a second wave in case the helos fail. The rescue mission goes down in a howling sandstorm. At the cost of two helicopters and crew, Carter abandons the mission. Ayatollah Ruhollah Khomeini, leader of the Muslim students, credits divine intervention on behalf of Islam. His prestige skyrockets, and the theocratic Iranian Revolution solidifies its hold on Iran. Watching this clusterfuck of military and political humiliation, Mattis and three thousand disgusted Marines spend sixty-five days sailing in a circle in the Indian Ocean, "training, doing PT [physical training] on the deck and sweating in the hold."[14] The Soviet Union sends more troops into Afghanistan, ignoring the feckless denunciations of American politicians.

The 3/3 sails to Perth, Australia, to recover from the morale-killing Operation Eagle Claw. The troops, including a lively group of young Marine lieutenants who, having shaved their heads, are known as the Coneheads after the *Saturday Night Live* sketch, descend on the pubs and sidewalks of Perth in a frenzy of pent-up frustration.

US Marines rampaging through Perth, like a combination of Mardi Gras and running with the bulls, has been a tradition since

World War II, when Marines turned the Japanese invaders back at Guadalcanal, saving Australia from imminent Japanese invasion and certain conquest. Australians, particularly the young ladies, have never forgotten what the Marines did, and maintain a tradition of offering a particularly warm welcome to them.

Jordan says of Mattis at this time, "He'd smile and joke with the men, have a drink or two, but never get wild or anything. He was just a good guy and heck of an officer."[15] Lieutenant Dave Pittelkow, one of the Coneheads, remembers, "He wasn't dancing on the tables like some of the guys. He was a Marine officer. He'd stay and have a laugh with us, then leave early."[16]

By late March, Mattis and the 3/3 are back in Kaneohe, Hawaii. On this Hawaiian island crawling with lonely Marines, Mattis finds an attractive and unattached young lady. Out of deference to Mattis's family, we'll call her only by her first name. His relationship with Alice begins slowly, so Mattis keeps it from most of his closest colleagues. However, because she shares his reverential worldview and has a deep appreciation for the Marines Corps, the romance grows.

He's ready for this romance. Now a thirty-year-old Marine captain, Mattis has traveled the world, met civilian and military leaders in dozens of nations, and seen much of what the world has to offer. He has tested himself in extreme conditions and passed those tests. Even as he continues his diligent study into the nature of mankind, he has found many of the answers he sought, particularly about himself. He has found his place among men in the brotherhood of arms. His obvious self-confidence and comfort in the simple, Spartan lifestyle of a Marine officer signals his maturity and readiness for a more serious relationship. He relinquishes command in matters of the heart to Alice.

The lovers' idyll is short-lived. In April 1980, the Thirty-First MAU, including Mattis and the 3/3, are at sea again, heading to ports of call in Africa, the Middle East, and the Philippines. They are deployed for over three months, returning to Hawaii in July. On August 4, 1980,

Mattis assumes command of the relatively new configuration of a weapons company for the 3/3. Until recently, Marine infantry battalions have possessed only four rifle companies, each with a complement of combined arms such as mortars and rifles. Now the 3/3 is to stand up a company that handles specialized weapons systems such as 60- and 81-millimeter mortars and Dragon anti-armor weapons.

Pittelkow commands weapons company's Dragon anti-armor platoon under Mattis. While reviewing the performance of Pittelkow's platoon, Mattis notices the young lieutenant giving orders to his men, but not pitching in quite as much with the physical work of setting up the heavy, dangerous equipment. He pulls his lieutenant aside and counsels him on the shared work ethic of the Marine Corps: "Y'know, Dave, the privilege of command is command. You don't get a bigger tent."[17]

With his natural talents for organization and his experience as an S-3 operations officer guiding him, Mattis earns this fitness report from Jordan on November 30, 1980: "As the weapons company commander, Capt. Mattis serves as the battalion fire support coordinator, where his duties require detailed knowledge of the control, capabilities and coordination of the supporting arms, in addition to the normal leadership responsibilities faced by a company commander. In all respects, Capt. Mattis consistently performs in an outstanding manner. He is intelligent, confident and highly principled, a stern but positive leader who commands a fine company."[18]

His preparation for married life is also moving ahead. Mattis decides to propose to Alice, and she says yes. They set the date for the ceremony in late June, to coincide with his return from scheduled exercises of the 3/3 in the East. They plan a quiet, private ceremony with close family and few friends. However, a few days before departure, Alice begins having doubts. Being married to a young Marine means a series of months-long deployments, interrupted only by brief periods of intense focus and long hours on Marine Corps business even when at home. There will be frequent moves to different parts of the world, and the constant threat of having officers knocking on her door one day in full dress uniform to deliver the worst possible news. As much as she respects the sacrifices that Marines make, she realizes that she's not prepared to do the same. The conversation they have will change the course of both of their lives.

She asks Mattis to resign from the military. His choice is simple: her or the Corps. He cannot have both. Mattis frets over the decision, but ultimately he chooses love. He agrees to resign his commission and begins the process. The upcoming float will be his last. Alarmed at the loss of such a rising star and well-liked leader, Mattis's Marines launch a love assault. Their wives and fiancées, some of whom have not before met her, visit Alice. Some bring their men to vouch for the realities of life with a Marine. The avalanche of support is overwhelming. Alice's deep misgivings subside with this new-found, extended Marine family, people who have pledged their love to her, to Jim, and to their family to come. She finally relents. With only hours before the 3/3 ships out, the June wedding is back on track. Mattis trashes his resignation forms, grabs his sea bag for a long deployment, and heads out the door. He likely stows his rioting emotions with the rest of his gear.

On February 21, 1981, the 3/3 and Captain Mattis departs on another West Pacific float. The Marines conduct partnered training exercises at sea and on land with elements of the Navy and Marine Air Force as they make ports of call in Okinawa, Korea, Hong Kong, the Philippines, Singapore, Sri Lanka, Diego Garcia, Thailand, and once again, Australia. Nothing stays private very long during months at sea in close quarters, so when they make landfall at various ports, Mattis is repeatedly subjected to hair-raising bachelor parties with the Coneheads and others, particularly in Perth. They are at sea this time for over four months.

On this deployment he receives the following fitness report from battalion commander Jordan on 25 May 1981:

Recommended for the Leftwich Award for outstanding leadership, Capt. Mattis exceeds all expectations for tactical knowledge, leadership ability and operational skill. A dedicated, hard-working, dependable officer, he was instrumental in assisting this BLT to attain a score of 97 on the recent CRE [Combat Readiness Evaluation], the highest score in the brigade. His company consistently excels in quantifiable areas, and he sets the example for his men. He is intelligent, and expresses himself well verbally and in writing.[19]

Back in Hawaii, the wedding proceeds with customary frenzy. As relatives from the mainland begin to arrive and caterers prepare, Mattis receives word that his bride-to-be has reconsidered. She realizes that Mattis is going to have an exceptional future in the Corps. His time will increasingly not be his own. She simply can't imagine their married life being anything other than an unhappy waiting game. She realizes she'll be a burden to him and his career.

This time only a few truly close friends rush to the couple's support. They beg Alice to reconsider and to be patient. Jim Mattis, they stress, is worth the wait. It won't always be as it has been recently. The men tell her, truthfully, that he hasn't looked at another woman since their engagement. Finally Mattis and Alice have an agonizing talk, but she is not swayed. The wedding is canceled.

On July 28, 1981, Mattis relinquishes command of 3/3 weapons company Kilo. He is promoted to the rank of major and leaves Hawaii to return home to the Pacific Northwest, where he takes command of a quiet Marine recruiting office in Portland, Oregon, near the banks of his beloved Columbia River. Like the first Marines, who remained unmarried while in the Corps, he returns to the simple, monkish life of reading and fishing that he knew before Alice and the 3/3, even before the Marine Corps.

He will never marry.

6

The Enemy of My Enemy

Until the Iranian people can get rid of this theocracy, these guys who think they can tell the people even which candidates they get a choice of, it's going to be very, very difficult. This is a regime that employs surrogates, like Lebanese Hezbollah to threaten Israel, to murder the former Lebanese prime minister, murder Israeli tourists in Bulgaria which caused the European Union to put more severe sanctions on Iran than the Americans have ever put on Iran.

. . . The Iranian people are not the problem. The Iranian people are definitely not the problem, it's the regime that sends agents around to murder ambassadors in Pakistan or in Washington DC. It's the regime that provides missiles to Lebanese Hezbollah or the Houthi in Yemen.

. . . So somehow, you don't want to unite the Iranian people with that unpopular regime because if you pressure them both then they will grow together. We've got to make certain that the Iranian people know that we don't have any conflict with them.

. . . I think that's mostly economic but it also includes a political counterweight so people who don't agree have a place to turn to other than picking up a gun.

. . . By having everybody feel like they've got a stake in the future, especially the young people, you can create a positive environment economically, politically, and diplomatically.

—*Mattis interview, the* MIHS Islander, *June 20, 2017*

0930 Hours—3 June 1982—London

Iraqi intelligence officer Colonel Nawaf al-Rosan loiters outside the five-star Dorchester Hotel on the corner of Park Lane and Deanery Street in London's exclusive Mayfair district. The colonel waits outside to greet Israeli ambassador Shlomo Argov, who is having dinner there. With al-Rosan is a notorious terrorist assassin for the Palestinian Liberation Front (PLF) and a Palestinian member of the PLF. Al-Rosan is the commander and paymaster of the group for Iraqi president Saddam Hussein.

The men are dressed in fashionable, dark-colored summer jackets and stand quietly together on the corner, keeping an eye on the front door of the hotel. In the assassin's jacket pocket is a loaded 7.62-millimeter Tokarev pistol, standard issue of the Russian and now Iraqi armies. Iraqi president Saddam has chosen this simple weapon and a very simple tactic to begin a war between Israel and the Palestinians. Saddam knows Israel is looking for any excuse to retaliate against him for financing and arming PLF's many terror attacks against Israel, and may take advantage of his current weakness. To deflect possible Israeli attack, he will simply feed his allies, the trusting patriots of Palestine, to the lion of Israel.

As Ambassador Argov and his bodyguard step from the front doors of the Dorchester, the assassin moves toward him, the others close behind. Argov's bodyguard opens the rear door of the waiting car as Argov steps to enter the car. The pistol is drawn, and the assassin fires one shot into the side of Argov's head, then turns and runs back toward the corner. Argov's bodyguard draws his weapon and fires one shot, hitting the fleeing shooter in the back of the head and knocking him to the sidewalk. The pistol clatters across the stone. Al-Rosan picks it up and runs after the second accomplice toward the corner, where a car waits to whisk them to the Iraqi Embassy. From the embassy, the two remaining assassins are taken to a safe house, where they are told to wait for further instructions. Within minutes of the embassy car leaving, the London police are at the safe house and arrest the two for attempted murder. Argov is still alive; although incapacitated, he will survive for another twenty-five years.[1]

Israeli general Ariel Sharon now has the excuse he needs, and the obvious culprits have been conveniently delivered while emotions are still high. The following day, the headquarters of the Palestine Liberation Organization (PLO) of Yasser Arafat are bombed in Lebanon. Within forty-eight hours, Israeli tanks cross the border into Lebanon, sweeping the defending Syrian armor aside as they attack the Palestinian headquarters in Beirut. Syria, Lebanon's armorer and ally, is now drawn into the battle as well.

Watching all this bloodshed with great interest is Iran's Shiite Muslim dictator, Ayatollah Khomeini, and the ruling mullahs, the lead actors in this drama. Through their stalwart support of certain suicidally aggressive Palestinian factions, the Iranians have kept their ultimate enemy, Israel, on the defensive. This surprising invasion of Beirut may be an opportunity. The mullahs watch patiently. If this is a typical Israeli lightning strike and quick victory, they won't have time to move against the Israelis. They quietly send weapons to the Palestinians.

After fast initial victories in the open desert against the antiquated Russian tanks of the Syrians, the sleek new Israeli Merkava tanks are almost useless in the narrow streets of Beirut. Days stretch into weeks, weeks into months. The Israelis are becoming bogged down in a house-to-house urban quagmire. The mullahs attack, sending 1,500 elite Revolutionary Guards to the Bekaa Valley near Beirut. Their mission: to mold the half dozen Palestinian and Lebanese factions inside Beirut into a unified Shiite guerilla army. Disguising the organization as a spontaneous people's resistance force to avoid any responsibility and possible retaliation, they call it the Party of God—Hezbollah.

Months of quietly manning Marine Recruiting Station Portland have allowed thirty-two-year-old Major Mattis to develop the comforting and regular routines of an office worker. He likely recalls the raucous pub crawls through ports of call around the world with the 3/3 with fondness and amusement. Memories of evenings with Alice may still sting but are probably becoming less sharp and less frequent. If he wanted to prove that he could hold down a real nine-to-five desk job like a normal, working man, he's done that. With the rest of America, he has seen terrorism erupt around the world. New players Iran and Russia are on rampages of conquest, killing thousands of innocent people in their wakes. The counterbalance of American military leadership is missing.

Almost like Mattis himself, America seems to be struggling out of a period of retreat. The legacy of Vietnam still stifles discussions of military power, even as the country is humiliated once again by a small group of oil-rich nations imposing an oil embargo. America has lost its nerve.

Mattis is very likely not surprised by any of this. From his reading of history he can probably see alliances form and then turn against each other, allies betraying and enemies helping each other. All of it would be instantly recognizable to Sun Tzu, Thucydides, or George Patton. The only thing new about war is that now everyone watches it on television.

0622 Hours—23 October 1983

Hezbollah kills 241 American Marines and sailors—the backbone of the multinational force acting as peacekeepers with the French[2]—and fifty-eight French peacekeepers in Beirut, Lebanon. The Marines are in Battalion Landing Team 1/8, East Coast Marines from Camp Lejeune, of the storied Second Division. Two trucks, carrying about five tons of high explosive each, detonate in front of the men's barracks. It is the most fatal day for Marines since the Tet Offensive in Vietnam, fifteen years before.

A previously unknown group calling itself Islamic Jihad claims responsibility. President Ronald Reagan retreats from Lebanon, but on his way out, in a spasm of impotent rage, he lobs three hundred 16-inch artillery shells from the USS *New Jersey* at the heart of Hezbollah in the Bekaa Valley. Reagan may have wounded Hezbollah slightly, but it had moved out of the valley long ago and now operates all over the world. For decades Iran will deny that it was behind the attack, but twenty years later, after the attack has been long forgotten, a statue commemorating the day and the two heroic martyrs who drove the trucks will be erected in central Tehran.

Mattis enrolls in the Marine Corps Command and Staff College, moving from quiet Portland to the busy campus in Quantico, Virginia, headquarters of the Marine Corps. He tackles a master's degree in military studies by analyzing and reminding the Marine Corps about what they do best—attacking from the sea. The title of his dissertation is "Amphibious Raids: An Historical Imperative for Today's Marines." In it he points to America's growing confidence under the leadership of President Ronald Reagan, arguing that Marines should maintain and expand their historical role as soldiers from the sea.

Mattis writes:

At a time when the American people are demonstrating their belief in the traditional need for a strong national defense, it is well that we in the Corps remind ourselves that it hasn't always been so. Only a few short years ago, after the Vietnam debacle, the need for any amphibious capability was questioned by many Americans, notably some highly placed, vocal critics, in and out of government.

Conversely, today we are living in the "Halcyon Days," as our expanded budgets provide equipment and capabilities we could only dream about years ago. Prepositioned equipment, additional mechanized vehicles, integration into NATO's command structure—all these show how widely the Marines' role has been accepted, and even expanded, beyond the forcible entry capability (the prepositioned equipment must be "married up" with airlifted troops in a benign environment where ship offload facilities and airports are available).

But as the political winds blow more favorably for us in the budget process, it is essential that we do not permit ourselves to be led astray from our primarily amphibious mission. Historical examples give credibility to this position, as the Marine Corps contributes its best when it performs in the amphibious role.[3]

In Baghdad, Mattis's future enemy Saddam Hussein resorts to World War I tactics by using mustard gas against the conscripted child soldiers of Iran's Ruhollah Khomeini. The two leaders, rather than learning from history, have repeated it, using the same barbed wire, trenches, bayonet charges, and human wave attacks that killed twenty million people within living memory in Europe. Shamefully, both Iraqis and Iranians resort to using children as combatants and civilian families as targets.

Although Saddam seized the advantage by attacking first, just after Khomeini's coup defeating the shah and backhanding American president Jimmy Carter, the war has devolved into a consuming stalemate, killing nearly five hundred thousand soldiers and civilians from both sides over six years. Finally, lacking ready military ground forces, Saddam rains his chemical weapons down on the northern Iraqi city of Halabja, recently taken by Iranian forces, killing and injuring about fifteen thousand Iraqi Kurdish civilians. The naked barbarism of Saddam and the Iranian mullahs is now on full display to the world through twenty-four-hour satellite news broadcasts showing the aftermath in Halabja and their stalemated trench warfare.

No doubt Mattis, along with most people, felt disgust at this brutality against civilians. It may have deepened his sense of responsibility toward the innocent victims of war. This sensitivity would become an essential element in his coming role of peacemaker in Iraq.

Also in Baghdad at the time, Abu Nidal, reliable assassin and collaborator, lives comfortably, awaiting contracts from Saddam or others seeking to destroy Israel. Realizing that Saddam is preoccupied with his own survival, Nidal initiates a freelance operation to maintain the high profile of his Palestinian Liberation Front.

On October 7, 1985, four PLF hijackers take control of the ocean liner *Achille Lauro* as it is sailing from Alexandria to Port Said, Egypt. They demand the release of fifty Palestinian militants from Israeli prisons. The next day, after being refused permission by the Syrian government to dock at Tartus, the hijackers single out elderly, disabled Leon Klinghoffer, a sixty-nine-year-old American Jew. They shoot Leon in the forehead and chest and throw his body and wheelchair overboard. They negotiate their escape with Moammar Qaddafi's Libyan regime on a plane out of Tripoli. In the air, President Reagan orders the interception of the plane with American F-15 fighters that force it to land at the American base in Sigonella, Italy. He finally has a chance to expose the connections of Palestinian terrorist networks such as Hezbollah and begin to retaliate.[4]

Italian authorities arrest the Palestinians and hold them while an extradition dispute is being decided. Before an American arrest warrant can be served, PLF founder Abu Abbas is released to Yugoslavia. The others are convicted and imprisoned.

Israel remains entangled in a low-intensity guerrilla war in southern Lebanon for the next five years. After the 1983 assassination of newly elected Lebanese president Bechir Gemayel, a Christian, Israeli allies in the Lebanese Christian militia kill three hundred suspected Palestinian fighters in the Shatila refugee camp. Israel is condemned by a United Nations commission for the war crime of genocide. Finally, recognizing the cost and futility of further engagement, Israel withdraws from Beirut, ceding control to rivals Syria and factions under Hezbollah.

Iran, through proxies like Hezbollah in Palestine, is now an unstoppable sponsor of Islamic terrorism. Based in the Middle East but conducting operations around the world, it is the inspiration and working model for organizations yet to come, like al-Qaeda, that will occupy the entire career of Jim Mattis.

9 November 1989

Major Mattis's focus on possible Soviet aggression in Europe shifts as the Berlin Wall collapses and the Soviet Union disbands into fifteen separate nations. The wary eyes of the world move toward the Middle East, where Soviet clients including Saddam Hussein are now without a nuclear-armed ally and business partner. Saddam is no longer even sure he can get spare parts for his Soviet-equipped army. The good news is that territories and resources once under Soviet protection are now available for conquest.

Suddenly Mattis's vision of maintaining a sea-based, highly mobile Marine Corps appears to be a vital component of American military power. Soon he will be called upon to integrate his vision into the doctrine of "maneuver warfare." This will become America's blitzkrieg, the shock and awe of the new fast and light footprint of American military power that Mattis will command on the battlefields of the Middle East.

Now, with his master's degree in military studies and rank of lieutenant colonel, Mattis takes command of the First Battalion, Seventh Marine Regiment, the storied "First Team" once commanded by Marine Corps legend Lieutenant Colonel Lewis B. "Chesty" Puller and first made famous at the Battle of Bloody Ridge by legendary gunnery sergeant "Manila John" Basilone.[5] The 1/7 is based at Twentynine Palms, California, the Corps' primary training ground for desert warfare.

In Baghdad, desperate for cash after eight years of fighting Iran and sponsoring Palestinian terrorists in Lebanon and Europe, Saddam engages neighboring Kuwait in a Melian Dialogue. He moves one hundred thousand of his most elite troops to the Kuwaiti border and then makes an offer that is elegantly simple and couched in the most innocuous diplomatic language. Kuwait will forgive the $14 billion in debt he borrowed to finance the Iranian war and give him another $1 billion in cash for the oil it had stolen by horizontal drilling into his Rumayla oil fields. In return, Saddam will not invade and kill them all. The naive Kuwaitis respond that the offer is not fair. They seem to think he is negotiating. They insult him with a counteroffer of $9 billion.

Checking his western flank first, on June 25, 1990, Saddam meets with American ambassador April Glaspie in Baghdad about Kuwait's oil theft. The American ambassador also seems to believe Saddam is negotiating. Glaspie says that America is "inspired by the friendship and not by confrontation . . . we have no opinion on the Arab–Arab conflicts." For further assurance, she says the United States does not intend "to start an economic war against Iraq."[6]

0200 Hours—2 August 1990— Kuwait-Iraq Border

Saddam invades Kuwait with special forces and three elite Iraqi Republican Guard divisions. By midday of the first day, the poorly prepared Kuwaitis have run out of ammunition and are overrun. Kuwaitis who can escape over land or sea to Saudi Arabia or by air to Bahrain and Qatar, run for their lives. By nightfall Ali al-Salem Air Base is captured, and the Iraqi flag flies over the capital of Kuwait City.

The Kuwaitis and Americans are both surprised. Like the ancient warriors of Athens, Saddam had not been negotiating. He had simply offered a reasonable choice. And like the militarily weak merchants of the island of Melos who rejected a similar Athenian offer, the Kuwaitis were crushed without mercy.

Lieutenant Colonel Mattis is about to lead the one thousand Marines of the 1/7 into harm's way. They will be a vital part of the coalition of thirty-four nations, including regional rival Syria, and will lead the attack at the "tip of the spear" against Saddam's battle-hardened, dug-in defenders in Kuwait City. As the first mission for a first-time battle commander, it is an ambitious trial by fire, one that forty-year-old Mattis has been preparing to face for over twenty years.

After their easy victory, Saddam's elite fighters are highly motivated. They are assured by Saddam that in spite of President George H. W. Bush's promise to defend Saudi Arabia, America "is a society which cannot accept 10,000 dead in one battle."[7] It will be months before the Americans arrive, if ever. Saddam directs his commanders to strengthen their fortifications and enjoy the spoils of war, including the Bentley and Mercedes sedans of Kuwait's fled or dead wealthy class. They have reclaimed Iraq's historical southern territory and struck a blow against the capitalist tyrants of the West and their Saudi collaborators.

Saddam has wide support in the Arab world as the "Sunni Shield" against the ethnically Persian and predatory Shiite Iranians and Wahabi Saudis. Tribally, he is seen as the strongman of one of the strongest tribes in the region, the Ba'athists (from the Arabic word for resurrection). With his conquest of Kuwait, he is also now one of the wealthiest. Politically, Saddam's Ba'ath Party is a socialist dictatorship calling for solidarity among Arabs. Ba'athists seek to erase the arbitrary borders drawn by the British and their puppets, the Saudis, in the 1920s. They want to restore the Ottoman Caliphate.

After eight years of conflict with the Persian Shiites of Iran, Saddam has lost over 150,000 men but still has nearly a million in his army. He has dragooned every able-bodied boy and man in Iraq to fill his ranks. Many have no weapons or even uniforms, but they are all well motivated to fight by commanders who will shoot them on the spot if they don't. Those who resisted joining the army, like the "Marsh Arabs" of the Fertile Crescent in the south, have simply been wiped out, their marshland drained and turned to desert so those who survive have nowhere to go but the army. There are few other industries in Iraq by this time.

For President George H. W. Bush, America's first objective is to secure Saudi Arabian oil fields. The industrialized world depends on an uninterrupted flow of Saudi oil. Saudi King Fahd bin Abdul Aziz al-Saud accepts Bush's commitment to defend his kingdom and dismisses the deep-seated national abhorrence toward foreign troops being on the same soil that holds Islam's holiest sites. In particular, thirty-three-year-old Osama bin Laden, heir to the multibillion-dollar Saudi-based bin Laden construction conglomerate, feels personally humiliated and enraged at his king. Just two years before, Osama formed his terror group al-Qaeda (in Arabic, "the Foundation") to finance and train fellow Muslim Afghanis in holy jihad against the infidel Soviet incursion. Now the entire infidel world will have troops and heavy armor just over a day's drive away from Mecca.

On August 6, 1990, US forces receive movement orders to Saudi Arabia. Two F-15 fighter squadrons, two carrier battle groups, and the ready brigade of the US Army's Eighty-Second Airborne Division scramble to the Saudi's defense. Central Command's General Norman Schwartzkopf begins planning for the largest and most complex projection of American military power since World War II. In the plans, the First Marine Expeditionary Force (I MEF), commanded by General Walter Boomer, along with the Army's Eighty-Second Airborne Ready Brigade, will be the immediate front-line defense against Saddam's three elite armored divisions.

Boomer picks the First Division, including Mattis's 1/7, to be the first to draw battle lines in the sand against Saddam. Mattis's immediate boss commanding the division is forty-nine-year-old Brigadier General James M. "Mike" Myatt. Myatt's task of moving the division to the front lines in the Saudi desert is complicated by the facts that it needed to happen fast and the division had not been deployed overseas since Vietnam. The First Marine Division at Camp Pendleton consists of three infantry regiments totaling twelve battalions, supported by one regiment of artillery, one tank battalion, one assault amphibian battalion, one reconnaissance battalion, and one combat engineer battalion. Mattis is about to receive a master class in real-world logistics from General Myatt. It is a lesson that will inform Mattis's development of "log lite," or "lightened logistics," a critical element of maneuver warfare.[8]

On August 8, Schwartzkopf gets Secretary of State Dick Cheney's approval of his initial plans. Together they begin to assemble a coalition force that will eventually exceed 956,000 people from 34 countries, including 700,000 Americans. The desert-trained First Marine Division, including Mattis's 1/7 and the ready force of the Eighty-Second Airborne, are put on alert. The maritime prepositioning squadron sails from the island of Diego Garcia with 14 supply ships filled with the Marines' equipment and weapons, including M60A1 tanks, amphibious assault vehicles (AAVs), high-mobility multipurpose wheeled vehicles (HMMWVs, more commonly known as Humvees), trucks, and 155-millimeter M198 artillery.

In California, Mattis receives movement orders for the 1/7. The battalion is about to play a critical role in what may be America's last heavy invasion force. Instead of taking the time to say goodbye with a family dinner and squaring away the dozens of personal details that need attention before a deployment, Mattis and his men pack everything they can carry into heavy combat packs, shoulder their personal weapons, and are bussed five miles from Camp Pendleton to the San Diego airport. They board waiting commercial charter airliners bound nonstop direct to Saudi Arabia.

The supply ships from Diego Garcia leave so quickly that the mechanics who are supposed to prepare the equipment en route arrive on the island after the ships are gone. This causes delays in Saudi Arabia getting the Marines into the field. Also, since the destination of Saudi Arabia's port of Jubayl is close to the border of Kuwait and could be under direct enemy attack at any moment, it is decided to stage combat units at the port until they are fully prepared to take up defensive positions in the field.

Over the next seven weeks, the US Army in Europe moves more than 122,000 soldiers and civilians and 5,500 pieces of heavy equipment from Germany to Saudi Arabia. Twenty-one barge loads, 407 trains with 12,210 railcars, and 204 road convoys totaling 5,100 vehicles converge on Germany's three main seaports and offload onto 115 ships bound for Saudi Arabia. The soldiers take 1,772 buses, followed by 1,008 vehicles carrying their baggage, before boarding 578 aircraft. As Lieutenant General William S. Flynn, commander of the Twenty-First Theater Army Area Command, puts it, "We usually plan all year long to unload two or three ships in one port. For Desert Shield we planned for a week and loaded some 115 ships through three ports and moved more than a corps worth of equipment through the lines of communication."[9]

At the height of the move, more tons of ammunition are moved in one day than the European theater normally ships in one year. Since its collapse, the Soviet Union is no longer seen as a threat against Europe. As a result, America practically empties Europe of defenses, shipping them all to the Middle East.

In spite of King Fahd's dismissal of concerns about foreign soldiers on holy ground, his government cannot completely ignore their restive people and Muslim neighbors. The Saudis are the unelected stewards of Islam's two most holy sites, Medina and Mecca, and must answer for any real or perceived defilement of the sites. Tensions are particularly high this year after 1,426 Muslims were trampled to death a few weeks earlier in a panic during the annual hajj pilgrimage to Mecca. Superstition crowds out reason. Is this evil omen Allah's warning about the heavy foot of infidel soldiers coming to their land?

On September 10, after delivery of America's huge military commitment to his nation, King Fahd verbally commits to comprehensive support of the troops. Another six weeks go by before Department of Defense negotiators conclude an agreement allowing "gifts" from Saudi Arabia to the United States, thereby avoiding formal ties. The Saudis agree to pay all costs of US forces—all freshly prepared meals, water, fuel, transportation within Saudi Arabia, and housing facilities, including construction—as of October 30. A first check for $760 million is personally carried back to New York for deposit by a military officer. The total Saudi commitment is valued at approximately $2.5 billion.

In spite of the financial cooperation, restrictions are placed on the Marines beyond the customary bans on alcohol and pornography, which includes any printed material showing women with bare arms or legs. They are not allowed to leave the port area. For weeks, while their heavy weapons are being offloaded and serviced for action, the Marines swelter in four overcrowded, overheated, filthy warehouses on a pier of al-Jubayl harbor.

As more units pour in every day, eventually over 9,000 Marines are jammed into the warehouses. The warehouses have no running water, no working toilets, and no significant ventilation to relieve the 120-degree summer heat. As each Marine unit arrives and is shoehorned into the warehouses, the levels of tension, noise, and discomfort ratchet up. Contractors hired to provide portable toilets are quickly overwhelmed and cannot service or provide sufficient new facilities. The smell quickly becomes horrendous. The warehouses are filthy with dust and rat and bird feces, threatening an outbreak of respiratory illnesses. The sheet-metal walls and iron frames hold the day's heat and radiate it out at night so that the men wake up drenched in sweat and exhausted. Nerves quickly fray, and the normally high Marine morale wavers.

Major Michael F. Applegate of the Third Assault Amphibian Battalion later said, "The time we spent in those warehouses was the worst experience of my life. At least in the desert you can move around, and you have the morning and evening breezes."[10]

Mattis's first combat deployment is a logistical nightmare. As the cases of diarrhea, heat rash, and coughing escalate, staying in the warehouses becomes a threat to the mission. Mattis gives his first public statement as Marine commander to the Alton Telegraph on 7 September 1990. "We've had some colds, some gastroenteritis," he says.

The unhealthy warehouses prompt a master class in leadership. Mattis's immediate superior, General Myatt, encourages his commanders to listen to every Marine, particularly the NCOs, the sergeants and lance corporals who carry the burden of the day-to-day work and drive morale at the platoon level. Mattis doesn't have to listen too closely to hear the mutiny brewing among his outspoken men.

While the politicians negotiate, the Marines take matters into their own hands. They meet with Saudi Army major general Saleh Ali Aloha and negotiate to move combat units out of the warehouses and into defensive positions north of the port. Mattis's 1/7 and the 1/5 are first into the field. They begin constructing defensive positions thirty miles north of al-Jubayl at what will become known as the "Cement Factory."

A second master class about cooperating with Middle Eastern hosts and fighting alongside them presents itself. Like Saddam's Sunnis, underneath the Saudis' affluence and modern infrastructure, they are essentially a religious tribal society. Strength, moral and military, is their most valued currency. With it, things like moving combat troops out of warehouses are negotiable. Without it, nothing is negotiable. Essentially it is the same martial code of honor that Mattis adopted as a Boy Scout, and that drew him to the Marines.

The Cement Factory is the only large structure in the otherwise mostly featureless Saudi desert, and a natural obstacle. It sits on an elevated ridge line and includes a series of gravel pits that sit on both sides of the coastal highway. Although September is generally the hottest time of year to be digging fighting positions in the desert, the conditions there are still better than in the warehouses. Morale improves as the 1/7 migrates toward a nocturnal schedule like that of most other desert-dwelling creatures. They dig all night and try to sleep during the suffocating 120-degree days, when swarms of flies torment them. Adding to their misery and exhaustion, they know that if Saddam attacks now with his massed armored divisions, casualties will be high. They refer to themselves as "speed bumps" on Saddam's way to the Saudi oil fields.

In his first televised interview as a commander, Mattis speaks with NBC's Tom Brokaw at the Cement Factory defensive line.

BROKAW: These are Marines but they're also young kids and they've never been in this situation before. Are you having to deal with nerves as well?

MATTIS: No. They're pretty calm, pretty matter of fact. They know what's expected of them and they're all pretty hard chargin' and they're ready to go.

Brokaw then narrates over shots of Marines filling sandbags and digging fighting positions,

BROKAW: The Marines are a little more candid.

Brokaw speaks to a young Marine on the front line,

BROKAW: You guys are what they call the trip wire, you're the forward elements after all. Make you a little nervous?

MARINE: Yeah. A little bit. You're nervous a lot at first but then you kind of get used to it. When I first found out . . . Now it's a week or two later. Now I'm not as nervous as I was when I first found out.[11]

Across the border, Saddam's commanders are not thinking of attacking just yet. They have been working since the invasion on their own defenses of entrenched infantry behind protective barriers, backed up by reserves of captured Kuwaiti tank and mechanized divisions. These are further reinforced by additional new divisions of Republican Guards. Altogether, hundreds of thousands of heavily armed, experienced fighters face the Marines, backed up by artillery, attack aircraft, and tanks.

Saddam is gambling that he can make the liberation of Kuwait more expensive, in blood, than the American public is willing to pay. From his tribal perspective, civilian control and popular opinion restricting America's military are exploitable weaknesses. He apparently believes that, as they demonstrated in Tehran in 1979 and have continued to demonstrate ever since, Americans don't really have the stomach for war, particularly a war of aggression.

Specifically, he taunts President Bush with his often repeated opinion of America's weakness: "Yours is a nation that cannot afford to take 10,000 casualties in one battle."[12]

Saddam calculates that Americans are still too timid to risk another South Asian land war like Vietnam. They've made their big show of force; now they can honorably withdraw. But he's miscalculated America's new resolve.

By mid-September, America's coalition force has secured the world's oil supply along a forty-two-mile front, just below Saudi Arabia's northern border with Kuwait. The front extends from the Persian Gulf inland west to the elbow where the border turns northwesterly. It controls King Fahad Road, the main north-south artery, which runs a few miles inland along the Gulf coast.

After several weeks of hard labor with pickaxes and shovels at the Cement Factory, the 1/7 has done such an excellent job of building their fortifications that they get to start all over again. They are repositioned twenty miles to the west and give the Cement Factory defense line to the Saudi Joint Forces Command of Arab coalition partners. The 1/7 is now in the center of the coalition defensive line, at the border elbow between the Second Marine Division and the Arab Joint Forces. Anticipating that their defensive posture is temporary, Schwarzkopf positions the Marines where they will be the tip of the spear when the order comes to attack. President Bush, a former military commander himself, agrees with Schwarzkopf. They know that this defensive line will protect Saudi Arabia only as long as the Americans maintain it. Saddam must go.

On his Thanksgiving visit to First Marine Division headquarters just behind the front lines, President Bush announces his intention to attack and drive Saddam from Kuwait. After frustrating months of sweltering in the desert and eating dust, this news is as welcome as a sudden rainstorm. The Marines are itching to take the fight to Saddam and go home. The mission is now to prepare for the invasion of Kuwait by January 15, 1991—the United Nations' deadline for Saddam's withdrawal.

With the UN resolution, Saddam realizes that America and her coalition partners are not only not going to retreat—they are now authorized to attack. But before they get too far in that line of thinking, he will draw first blood from America's soft spot. He will send a few dozen Americans home in body bags and see how the fragile American public likes that.

On January 17, 1991, the American coalition begins air and artillery raids on Iraqi positions, as well as a series of masking maneuvers to confuse the Iraqis about the real point of attack. Mattis's 1/7 readies itself to lead the attack, with newly added companies of combat engineers and special breaching equipment. The engineers will clear paths through Iraqi minefields with specially equipped tanks and blow holes through fixed fortifications. Mattis's first combat action, his baptism by fire, will be at the tip of the spear.

On January 27, Saddam meets in Basra, Iraq's southernmost city, with Major General Salah Mahmoud. Mahmoud assures his president that the Saudi Arabian coastal city of Khafji, seven miles inside Saudi Arabia, will be his in three days, and he will have dozens of dead Americans for propaganda purposes. Saddam returns to Baghdad by armed convoy. As an omen of things to come, on the way his convoy is attacked by coalition aircraft, and Saddam narrowly escapes.

The following day, coalition intelligence sees Iraqi movement at the border in the Arab Forces sector above Khafji. Coalition air and artillery strikes escalate throughout the day. Warnings about a possible attack are forwarded to Schwarzkopf at Central Command. Coordinating the pre-invasion air campaign is taking priority with Schwarzkopf and his staff, so the warning is relegated to lower importance.

Cross-training with the Arab coalition forces began soon after the First Division finished building the Cement Factory defense line. In assuming the line at the Cement Factory from the division, the Saudis became responsible for protecting the division's right flank. Recognizing the Saudis' now vital role in the war, General Myatt assigned the assistant division commander, Brigadier General Thomas V. Draude, to coordinate the critical cross-training between Marine and Saudi fighters. The training included the Royal Saudi Army, the fledgling Saudi Marine Corps, and the Saudi Army National Guard, as well as Qatari, Pakistani, Moroccan, and Bangladeshi units.

Training with the Saudi Marine Corps meant sharing training ranges, equipment, and sensitive military intelligence. It was a reciprocal effort: the Saudis taught the Marines desert tactics, desert survival, and desert navigation. Training included individual combat skills and participation in full scale Central Command–directed exercises. The emphasis was on perfecting tactics of the mobile defense until UN Resolution 688 passed in November, demanding Iraq's withdrawal.

Training then immediately switched to offensive operations,

especially breaching techniques. Mostly American and Arab commanders conducted tactical exercises without troops on sand tables representing the battlefield. Large-scale exercises involving entire units were minimized to avoid wear and tear on the equipment. The intent of the training was to make sure everyone was prepared for different possible combat situations. It was also where Mattis's and his future Arab allies worked closely together, taking the measure of each other and gaining the trust they needed to put their lives and the lives of their men in each other's hands.

These critical bonds were forged in these often intense and repetitive trainings and would soon be tempered under fire. The Arab coalition forces, invited to celebrate the Marine Corps' 215th birthday on November 10, 1990, with their new brothers-in-arms, accepted graciously. In a very real sense it was the first birthday of the Saudi Marine Corps as well.

Over the next weeks, the First Marine Division slowly moves north toward the forty-nine-foot-high sand berm just a few miles south of the Kuwaiti border with Saudi Arabia. It has been nearly four months of constant preparation and training since Mattis and the 1/7 made port at al-Jubayl. Cooler weather, rain, and howling dust storms called *haboob*s replace the oppressive summer heat. Daytime temperatures drop into the seventies, and nights are often a frigid and sometimes wet fifty degrees.

General Boomer is not in a hurry to move forces closer to the border. Iraq's well-prepared defenses mean the Marines no longer have the advantage of surprise. They are left with only the selection of the time and place for the attack. In early January, intelligence reports identify gaps between Iraqi divisions. The most exploitable gap appears at the strategically critical southwest corner, the elbow of Kuwait, a few miles to the east of Mattis and the 1/7. If the reports are true, the gap offers a direct avenue of approach to Kuwait City.

The First and Second Marine Divisions begin moving to the border assembly areas while the US Army relocates its entire VII Corps fifteen miles to the northwest Saudi-Kuwaiti border. The Army plans an envelopment maneuver through the trackless western desert against Saddam's unprotected right flank. This maneuver was to be led by the nine Abrams tanks and several armored vehicles of Eagle Troop, commanded by Captain H. R. McMaster. It would prove to be the last great tank battle of the twentieth century.

The Iraqis' right flank was unprotected because they thought a mechanized force could not navigate the empty desert and find them in time as part of a synchronized, multifront attack. The coalition's secret weapon that made this maneuver possible was the recently developed GPS. This technology, combined with the vastly superior coalition M1A1 Abrams tanks, rendered the Iraqis' defense strategy and Russian tanks obsolete.

Mattis's 1/7 and other Marine regiments are done with digging fighting holes; now they conduct raids or "ambiguity operations" to confuse the Iraqis as to their positions and intentions. Mattis's job now includes determining raid timelines, force routes, checkpoints, assembly areas, and tentative firing positions. Division command selects targets, coordinates air support, and raid forces movements during the day to be in firing positions for the raids by nightfall. Twelve raids are conducted. They damage Iraqi forward positions, but the division suffers its first casualties with four Marines killed and two wounded in accidents and friendly fire.

1926 Hours—29 January 1991

It is a frigid, overcast night at Observation Post 4 (OP 4), at the elbow of the Saudi-Kuwaiti border. Without even a partial moon, the flat, empty desert disappears beyond a few hundred yards. OP 4, known as the as-Zabr police station to the locals, is a small office and barracks with a forty-foot stone tower overlooking the border a mile or so north.

In the tower, Second Platoon, First Recon Marines spot a column of about thirty Iraqi armored vehicles moving toward them out of the blackness, including five T-62 tanks. This sector of the border is defended by Task Force Shepherd. After being reassigned from a defensive force to an attack force, First Division reorganized into separate task forces, each with a distinct composition and mission. Task Force Shepherd will be a blocking force in the coming attack into Kuwait. Its mission is to breach the first minefield and obstacle belt protecting the Iraqis, then act as a screen or blocking force defending the left flank of Task Force Ripper as Ripper breaches the second minefield and obstacle belt and attacks the al-Jaber airfield beyond. Mattis and the 1/7 will be up front, at the point of Task Force Ripper.

As the Iraqis are moving against OP 4, three Iraqi mechanized brigades are also moving south on the coastal King Fahad Road toward the Arab sector of the border on Mattis's right flank. This sector is defended by the Second Brigade, Saudi Arabian National Guard, a mechanized infantry unit. The only Marines in the Saudi sector are liaison officers, training advisers, and reconnaissance teams, including two teams positioned inside the town of Khafji, nine miles south of the border.

At OP 4, the recon platoon calls in an airstrike against the fast-approaching Iraqi armor. The first aircraft arrive and attack. Met with heavy anti-aircraft fire, they fail to stop the Iraqi advance. Once within small-arms range, the recon platoon opens fire with a combination of grenade launchers, shoulder-fired antitank rockets, and machine guns. One tank is stopped by the rocket fire. The Iraqi tanks return fire with armor-penetrating missiles that go through both stone walls of the observation tower. The recon platoon withdraws a little over a mile to a horseshoe-shaped berm behind the post and reengages the tanks and Russian-made armored vehicles. Platoon commander Captain Roger L. Pollard calls in another air strike as the Iraqis take the observation post in force. General Myatt is informed that the Iraqis have taken OP 4 and are also moving against OP 5 and 6, as well as the Arab sector to the east. He mobilizes artillery and the Third Marine air wing in support of Task Force Shepherd. Mattis and Task Force Ripper, on high alert, wait in sector for orders as they monitor the attacks on either side.[13]

At 2100 hours, the Iraqis break through at the Arab sector and charge toward Khafji, driving back reconnaissance teams from the border. In Khafji, US Army Special Forces, the Saudi National Guard, and reconnaissance units withdraw to nearby Mishab, but two First Marine Division reconnaissance teams are trapped in Khafji by the fast-moving attack. The coalition didn't anticipate an attack in this sector, since there is no strategic value to Khafji. But Saddam doesn't want Khafji; for publicity he wants the dead bodies of the Marines now trapped there.

Fierce fighting continues at OP 4 as artillery and sorties of A-10 attack aircraft slow the advance of the Iraqi armor. Through the dust and low clouds, it is difficult to distinguish coalition from enemy vehicles. An illumination flare dropped from an A-10 that is meant to mark the lead position of Iraqi forces instead falls behind the Marine position, putting the Marines in the gunsights of their own air cover. Moments later a Marine LAV explodes, killing the entire crew. Captain Pollard will later recount, "It was the only time I got scared. I was in the center of the line looking for the flare to land in front of me, when all of a sudden there was this huge explosion on my right. I thought we had been flanked and had lost a vehicle to enemy tank fire."[14]

It has been a two-hour continuous gunfight, with the Marines maintaining discipline, staying off the radio, and maneuvering in total darkness. As Pollard describes it, "Normally it is difficult to keep chatter off the radio, but throughout the battle, they maintained perfect radio silence. The only voices to be heard were those of myself, the XO [executive office], my FAC [forward air controller], and occasionally the platoon commanders. However, when the LAV-25 went up, there was pandemonium over the net and it took a moment to settle everybody down."[15]

The A-10s correct for the errant illumination flare, and an Iraqi T-55 tank explodes just yards in front of OP 4. It creates an illuminating reference point for attacks against other Iraqi armor. The assault begins to waver as two tanks break formation and drive blindly into a berm. Their crews abandon the tanks moments before they are destroyed. Artillery is zeroed in on dismounted infantry and scattering BMPs.

Unnoticed at the time is the lack of continuing Iraqi artillery to support the assault, and particularly ineffective commanders as the initial attack falters. These two indicators eventually reveal to every Marine commander the critical flaws in Saddam's military—flaws that will increase over time and drive current and future military doctrine in the Gulf War yet to come. These flaws will prompt the future, typically humble General Mattis to say, "It's not that I'm such a great general, it's that the other guys [the enemy] really suck."[16]

As dawn breaks on January 30, the Iraqis occupy Khafji. They hurriedly prepare defenses against the inevitable counterattack. The two trapped Marine reconnaissance teams continue to report from inside the city. They estimate they have a day, possibly two, until the Iraqis sweep the city and discover them. Unfortunately, Myatt is now in a politically difficult position, since the city is in the Arab sector. A unilateral Marine counterattack will embarrass his new Saudi allies as weak and jeopardize the new coalition. Instead of the direct military approach, Myatt takes the indirect political route of sending his emissary Colonel John H. Admire, commander of Task Force Taro, to the commander of the Saudi National Guard, Colonel Turki.

Admire's extensive cross training with Turki has created a special bond that the Marines now call upon with a respectful offer of infantry and artillery support. As expected, the Saudis view the taking of Khafji as a humiliation, and rescuing the reconnaissance teams as a matter of honor. It is a fundamental tribal custom that guests, like any other tribe member, are under the absolute protection of their hosts. Enraged at the Iraqi attack, the Saudi government orders Colonel Turki to immediately retake the city at all costs and rescue the Marines.

At OP 4, reeling from the overwhelming Marine defense, the Iraqis begin to retreat back across the border to Kuwait. Even after ten hours of full-bore combat, seeing the remaining T-55 and T-62 tanks pulling back energizes the Marines. For the next two hours, they chase the invaders back under a hailstorm of flying metal and fire. When it is over, twenty-two Iraqi tanks lie in pieces, and several hundred enemy prisoners of war are offering everything they know about Saddam's army to intelligence officers in return for food and water.

For the next few days, Iraqi mechanized units harass the line of Marine observation posts along the border but do not attempt to breach again. Intelligence reports note the poor performance of the enemy's artillery and air force in the January 29 attacks. Without this combined arms support for the mechanized ground forces, the Iraqis never penetrated beyond the "trip wire" defenses at the border that might have revealed the position of coalition main forces forty miles farther south.

The Marines learned that many of the Iraqi soldiers were hungry, badly trained, and poorly led. The division's offensive plan changed as the true state of Saddam's infantry became clear. Based on this knowledge, Myatt ordered new surveillance of the obstacle belts inside Kuwait. This revealed weaknesses not seen before, including a gap in the Iraqi air surveillance capabilities where Task Force Ripper, led by Mattis's 1/7, could move to the border undetected. The Marines were now reading Iraq's defenses like an open book. It became an essential textbook in Mattis's mental library.

The retaking of Khafji became the cement in the already strong Saudi/Marine Corps alliance. Entrusting the lives of its recon Marines to the Saudi National Guard was proof of the confidence the Marines had in the Saudis. Deft negotiations at the battalion commander level from Admire allowed his Marine units to shadow the assaulting Arab battalions—just in case. Colonel Turki, his commanders, and other Arab allies in the sector planned and executed the mission using the full complement of Task Force Taro's combined arms assets, including anti-armor detachments, infantry security forces, air and naval gunfire liaison teams, and critical artillery and air support.

0230 Hours—31 January 1991—North of Khafji, Saudi Arabia

Another cold, moonless night of low cloud cover and poor visibility. The Saudis launch a probing attack to determine Iraqi positions and their reaction strength. Some initial confusion sputters across the net as inexperienced, excited Arab gunners overreact, seeing threats in the darkness that don't exist. Colonel Admire and his commanders monitor the radio traffic but hold their positions. They understand that the new fighters are having a case of nerves, and allow the Saudi commanders to sort out their problems.

At 0630 hours, as the sun begins to rise over the Persian Gulf, Saudi and Qatari units attack north and northeast into Khafji. Two Marine AV-8B Harrier jets destroy three Iraqi vehicles at the point of attack for the Second Battalion of the Saudi Army National Guard as it punches through the outer edge of the city. They capture seventy-five Iraqi soldiers.

Inside the city, the trapped recon Marines continue to direct Harrier jet attacks against targets near them and against enemy armor attempting to move into the city along King Fahad Road. By 1200 hours, the Saudi's Seventh Battalion fights through the city to the Marines. It loads them into armored vehicles and moves them to secure forward air controller positions to advise on additional fire missions against the Iraqis. It is a huge victory—a redemption of their honor and a vindication of their alliance with the Americans for the Saudis, and a testament to the intellectual standard of Marine commanders like General Mike Myatt and Colonel John Admire, who understand and can apply the political as well as military dimensions of war.

As night falls, the Saudis, Qataris, and other Arab allies consolidate their positions inside the city. The recon Marines remain with the Arab contingent to assist with targeting missions to come in the morning. It isn't yet time for celebration while the city is still in Saddam's grip.

By 1600 the following day, the Tenth Battalion of the Saudi Army National Guard sweeps the Iraqis out of the city and links up with the Fifth Battalion at the northern edge of town. The Iraqis are chased back across the border, with heavy losses of over 90 percent of their original force. The Saudis and Qataris have captured over six hundred enemy soldiers and, with coalition assistance, destroyed over ninety Iraqi tanks and armored vehicles.

Major General Salah Mahmoud's mission for Saddam is a total, humiliating failure. The inexperienced Saudis took on Mahmoud's highly experienced and much larger force, defeated it, and sent it scurrying home. No territory was captured, and no dead Americans would be delivered to Saddam for publicity.

Based on the Saudi performance in Khafji, Marine command creates combat assignments for them in the coming Kuwaiti offensive. Previously the Saudis were assigned only to defensive positions, and only inside Saudi Arabia. Now they will fight alongside American and other coalition attack elements as one unified force. Now it's time for celebration. Without alcohol of any kind in the kingdom, the Marines are temporarily at a loss, but characteristically quickly adapt. Small groups of proud Arab warriors with their American and European brothers-in-arms hunker down together to share fruit juice, rock and roll, and war stories.

7

Task Force Ripper

From a purely numbers perspective, the odds seemed to be stacked against Task Force Ripper, the first coalition ground unit to assault Kuwait. "From the intel we had, we were way outnumbered, and figured it would be a pretty tough fight," said First Lieutenant Brian C. Hormberg from Houston.

Before the air war began on January 17, the ratio of Iraqi troops was estimated to be a whopping seven to one. Enemy tanks enjoyed a numerical advantage of at least four to one. And since Central Command didn't make public an estimate of the number of Iraqis killed by bombing, no one was certain what was waiting for Marines beyond the two minefields.

—*Claude W. Curtis, "The Tip of the Spear,"* Leatherneck, *August 1991*

0330 Hours—24 February 1991—Task Force Assembly Area Near the Saudi-Kuwaiti Border

The commanders of Task Force Ripper wait silently in their armored vehicles. An occasional comm check comes over the net. Fourteen thousand Marines in six task forces stand by with their weapons in Condition 1: magazine inserted, round in the chamber, safety on.

Some visualize the actions they will take in a few moments, some pray, some focus on home and loved ones.

Lieutenant Colonel Mattis has already lost his first Marine and written his first letter home to a grieving Marine family. Two days before, an accidental discharge of an M-16 rifle killed one of his men.[1] The casualty estimation for Mattis's 1/7 battalion in the coming attack is 10 percent, or about forty men. Privately he confides to a friend back home, "They expect heavy casualties."[2]

He expects to have many more letters to write by the time they get to Kuwait City.

Hours earlier, Task Forces Grizzly and Taro crossed the line of departure at the border and opened two lanes through the first minefield and obstacle belt inside Kuwait.[3] They now wait in blocking positions to protect the left and right flanks of Task Forces Ripper and Papa Bear as those two task forces pass through the lanes and breach the second minefield and obstacle belt farther north. General Myatt's worry, as he monitors weather reports in his headquarters tent at the border, is that Ripper and Papa Bear will have trouble getting through the second obstacle belt and get stuck in between the first and second belts. This is a kill zone zeroed in on by Saddam's deadliest weapon, his artillery.

Myatt needs air cover to protect Ripper and Papa Bear as they work through the second belt, but the weather is not cooperating. Low, drizzling clouds obscure the battlefield. Every minute that ticks by gives Saddam time to move his forces to the now obvious point of attack. Every minute waiting ensures more casualties for the coalition. The distant thunder of B-52 bombardment reassures Myatt that at least some part of Saddam's artillery is being destroyed.

Task Force Ripper, composed of Mattis's 1/7 and Christopher Cortez's 1/5, assuming they quickly breach the second belt, will be the main maneuver element inside Kuwait. The task force's plan of maneuver will rely on the speed and mobility of the relatively new doctrine of maneuver warfare over massed firepower.[4] Mattis will be among the first field commanders to use it in desert combat with heavy armor. Although their maneuvers have been rehearsed on sand tables many times, they couldn't know exactly what Saddam has hidden beyond the minefields. The only thing they know for certain is that the 1/7 and the 1/5 will meet the brunt of Saddam's armor, so two companies of M60A1 tanks roll in front of them, forming the twin steel spearheads of their attack.

The Army, sweeping in a left hook through southern Iraq against Kuwait City, has the newest, most technologically advanced Abrams M1A1 tanks, which can shoot and hit any target within a mile while charging over rough terrain at up to forty miles per hour.[5] The Marines' M60A1s, which were developed during the Korean War and used extensively in Vietnam,[6] are a much closer match to Saddam's aging Russian T-55s and T-62s.

Myatt can't wait any longer for the weather; he issues the command to assume attack positions. The net relays the code word "Coors" to all units.[7] Radio silence ends with the sudden chatter of coordinates and sharp commands, a thousand diesel engines roar to life, and Task Force Ripper rolls over the line of departure several miles south of the Kuwait border toward its attack position inside Kuwait. Colonel Carlton Fulford orders Ripper's two mechanized infantry battalions and tank battalion into a "tanks forward" wedge formation. AAVs with commanders and infantry troops fall in behind the iron phalanx of tanks as they move cautiously northeast across the desert, using night vision devices to navigate.

0410 Hours

Ripper crosses Phase Line Black at the Kuwaiti border and is soon within range of Saddam's artillery. Scouts see no sign of the enemy until Fulford gets an aerial surveillance report of four tanks, six BMPs (Russian armored vehicles), and a suspected command post in front of the task force. As it continues to move forward, pre-positioned special teams—forward air controllers, artillery observers, naval gunfire teams, a surveillance and target acquisition platoon, and mine-clearing tanks—fall in behind Ripper's steel wedges. Fulford deployed the teams the day before to check the route and secure their attack position.

A squad of A-6 Intruder jets strike the four Iraqi tanks and BMPs reported in Ripper's sector. The tanks withdraw north, drawing the fire of Task Force Grizzly into Ripper's sector. Ripper holds its fire and continues in wedge formation to Phase Line Saber, the edge of the second minefield. At 0500, Ripper is an hour ahead of schedule. Fulford orders a halt. The enemy has fled their sector. Engines idle in the dark while Fulford reports to Myatt that he is in position and has met no resistance. Engines shut down, and near silence descends as Task Force Ripper waits for the order to begin the attack. They send up a series of red star cluster flares, signaling that they have reached the second minefield.

Tanks equipped with mine plows come from behind the protection of the forward tanks and begin clearing lanes through the minefield. A light drizzle turns to rain, blinding the air cover and soaking the dismounted infantry of Grizzly and Taro protecting Ripper's flanks as they march toward their forward blocking positions. The Marines are now partially blind to Saddam's movements, but Saddam knows exactly where the Marines are and which way they are coming—the direct route northeast toward Kuwait City.

At dawn, Task Force Grizzly, preceding Ripper toward its blocking position, again fires on three T-72 tanks and three BMPs in Ripper's sector. Ripper's Third Battalion tankers, who have moved through the breached minefield, are unaware that Grizzly has been delayed in its advance and is still in Ripper's sector. They think the distant, indistinct silhouettes are Iraqi. They open fire, and Grizzly begins taking casualties. Grizzly's Colonel Fulks and Ripper's Colonel Fulford quickly figure out that it is Ripper's friendly fire hitting Grizzly. General Myatt jumps into the conversation and orders constant communication between task force commanders to avoid more friendly fire incidents.[8]

1030 Hours

A constant stream of Iraqi deserters begin to enter the lines.[9] They wave white T-shirts of surrender and hold paper "Get Out of Iraq Free" flyers over their heads. The flyers are instructions in Arabic on how to surrender to the Marines, dropped the day before by B-52 bombers. Complicating matters for Mattis and the 1/7, while making its breach of the second obstacle belt, they run into their first significant firefight as scattered bunkers and armored squads open fire. At the same time, thousands of enemy soldiers are leaving their positions and approaching the Marines. Mattis's first battle is a muddle of combat and humanitarian assistance. "At this time," writes Gunnery Sergeant Paul S. Cochran, Third Tank Battalion, "POWs started appearing from everywhere. A total of approx 300 to 350 were credited to 2nd Plt [Platoon], because the[y] surrendered to our t[an]ks in our sector. POWs were blowing us kisses, waving American flags and ask[ing] for food and water."[10] Major Drew Bennett, 1/7 operations officer, reports "hundreds upon hundreds of Iraqis sporting white flags . . . converging on the breach sites, especially lane-3."[11]

The 1/7 is still working its way through the second minefield, but the number of surrendering Iraqis threatens to slow the battalion's advance. Mattis orders an infantry platoon to set up a prisoner holding area about three hundred yards south of the breach. At the same time he monitors the sporadic fighting to his front and orders artillery and air fire missions on enemy positions.

Within minutes the situation gets worse. The lanes get so congested that the attack completely stops—exactly as Myatt feared. Mattis immediately replaces his dismounted Marines guarding the enemy prisoners with Marines from the battalion supply trucks behind him. Then, judging the starving Iraqis to be no threat, he instructs the 1/7 not to stop for surrendering soldiers. Instead, the Iraqis are pointed toward the rear and waved on.

Mattis clears lane 3, then directs his Team Tank platoon through lane 4 to continue covering Task Force Ripper's right flank. Team Tank and a combined anti-armor team, CAAT 2, immediately find and turn to attack two enemy tanks. They close with the enemy, exchanging heavy fire that kills both tanks but carries them dangerously into Task Force Papa Bear's sector. Mattis orders Team Tank to correct course and return to formation, continuing the advance on the first day's ultimate objective, the al-Jaber airfield.

Shifting his attack orientation from northeast to west, Mattis halts south of a tree-covered area with several buildings known as Emir's Farm.[12]

1400 Hours

Mattis attacks Emir's Farm. Dismounted infantry Company C and a mechanized infantry company he calls Team Mech envelop the position from west to east, while Team Tank covers their movement with fire. Hovering just above the trees, the Gunfighters squadron of Cobra helicopter gunships relay to Mattis which bunkers have enemy troops in them.

Team Mech moves in close, dismounts, and attacks the farm, supported by machine-gun fire from its AAVs and the Gunfighters above. The area was already swept by artillery fire during Ripper's breach of the obstacle belts. The enemy force begins to disintegrate as Team Mech moves to within 1,800 yards, covered by a smoke barrage. Sweating profusely in their level 4 MOPP suits—full hood cover, rubber boots, and gas masks—they move slowly, too slowly for Mattis. He seems convinced that the defenders want to surrender. Frustrated with the pace of the attack, he assaults the farm from the opposite side with his own headquarters vehicles and directs the final envelopment from there.

Mattis guessed partly right. Headquarters and Team Mech companies capture two hundred prisoners. Mattis calls up the entire battalion to sweep the area, but soon realizes that the fight for Emir's

Farm is far from over. The Marines start engaging camouflaged Iraqi bunkers, tanks, rocket launchers, and armored personnel carriers. Mattis calls in the Gunfighters overhead against the Iraqi armor, with their Hellfire and TOW missiles. In the bunkers, Iraqi infantry are buried alive, literally plowed under by tanks rolling over them, fitted with mine plows that resemble fire-breathing, razor-toothed dinosaurs.

By 1530 the Iraqis are dead, fled, or begging to be fed. Now behind schedule for the main assault on al-Jaber, Mattis directs Team Tank to move ahead to their attack position northeast of the airfield. The rest of 1/7 will catch up.

1630 Hours

General Myatt forms up the spearhead of Task Force Ripper's attack west of the airfield, with the Third Tank Battalion in the center, Mattis's 1/7 on the right, and Cortez's 1/5 on the left. Mattis and Cortez are also in wedge formation with their tank companies in the lead, mechanized companies on their left, and infantry companies on their right. Mattis and Cortez are in the center of their wedge in their armored vehicles behind the tanks. As they advance, artillery bombards the airfield. For the first time, the burning oil wells of the nearby al-Burqan oil field are a tactical problem.

Major Drew Bennett, operations officer of the 1/7, notes in his journal, "All hands were awestruck by the ominous pall of smoke emanating from over 50 wellhead fires in the Al Burqan oilfield. Commanders whose senses were sharply focused found that the rumbling from the burning [well heads] played tricks on their hearing, sounding almost like columns of armored vehicles approaching our right flank."[13]

Task Force Ripper maneuvers north to envelop the airfield from the rear. At 1734, with visibility down to 300 yards, two T-62 tanks approach the right flank of the 1/7. The CAAT protecting the 1/7's right flank spots the tanks and takes them out. In front of 1/7, Team Tank finds and destroys three more T-62s dug into revetments. As the 1/7 fights its way to the airfield perimeter, six more enemy tanks are taken on and destroyed.

1800 Hours

Task Force Ripper halts at the al-Jaber airfield perimeter, awaiting further orders. Under low clouds of rain and drizzle, wind blows thick plumes of toxic oil smoke over the men, who are still in their gas masks and full chemical protection suits. Iraqi resistance dwindles as dusk turns to night. Intelligence from newly captured Iraqis informs Myatt that the airfield is now abandoned. He issues Task Force Ripper new orders. Their objective is no longer the al-Jaber airfield. The task force turns from facing al-Jaber to facing northeast toward Objective C, Kuwait City. They form up into protective circle formations for the night and set the first watch. In the morning, they are to lead the fight across twenty-five miles of open desert through Saddam's best Republican Guard divisions and kick in the front door of his most prized possession, Kuwait International Airport, unfortunately abbreviated as KIA, the military abbreviation for Killed in Action.

Lieutenant James D. Gonsalves, Company C, Third Tank Battalion, encounters an enemy tank soon after moving into position: "We had pulled up to our 2nd day's objective and were awaiting further orders. The smoke clouds from the burning oil wells were closing in fast, reducing visibility to less than 1,500 meters. All of a sudden my loader, Lance Corporal Rodrigues, yelled: 'We got a T-62 out there! Look! Gunner! SABOT! Tank! Range 1100 meters!' The first explosion was small but then its ammo started cooking off. I counted 14 secondary explosions."[14]

Reports of a full-scale enemy counterattack from battalions

hiding inside the burning oil fields never materialize. Gunnery Sergeant Cochran would write about that first night inside Kuwait, "It turned to midnight, had to use night vision goggles to see. Did not work. By 6PM Iraq troops PCs [personnel carriers] and tks were reported 3 [kilometers] from us and moving closer. They finally stopped 2 short of our pos because of total blackout. I could not see the end of my 50 barrel 4 ft away."[15]

Firefights including nearby cannon fire erupt throughout the night as Mattis and most of the exhausted 1/7 sleep through the lullaby of warfare. Some sleep sitting up in their vehicles; some lie on the ground underneath them or nearby, under a light drizzle of rain mixed with crude oil. They will not be there long enough to rest, just long enough to get covered with oil.

Myatt moves his command post forward through the second obstacle belt to be in position for directing the next day's attack. Reports filter in that two enemy armored brigades are positioning to strike the division's front and right flank. These reports corroborate each other, not like the scattered reports of roaming Iraqi units he has been receiving. He wakes up his commanders, and they position tanks and antitank teams to the front. Myatt's analysis of the reports is correct.

0515 Hours—25 February 1991

The Iraqi counterattack begins from the west with a feint against Mattis and the 1/7 on the left flank of Task Force Ripper, followed by large-scale assaults against the right flank and center of both Task Forces Ripper and Shepherd. By 0620, Ripper's Third Tank Battalion is in an intense firefight with twenty vehicles and an unknown number of infantry. The tanks knock down the first wave of the attack. Dense fog has rolled in with the drizzle and oil smoke, cutting visibility to less than three hundred feet.

Successive waves can't coordinate their attacks in the low visibility, so instead of massing against a point of attack, they disperse across the front, some of them drifting into Task Force Papa Bear's sector, which guards the right rear flank of the division. Some Iraqi units collide, while some slip through the lines, penetrating to the headquarters company at the center of Papa Bear. At that moment, Papa Bear is engaged in the largest tank battle in Marine Corps history, with a large armored force attacking from the west.

At 0800 Colonel Richard Hodory, commander of Papa Bear, and his staff are in their headquarters vehicles as an Iraqi T-55 tank and three armored personnel carriers emerge from the fog and halt about fifty yards away. The tank sits motionless, its gun sighted exactly on Hodory's command vehicle. But instead of firing, the Iraqi commander gets out of his armored vehicle and surrenders.

The Iraqi commander says he is part of the brigade that attacked the right flank earlier. Within minutes, the rest of the commander's force also finds Hodory but attacks the command post. Major John H. Turner reports, "We had main gun rounds, machine gun tracers and even 5.56-millimeter fire [from India Company 3/9, friendly fire] coming through the CP [command post]. I remember hitting the deck for the first time during the war and I saw tracers going through the CP from east to west at knee height.[16]

The headquarters company counters with grenade launchers, heavy machine guns, and antitank weapons. They kill one enemy tank and several armored personnel carriers. The remaining Iraqis retreat into the fog.

1100 Hours

The Iraqi counterattack is over, and the First Division again controls the battlefield. Remnants of the Iraqi force surrender or withdraw north and west into the smoke of the burning al-Burqan oil field. In a pitched battle lasting three hours, the enemy has lost seventy-five tanks and twenty-five armored personnel carriers and had three hundred prisoners taken. No Marines were killed or injured.

Mattis and the 1/7 are ordered to stay in position at al-Jaber while the rest of Task Force Ripper moves north. Task Force Grizzly is ordered to move up from its blocking position behind the second obstacle belt and relieve Mattis at the airfield. They are delayed by the traffic jam in the lanes and sporadic skirmishing with separated, lost Iraqi units along the way.

After about three hours of sleep and thirty hours of maneuvering, interrupted by four hours of intense firefights in heavy, unventilated MOPP suits, Mattis and his men are just at the leading edge of exhaustion. Mattis allows most of the men to rest as they wait and again sets the first watch. As the sun begins to warm them in their steel vehicles, the Marines on watch ward off sleep with instant coffee poured directly from the packet onto their tongues and whatever sugary treats they can find in their MREs. The morning wind has changed, lifting the fog and oil smoke around them, relieving some anxiety about being surprised by tanks rolling up on them.

Hours tick by, and still Grizzly is not in place to relieve them. Mattis is going to have to drive hard across probably mined and defended territory to catch up with the rest of Ripper after Grizzly does arrive. There is nothing to do but wait in the stifling vehicles until then. Many of the men and all of the vehicles are covered in a light film of crude oil encrusted with grit and sand. They have been sweating, swearing, and farting in their MOPP suits for over a day. They are beginning to stink horribly.

0230 Hours

Task Force Grizzly arrives at the al-Jaber airfield and relieves the 1/7. Mattis gives the command to move out, and the 1/7 advances double-time to the northeast to catch up with Task Force Ripper.

The wind changes direction again, enveloping the battalion in a thick blanket of toxic oil smoke. By 1500 the sun has vanished into a darkness so black that even night-vision devices are useless.

Mattis positions CAAT 1 and CAAT 2 forward, protecting the battalion's left and right fronts, as he keeps the companies into a tight wedge formation with Team Mech at the point, Company C on the left, and Team Tank on the right. Gunnery Sergeant Cochran will note that "It was like being in a black hole."[17]

Driving blind to the possible threats around them and relying entirely on GPS, the 1/7 manages to find and rejoin Task Force Ripper. The task force is now ready to attack Kuwait International Airport.

0654 Hours

Continuing smoke and cloud cover eliminate fighter-attack aircraft and limit the use of Cobra attack helicopters. Reports at headquarters indicate that the Iraqi III Corps are receiving orders to withdraw. Commanding general Boomer of the First Marine Expeditionary Force wants III Corps caught and wiped out. He orders First Division commander Myatt to start the attack.

The battleground approaching the airport is littered with immobilized enemy tanks and abandoned vehicles. But some Iraqis remain in their vehicles, lying in ambush for the Marines. As Task Forces Ripper and Papa Bear advance, scout detachments use thermal sights to determine whether the vehicles have a "hot" or "cold" signature, indicating whether their systems are turned on. Hot vehicles survive only seconds after discovery. It is stop-and-start fighting as Ripper and Papa Bear crawl forward. Ripper is ordered to halt ten miles south of the airport. Myatt orders Papa Bear into a flanking position for the final push through Saddam's front door. All units are ordered to halt for the evening.

0615 Hours—25 February 1991

Task Force Ripper advances in a wedge formation, with the Third Tank Battalion in the lead. Gunnery Sergeant Cochran journals:

> Moved out 0615 for next obj[ective] which was Kuwait International Airport. Ambushed by small arms fire from l[eft] flank. We returned fire, they disengaged and fled. We are getting reports of Iraq units surrendering in mass now and leaving equip[ment] abandoned in place. Encountered many abandoned inf[antry] positions and tanks as we move on north, and recon by fire. Move into small bunker complex. Destroyed 1 bunker. Stopped at LOA [limit of advance] for resupply and orders. Visibility very bad all day. Can't see well [and] can't range to tgets [targets]. Must fire all engagements from established battlesight SOP [standard operating procedure].[18]

0904 Hours

Task Force Ripper is attacked by small-arms fire on their left or western flank. They return fire at the attackers while continuing to advance northeast. It is only harassing fire by a band of disorganized, poorly led infantry and quickly dissipates. Saddam's reign of terror over senior military commanders, who are constantly suspected of plotting against him, has left many demoralized officers in charge of timid and unmotivated troops. This weakness at the very heart of Saddam's army is causing the uneven resistance and collapse the Marines are finding all around them. Many brave Iraqis maintain military discipline and fight, some even valiantly. Others, poor farmers and tradesmen pressed into service and motivated only by the threat of being shot by their commanders, decide to shoot their commanders instead and surrender.

About an hour into the attack, Mattis's 1/7 runs into a large un-mapped quarry directly in front of it. Mattis shifts the 1/7 left into Third Tank Battalion's zone to get around the quarry. He confirms his identity with Third Tank to avoid a friendly-fire incident. CAAT 2 and Team Mech, up front at the point, pour heavy machine gun fire into the quarry as they pass, probing for hidden enemy. The quarry is quiet.

As they pass the quarry to resume their position in the advance, a hailstorm of steel slams into them from barely visible dug-in positions in front of them as the train of unarmored supply trucks trailing them is attacked from behind. It is a trap. Enemy troops and armored vehicles pour out of the quarry and tear into the soft-sided trucks. The 1/7 is surrounded.

Mattis halts and, under heavy fire, organizes a rescue of the supply vehicles behind him. With the low visibility and spotty air reconnaissance, he has no idea of the size of the attacking forces in front or in back of him. He pulls a section of the CAAT 2 anti-armor company and Company C mechanized infantry from his front and sends them to take on the quarry attackers. For some time, as in a venerated story of the 1/7 in a previous war, the battalion is fighting in several directions at once. At that battle, the commander of the 1/7 at the time, the Marine legend Lewis B. "Chesty" Puller, shouted to his executive officer, "They're on the left of us, on the right of us, they're behind us and in front of us. They won't get away from us this time!"[19]

Following Chesty's example of explosive aggression, Mattis attacks to his front as Company C attacks to the rear. Mattis sees several enemy cannon shells skip harmlessly along the ground through his formation, missing every vehicle and exploding behind them. Colonel Fulford will later say that divine inter-vention prevented the Iraqis from hitting anything in several engagements. Mattis felt he was simply up against "the gang who couldn't shoot straight." In any case, Mattis is beginning to be rumored as having that most important quality in battlefield commanders, the one that the Emperor Napoleon insisted upon before commissioning his leaders. He is lucky.

Company C finishes cutting the quarry attackers to pieces behind them, killing dozens of dismounted troops and destroying several vehicles. They pursue the retreating Iraqis into the quarry and finish them off.

As the guns go quiet in front and the quarry becomes a silent graveyard, Mattis halts again to assess casualties and allow CAAT 2 and Company C to rejoin the steel spearhead. Then 1/7 rolls on again over the broken bodies and burning machines of some of Saddam's best fighters. They continue toward their attack position near Kuwait International Airport.

Halting at their attack position, Task Force Ripper and the 1/7 again wait for Task Force Papa Bear to join them. Papa Bear has swept the al-Jaber airfield and is on its way north. Near Kuwait International, CAAT 2 begins taking sporadic small-arms fire from a group of buildings 650 yards to the northeast. Mattis, perhaps still edgy after driving into the ambush at the quarry, unleashes the full fury of his weapons against the building—artillery, mortars, machine guns, 40-millimeter MK-19 grenades, and light anti-armor weapons (LAAWs). Thousands of glowing orange-yellow tracer rounds rain fire into the buildings, and explosions blast gaping holes in their sides, rocking them on their foundations. In moments the burning, shattered buildings collapse, burying the dead and wounded attackers inside together.

They have picked the absolute worst time to shoot at Jim Mattis and his men. While other units have been running into bunkers of Iraqis ready to surrender after brief firefights, Mattis has been running into well-planned and competently led ambushes. By the time he and the 1/7 get to the airport, shooting at Mattis is like poking a mad dog with a stick. The first layer of his reputation, along with his personally disliked nickname, "Mad Dog," has been created.

1530 Hours

The final advance toward Kuwait International begins in spite of clouds of black oil smoke obscuring nearly everything around them. Minutes into the action, Lance Corporal Peter Ramsey of CAAT 2 spots two "hot" T-54s through his thermal sights, about seventy yards away. Before the Iraqi tanks can even see Ramsey and CAAT 2 through the smoke, a pair of TOW missiles blows both of them to pieces. Another 1/7 crew spots another "hot" T-62 and takes it out with a TOW missile.

Just fifteen minutes into the attack, they roll up on an unmapped obstacle belt that begins with three bands of double-strand concertina wire. Mattis notifies Fulford of the obstacle in his sector, and before Fulford can reply with instructions to go through or around it, Mattis orders a quick breach. He's going through it. Heavy enemy fire across their entire front mixes with a windstorm that blows another coat of sand and crude oil over every machine and every exposed turret gunner. The gunners have to use their fingers to scrape the oil sludge off the glass eye ports of their gas masks to see anything.

By 1609 the 1/7 has destroyed eight armored vehicles. They lay down suppressing fire to protect the engineers who run from cover into the fire zone to manually prime the line charges, forty-foot-long steel chains studded with high explosive. When these are shot out in front of a vehicle across a minefield or other obstacle, the detonator wire frequently snaps, breaking the connection to the remote-control detonator. Combat engineers then have to execute one of the most dangerous assignments in combat: run from protective cover, sometimes under fire, and manually light the fuse to set off the charges.

Two Iraqi tanks suddenly roll out of the smoke two hundred yards to the front and begin raking the engineers with machine-gun fire. They dive for cover. Team Tank zeroes in the Iraqi tanks and blows them away. The engineers repeat their dangerous ordeal three times to open the three lanes that Mattis orders. Team Tank with its mine plows clears two additional lanes so the battalion can pass through more quickly.

When the Iraqis realize that Mattis's 1/7 has just rolled through their best defenses under heavy fire, they begin to disintegrate as a fighting force. As Mattis reported later in *Leatherneck*, the magazine of the Marine Corps, "I think they thought it would take us 24 hours to reach the second breach, giving them enough time to move guns and reposition ammunition supplies, but they guessed wrong. It took First Battalion 40 minutes to clear a path through the first minefield, but only eight minutes to make it through the second breach. That was twice as fast as we did during rehearsals and this was with the added factor of 82mm mortar, 122mm artillery and machine-gun fire."[20]

Mattis and his 1/7 chase fleeing Iraqis north along the western airport perimeter, rolling over and crushing their positions as he goes. He orders a hailstorm of artillery to run ahead of him and then cuts through the surviving enemy like a scythe through wheat. The wind builds into a raging sandstorm, blinding the 1/7 and isolating it from the rest of Ripper. Mattis's GPS navigation fails. He continues the attack. Moments later, the GPS backup system also fails. Mattis continues the attack, navigating with only a compass, a paper map, and odometer readings.

He will never again trust complex electronics in battle, always referring to paper maps. Notoriously spotty radio communications are also not to be trusted. Instead, under Mattis's command, each Marine must know the general's commander's intent before the battle. When communications fail in battle, as they always do, each man knows the strategy, tactics, and objective without further discussion.

Partially blind, with visibility between ten and a hundred yards in all directions, Mattis attacks through the oily darkness, killing everyone in his path who resists but showing mercy to those who surrender. "We did a number of things to lessen their will to fight," Mattis will say later. "We wanted them to know we weren't going to

kill them and when Iraqis hiding in trenches saw their comrades being herded to the rear and the wounded being treated, that lessened
their will to fight even more."[21]

But those who fired on Task Force Ripper were shown no mercy.
They were crushed under the task force's tank treads, plowed into
their graves while still alive, and had their will to fight permanently
shattered by images of violent death that would haunt their nightmares for decades.

1720 Hours

Seven hundred yards south of Kuwait City and four hundred yards
west of the airport perimeter, Mattis halts and orders his infantry
to dismount into the crude-oil-and-sand storm. They take positions
along Highway 6, the main artery into Kuwait City. No one can see
the city less than a half mile away through the storm. The Marines
dig in as the storm pelts them with greasy grit from the bowels of
the earth that stinks of tar and rotten eggs—a genuine shitstorm.

Mattis has outrun the rest of Ripper, exposing his right flank.
As he repositions and waits for Ripper's elements to catch up, his
immediate concern is for his obstacle-clearing vehicles, which are
carrying full loads of high-explosive line charges. A rocket or
mortar hit on any one of them would be lights out for dozens of
Marines. He waits in a defensive formation until the rest of Ripper
and all of Task Force Shepherd catch up, using the thermal sights
of his tank and TOW gunners to see through the shitstorm in all
directions.

Task Force Shepherd, normally covering Task Force Ripper's
right or eastern flank, has been fighting its way up coastal highway
40. About an hour after the 1/7 reaches Highway 6, Shepherd finds
the airport's eastern perimeter fence, turns north and fights its way
up the east side as Ripper had done along the west. Driving north
all the way to the city racetrack, Shepherd hits more Iraqi units at

1830. By 1930 it controls the racetrack and is once again covering Ripper and the 1/7's right flank. General Myatt lets Shepherd rest in place for five hours.

0230 Hours—26 February 1991

Task Force Shepard pulls out from Highway 6 next to Ripper and moves south to assist in the attack on Kuwait International, leaving Ripper in place against any attempted counterattack coming from the city.

0430 Hours

The attack on the airport begins in complete darkness. At 0645, the Marines raise the Marine Corps colors on the flagpole in front of the airport terminal. Fighting has stopped all across the division front. Myatt orders a halt for all units. For Mattis and the 1/7, the war is over.

1615 Hours

Myatt downgrades the MOPP level to zero, allowing the Marines to get out of their chemical protection suits for the first time in almost four days. An hour later the order comes down to stop taking the nauseating nerve agent protection pills (NAPP) and Cipro antibiotics that have been required since August.

The First Division has lost eighteen Marines killed in action, and fifty-five have been wounded. They've lost one tank, one truck, one howitzer, and one Humvee. Saddam has lost 10,365 troops by surrender, an unknown number killed and wounded, 600 tanks, 450 armored vehicles, and 750 trucks. As Mattis and his 1/7 stand at their post south of Kuwait City, Saddam's remaining 70,000 troops are in full retreat across the border, headed north back to Iraq on Highway 80. There they meet the Marine Third Air Wing and a battalion of the US Army's CH-64 Cobra helicopter gunships in what is officially known as the Battle of Rumaylah, for the oil fields nearby, but unofficially known as "the turkey shoot." Highway 80 unofficially becomes known as "the Highway of Death."[22]

As the sun comes up on February 27, 1991, Saddam's elite Republican Guard Divisions lie defenseless and strung out along eighty miles of the highway without cover or air defenses of any kind. They never make it back to their barracks in Baghdad. Saddam will lose another seven hundred military vehicles and estimates of up to ten thousand additional men along the Highway of Death that day.

Apparently, Saddam leads a country that can survive ten thousand deaths in one day—as he had taunted President Bush that America could not do. Saddam's Iraq not only survived ten thousand deaths that day, it was invigorated by them.

This humiliation at the hands of the Americans has revealed the weakness of Saddam's Sunni tribe. To survive among their enemies, they immediately begin to rebuild their army. Over the next decade, Saddam will foment and finance terrorist covert operations to internally weaken America and other enemies, stockpile more chemical weapons, begin developing nuclear weapons and a gigantic science-fiction creation last attempted by Adolf Hitler, called a Super Gun. For Mattis, the war against Saddam Hussein, which he thought ended at the Kuwait International Airport, in fact has just begun.

8

The Sleeping Enemy

My philosophy of command has several basic assumptions.
First, all Marines want to do the job. Second, mission accomplishment in the Marine Corps requires the combined
efforts of all hands. Last, I assume that all Marines can be
trusted.

—Captain Jim Mattis, "Concept of Command," 1983

Lieutenant Colonel Jim Mattis and the Marines enjoy a hero's welcome back in the United States. The first military parades since the
end of World War II shower Desert Storm veterans in New York
City, Washington, DC, and California with honor and ticker tape.
The 1/7's Marine Corps Band marches through Oceanside, California,
home city of Camp Pendleton, playing the "Marines' Hymn" for
adoring citizens waving yellow ribbons and American flags. The
stain of disgraceful retreat from Vietnam is suddenly bleached from
memory by the glaring sunlight of victory. America has formed a
powerful fist of allies and crushed a snarling Iraqi braggart like a fly,
liberating the Kuwaiti people and creating the beginning of a new
world order with America as the clear leader.

In Saudi Arabia, it is the feast of Eid al-Fitr, the beginning of
Islam's holiest season. Twenty-four thousand mostly American
coalition troops remain in Saudi Arabia, keeping a watchful eye
on Saddam Hussein and other threats against the kingdom. The
postwar calm in Saudi Arabia is roiled by the rest of the Islamic
world exploding into turmoil. Riots of rage warn leaders of the

vengeance intended toward them. By not supporting Iraq, they have strengthened the foreign invaders. They are apostates of the true Islam, they have humiliated their citizens, and most unforgivable of all, they have shown weakness.

Five thousand enraged demonstrators in Algiers wave new Iraqi flags in solidarity with Saddam. The green in the flag of Iraq is now black, indicating mourning, and inscribed in the center in Saddam's own handwriting[1] is "Allahu Akbar" (God is the Greatest), the ancient battle cry of faithful Muslims not heard for centuries. The committed secular socialist suddenly transforms himself into a religious leader. His propaganda ministry floods the Muslim world with the devotional story of Saddam transcribing a personal copy of the Koran with his own blood. This is to thank Allah for giving him the strength to beat back the new infidel crusaders and chase them from Iraq. Saddam calls all faithful Muslims, the dispossessed heirs of the great Ottoman caliphate, to jihad. Avenge this new infidel crusade that has torn Kuwait once again from the motherland, he urges. The Islamic world has begun to fracture. On one side are the jihadi or Saddam Muslims; on the other is the Saudi King Fahd, and the infidel Muslims.

In the holy city of Medina, Saudi Arabia's final preparations are being completed for the coming feast and holy month. An angry young man supervises the finishing touches to the holy mosque for his family's construction company—a global conglomerate that has been given the exclusive contracts to renovate all of Islam's holiest sites, including Mecca. A fervent Muslim, he broods over a recent insult from his king. He offered his own army of one hundred thousand devout Muslim fighters to Saudi King Fahd to help push Saddam from Kuwait but was rejected in favor of the Americans. Now the angry young Osama, heir to the bin Laden family construction business, will not forgive his king. Instead, he will side with the defiant strongman and visionary of a new Islamic caliphate, Saddam Hussein, and devote the rest of his life to the promotion of jihad.

★ ★ ★ ★

In Twentynine Palms, California, forty-one-year-old Lieutenant Colonel Jim Mattis squares away the men and equipment of the 1/7 who have just returned from war. Readiness exercises are routinely scheduled and conducted by the combat veterans of Desert Storm to set the lessons of Kuwait in muscle memory for new Marines coming into the unit. Maneuver warfare—shoot and scoot—is now the operating principle in training that the vets drill into the new men recruited into the 1/7. The pace is relaxed and steady, and motivation remains high. No one believes they are going to avoid another fight for very long. Many feel they should have gone all the way to Baghdad and taken out Saddam while they had the chance. Few doubt that when they are called upon again, they will be headed back to the Middle East.

At his headquarters desk, Mattis chips away at the mountain of post-deployment paperwork. His focus on "brilliance in the basics" in the field is now applied to his office work. He devours post-operation literature on lessons learned in Desert Storm in articles like "The Corps' Potable Water Capability—Assessing the Corps' Manufacture and Provision of Potable Water in Middle Eastern Deserts" in the *Marine Corps Gazette* and "Options in the Middle East—A Presentation of Policy Options Available to the US and Allied Countries, and to Iraq, in the Middle East Crisis" from the US Naval Institute's *Proceedings.*

It is well above his current pay grade to be considering policy options, but completely within his grasp. He has just helped create history, firsthand, on the ground. From his devoted study of the subject, he knows that nothing about the Kuwait campaign, other than the new weapons, would surprise previous campaigners, from Alexander to T. E. Lawrence, better known as Lawrence of Arabia. With time now to reflect on what just happened and what it predicts, he likely knows he has something to say about it, something important to contribute.

He maintains a daily ritual of interacting face-to-face with the men of the 1/7, infusing them with his quiet energy and keeping their motivation high. But at the end of each day, the empty, endless Sonora desert of California is there to remind him that he is stuck in a remote outpost, far away from where decisions are being made.

At forty-one, he has put in his twenty years with the Corps. He has proven himself in combat as a fierce and effective commander. He is the warrior he sought to become. He could walk away now and enjoy the hell out of a life safely beyond the Rocky Mountains, fishing on the Yakima River, working in the food bank in his hometown, and entertaining the local ladies. But it's not to be. America's new enemies in the Middle East are well known for maintaining blood vendettas over centuries. They are working even now, patiently and diligently, to avenge their recent defeats. Mattis seems to understand this and decides that his next years will not be spent entertaining women or fishing on the Yakima. Instead he will stand watch as America's gathering enemies prepare for battle. When the order comes, America's enemies will again become his enemies. And again they will not succeed, not on his watch. He applies for a position at Marine headquarters in Virginia, in the Enlisted Assignments Branch.

May 1991—Marine Headquarters— Quantico, Virginia

Mattis reports for duty as assistant head of the Marine Corps Enlisted Assignments Branch. He has his foot in the door of the nerve center of the Marine Corps, where the big decisions are made. His experience as an effective recruitment officer in Portland makes him the ideal candidate for the job. In reviewing his application for the position, heads of the enlistment branch no doubt have pulled his concept of command paper about the Portland recruiting post from his service file. In his concept of command, the then thirty-three-year-old Mattis wrote:

My philosophy of command has several basic assumptions. First, all Marines want to do the job. Second, mission accomplishment in the Marine Corps requires the combined efforts of all hands. Last, I assume that all Marines can be trusted. While there may be individuals in my command who do not live up to my assumptions, the tone of my command group will be in step with my assumptions. Marines who fail to live up to my expectations will be dealt with directly, and on an individual basis, but the character of my command will not be affected by those who fail.

My responsibilities as commanding officer will be to set the tone for the station, imparting the necessary sense of urgency while remaining positive at all times. This will best be accomplished by ensuring my personal example is above reproach, my performance is competent, and exceeds the standards I set for subordinates. It is also my responsibility to define the mission in such a manner that each Marine knows what part of the mission is his individual responsibility.

After two pages of precise goal-setting and anticipated challenges, Mattis concludes:

Recruiting is a vibrant, people-oriented assignment. The ultimate goal I have is to know that all Marines assigned to me in stations from Pocatello, Idaho to Coos Bay, Oregon to Vancouver, Washington are working in the best interests of our Corps, and, while giving 100 per cent effort in accomplishing their mission, do nothing to bring discredit on the Corps.[2]

Within a year, Mattis will be head of the Marine Corps Enlisted Assignments Branch at headquarters, with a secure career track far from the torments of the battlefield.

1218 Hours—23 February 1993

Perhaps just as Lieutenant Colonel Mattis is thinking about what to have for lunch, his secure career track gets derailed. The battlefield has followed him home. A high explosive truck bomb has ripped through the underground parking garage of the World Trade Center in New York City. Six are dead, thousands injured, and $1 billion in damage done. Osama hoped it would be worse. With his knowledge of construction, he thought the Twin Towers would topple, or at least be made unstable and uninhabitable, a crippling blow to the US economy. The Americans would retreat within their borders and leave his Saudi king and the Jewish stone in his shoe, Israel, unprotected and vulnerable.

Osama stays hidden, issuing a statement through proxies proclaiming a new Islamic army and promising more attacks if the United States does not leave the Middle East and abandon Israel. Mattis is suddenly in a beehive of speculation. Immediately thoughts at headquarters turn to Saddam, but within days the Blind Sheik, Omar Abdel-Rahman, is caught, and a different picture emerges. The sheik is a genuine Muslim leader, not a calculating poseur like Saddam. There is a genuine Islamic army out there somewhere. Suddenly Mattis's job, like that of every person in uniform, is to figure out who, exactly, has declared war on the United States, and where they are.

While Mattis is working overtime to understand the levers of power at headquarters, his 1/7 Marines ship out for Operation Restore Hope to Mogadishu, Somalia. They live in the Mogadishu Stadium Complex and conduct peacekeeping operations in the city and surrounding cities, patrolling the same areas where Army, Air Force, and Navy special operators will soon fight and lose the First Battle of Mogadishu to Muslim militiamen, a battle that will be dramatized in the movie *Black Hawk Down.*

23 April 1993

The 1/7 returns to Twentynine Palms from Somalia. Perhaps spurred on by the stories his friends bring back and the recent World Trade Center attack, Mattis makes his move to engage in military foreign policy conversations at the highest levels. He leaves the Enlisted Assignments Branch and enrolls in the National War College to pursue his second master's degree, this one in international security affairs.

As Mattis pursues his studies in quiet, bucolic Virginia, Somalia continues to slide deeper into murderous chaos under militant Muslim control. At the same moment in Europe, Yugoslavia suddenly explodes into a genocidal frenzy, much of it against Muslims. In news reporting it is known as the conflict in Bosnia and Herzegovina, or the Bosnian War. In military detail, it is actually ten small wars, each deadlier and more barbaric than the last. Eventually they escalate into the ethnic cleansing campaign of the Serbian Christians against the Bosnian Muslims. Before American air power and diplomacy bring the campaign to an end, 140,000 people will be killed. Current international policy becomes the urgent topic at the National War College, and Mattis is in the middle of the discussion.

In his paper *The Macedonian Conundrum*, published by the National War College that year, Army General Lawrence Adair writes, "The outbreak of war in the former Yugoslavia has presented the United States with a glaring denunciation of its ineffectual efforts to espouse a comprehensive policy towards this complex region. Foreign policy leaders have been increasingly reactive to shocking developments in the Balkans and seem especially impotent to promote even the most modest calls for stability."[3] Clearly Adair feels there is a pressing need for new American military strategy and strategists. He continues, "It is essential that the present hostilities not migrate south, endangering not only Greece and Turkey, but perhaps inviting the threat of Islamic extremists of the Middle East as well."[4]

But it is already too late to avoid the threat of Islamic extremists. To Osama and Saddam, the Muslim blood spilled in Bosnia is an invigorating tonic. The Crusades have returned, but the crusaders aren't coming for the Holy Grail: they are coming for the Holy Land itself, and the oil underneath it. Across the economically depressed and culturally isolated Middle East, religious jihadis and economic soldiers of fortune are recruited by the thousands.

Mattis's moves from battalion commander to headquarters staff to student of international defense policy have put him squarely in fortune's favor. While in his studies at the National War College, he is promoted from lieutenant colonel to colonel. The number of unforeseen regional conflicts in Europe and the Middle East make finding experienced new leaders like Mattis urgent. He is an engaging young man, full of incisive ideas grounded in an encyclopedic understanding of history. He has an easygoing, confident manner. His classwork is well regarded, garnering attention from his influential instructors and guest lecturers. Good fortune ushers his writings and reputation into the halls of power in nearby Washington, DC.

Graduating with his master's degree in international security affairs, Mattis enjoys a reunion with his old outfit, but now as its regimental commander. He now commands the three battalions of the Seventh Marine Regiment, including its first battalion, the 1/7. The regiment's mission is to be ready on forty-eight hours' notice to go anywhere in the world and hit the ground fighting. Mattis steps up an already rigorous training schedule, alternating between desert and amphibious exercises on the sand dunes of Twentynine Palms and the beaches of Camp Pendleton in Oceanside, California.

But at the end of each training day, the endless, parched Sonora desert or dusty hills of Camp Pendleton offer Mattis only solitude. He is mostly out of the loop of policy discussions back east. As regimental commander he is now desk-bound, limited to talking on the phone with headquarters about his regiment's day-to-day operations. The nearby desert town of Joshua Tree, population 7,414, offers cold beer and little else. He reads, he trains, he waits for orders. After two years of waiting by the phone, it finally rings with orders for Mattis himself to report to the Pentagon. The secretary of defense, William Perry, wants to speak with him.

Just as Mattis was graduating from the National War College, Perry, along with coauthors Ashton Carter and John Steinbruner, published *A New Concept for Cooperative Security*, laying out America's unique position in the post–Desert Storm world. In this highest of high-level policy papers, Perry calls for new thinking about America's defenses, just as Adair did in *The Macedonian Conundrum* during Mattis's previous time at the college. "For US security policy in particular, the conceptual crisis is acute," Perry suggests. "The USSR is gone; Iraq's military machine is defeated. The absence of immediate threat is welcome, but also disorienting. Countering threats and deterring through readiness are the traditional bases for defense planning. Yet in both conventional and nuclear realms, today's defense policy problems are not anchored in immediate threat."[5] He goes on to indicate how Mattis's on-the-ground experience and grasp of military history may have attracted Perry to the "lucky" Marine colonel:

> In the aftermath of the Persian Gulf War, the United States is generally conceded to possess a power projection capability, based on the reconnaissance strike complex [the ability to see and fire on targets hidden and beyond conventional ranges] that no other military establishment can match, not without also matching the lengthy and intense investment that created it.
>
> For more than a decade to come, therefore, no other military establishment will be able to contemplate any major offensive without acknowledging that the United States is capable of decisive countermeasures. That inevitability

makes the United States, in the estimation of most countries, the ultimate answer to acts of aggression; for some it also makes the United States a potential problem.[6]

Obviously, Perry is thinking of the vanished Russian threat, similar to Mattis's concern years before in his first student paper at the Command and Staff College. Perhaps this was another point of agreement that brought Mattis to Perry's attention.

Unfortunately for America, Perry had little concern about the danger rising in the Middle East that had just hit the United States at the World Trade Center. Asymmetrical warfare from private Islamic militias was not a concern for top-level planners in the Pentagon yet. In Saudi Arabia, Osama bin Laden's repeated threats against the kingdom and its American allies were downplayed. Defense minister Prince Sultan bin Abd al-Aziz al-Saud called the small attacks carried out by Osama's jihadis the previous year as "boyish," and stated that "the Saudi Kingdom is not influenced by threats."[7]

For the next two years, Mattis learns the job of secretary of defense at Perry's elbow. As Perry's executive secretary, he helps him prepare for policy battles with Bill Clinton's White House, funding battles with the 104th Congress, political intrigues in Washington, and the inertia of a bloated defense bureaucracy that is the nation's largest employer. Every week the department meets a payroll of 1.7 million active duty service members and 1.1 million civilian employees. Toward the end of Perry's tenure, while America is looking the other way, Osama's dismissed jihadis strike.

2220 Hours—25 June 1996—al-Khobar, Saudi Arabia

An enormous bomb concealed in a diesel-fuel truck explodes at the perimeter of the King Abdel Aziz airbase near Dhahran. The blast is so powerful it is felt twenty miles away in the country of Bahrain. It kills nineteen US Air Force pilots and mechanics whose mission it was to enforce Operation Southern Watch, the no-fly zone in southern Iraq, as they sleep in their beds. It injures another four hundred people in and around the airbase's tower.

Again, Osama stays hidden, letting the Saudis blame Iran and Hezbollah for his handiwork. Journalist Abdel Bari Atwan writes in *The Secret History of Al Qaeda*:

> In May 1996 Bin Laden and his entourage moved from Sudan to Afghanistan. As if to make the point that they might have been chased out of Sudan by Saudi Arabia and the US [but] they were not leaving with their tails between their legs, al Qaeda struck again: The June bombing of Khobar Towers. The Saudi authorities were at pains to implicate Shi'a militants backed by Iran in this attack, since the embarrassing truth that they had their very own homegrown militancy problem was inadmissible; they did not want to give the impression that there was domestic opposition to the deployment of US troops on Saudi soil.[8]

The pursuit of the Khobar bombers strains the battle-tested friendship of the United States and Saudis. Suspicion that the Saudis have a rat in their house grows in the United States.

William Perry leaves shortly after the reelection of Bill Clinton for a second term, and in the midst of the Monica Lewinsky sex scandal. He is replaced by Maine senator William Cohen. Mattis stays on through the transition period at Defense, and then flees Washington for Marine headquarters in Quantico, Virginia. Fast-tracked now as an up-and-coming policy wonk and operations whiz who is an adept player in the political big leagues, he is assigned as director of Manpower Plans and Policy division and, on October 1, 1997, promoted to Brigadier General.[9]

For the first time, Mattis controls a significant lever of power. He reports on and recommends the number of Marines recruited, trained, and deployed and has a seat at the table for many major policy decisions. He cuts staff in his division and instills a high-energy, high-efficiency work tempo that creates order by its momentum. To the amusement and admiration of his colleagues, Mattis rejects the privileges of power. He makes his own coffee, carries his own bags—if traveling overnight, a standard-issue green canvas sea bag—and largely handles his own filing and office work. His style is what Pentagon reporters call "unaffected."

Down the road at the White House, Bill Clinton is succeeded by President George W. Bush. Cohen is out at Defense, and Donald Rumsfeld and Assistant Secretary of Defense Paul Wolfowitz are in.

Temperamentally, Secretary Rumsfeld is like Mattis. They both work fast and like things lean and efficient. Bloated staffs, gone. Extra paperwork, gone. Long meetings, gone. Rumsfeld gets into the office early and works at a stand-up desk, handwriting notes at a furious pace, often late into the night. He attacks the Pentagon bloat, cutting over a hundred thousand civilian staff jobs and saving the department hundreds of millions of dollars a year. He is aggressive, combative, and unapologetic. Suddenly, the tone in the secretary of defense's office and in the George W. Bush White House is once again on Mattis's wavelength.

Philosophically, the new deputy secretary of defense, Paul Wolfowitz, is a near perfect match for Mattis. Wolfowitz has followed Mattis's career since Desert Shield and Desert Storm, when Wolfowitz was undersecretary of defense to Dick Cheney. In Cheney's office, Wolfowitz's team raised $50 billion in allied financial support for the operation.[10] Wolfowitz was in the room with Cheney, Colin Powell, and President George H. W. Bush when they decided on February 27, 1991, to destroy Saddam's army on Highway 80 but leave Saddam alive in Baghdad. Wolfowitz later publicly regretted that decision, testifying before a congressional committee that "the best opportunity to overthrow Saddam was, unfortunately, lost in the month right after the war."[11]

In that month after the war, Wolfowitz was horrified when "Saddam Hussein flew helicopters that slaughtered the people in the south and in the north who were rising up against him, while American fighter pilots flew overhead, desperately eager to shoot down those helicopters, and not allowed to do so." He went on, "Some people might say—and I think I would sympathize with this view—that perhaps if we had delayed the cease-fire by a few more days, we might have got rid of Saddam Hussein."[12]

Wolfowitz and Mattis see eye to eye, generally, on matters of warfare. Through dedicated study, they both have come to appreciate Eastern culture and empathize with the ordinary people in those regions. Wolfowitz, as ambassador to Indonesia under George H. W. Bush, a Jew in a majority Muslim country, fully embraced the culture, even learning the language. He was a highly effective and well-liked envoy with a "keen personal interest in development, including health care, agriculture and private sector expansion," according to a *Washington Post* interview.[13]

During George W. Bush's 2000 presidential campaign, Wolfowitz helped produce an influential ninety-page report called *Rebuilding America's Defenses: Strategies, Forces and Resources for a New Century*.[14] Although he is uncredited in the report, Mattis, with his intimate knowledge of current defense manpower and resources, may have been a significant contributor to Wolfowitz's thinking. Echoing the recommendations in *The Macedonian Conundrum*, the report states, "At present the United States faces no global rival. America's grand strategy should aim to preserve and extend this advantageous position as far into the future as possible."

The report's concepts find their way into Bush's campaign speeches and begin to form the Bush Doctrine, an aggressive national defense policy eventually including the concept of preemption, the justification of a first strike against perceived threats.

Through April 2001 Mattis helps Wolfowitz and Rumsfeld detail the emerging policy. Finally, the rebuilding of America's defenses is set into motion after years of the Clinton "procurement holiday," billed publicly as the "peace dividend" and credited to the president's economic and diplomatic successes. The truth is that Mattis, working behind the scenes at the highest levels of political power, helps pull the lever to dismantle and reverse Clinton's defense policy.

Now that he is actually working the controls of military power, Mattis is required to complete a mandatory course of instruction called Capstone for all new generals and admirals, taught over one month at the National Defense University. Through Capstone, Mattis is armed with the knowledge of how all the elements of national power are integrated. He learns the protocols for executing military strategies with interagency and multinational operations. At the age of fifty, he has been given the keys to America's armory and the operating instructions.

Perhaps this achievement of power in 2001 is just one more instance of Jim Mattis being lucky, as Napoleon would have seen it. Or maybe, if you believe in such things, it is something closer to his destiny.

0846 Hours—11 September 2001

On this day 2,605 Americans—along with 372 foreign nationals from over 50 countries—are burned or crushed to death in Osama's attacks against the Pentagon in Washington, DC, the World Trade Center towers in New York City, and United Airlines Flight 93. The victims include a group of children on a school trip and elderly grandparents returning from a family reunion.

It has been ten years since Desert Storm, but Mattis makes it plain to his superiors that he is a combat commander. Given command of the First Marine Expeditionary Brigade[15] and assigned to conduct exercises with Egyptian forces, he forms up his command staff, starting with Marine lieutenant colonel Clarke Lethin.

As a young lieutenant, Lethin helped Mattis rejuvenate the failing recruiting station in Portland, Oregon. Working together, they maintained a vision and offered themselves as living examples of what a young man could make of himself as a Marine. They inspired their junior officers to exceptional efforts and turned the station around from barely adequate to remarkable success. But that was fifteen years ago, and Lethin is now looking forward to retirement from the Marine Corps. Mattis calls his old friend to recruit him for a new difficult and dangerous assignment with absolutely no upside that is beginning to percolate up through channels. At first, Mattis doesn't even tell Lethin where they are going. "I don't know where it is," he says, "but we are going to do something, and I want you to come along."[16]

Later, when Mattis is briefed on the coming expedition, he asks to have a private conversation with Lethin's wife, Wendy, both to take some of the weight of explanation off his friend and to make sure Wendy and their young boys are on board. In his talk with Wendy, Mattis says, "We are going to go to Afghanistan and we're going to kill those guys. This is going to be a long war and a lot of people are going to die. Are you ready?"[17]

All Mattis has to offer the family in return for Lethin's hazardous duty and at least one year away from home is gratitude. The Lethin family once again answers the call to duty, agreeing to postpone Clarke's return to civilian life.

With Lethin as his chief of staff, Mattis begins to form his core group of leaders, who will take a task force halfway around the world to fight in primitive, unforgiving Afghanistan. The force will include Mattis's Marine Expeditionary Brigade and two amphibious ready groups of the Navy, organized around the warships USS *Peleliu* and USS *Bataan*.

Mattis tells his group, "Okay, this is what we're going to do. We're going to get over there and form a very small team . . . and we're going to start thinking about what we are going to do to go kick some ass."[18] Typically, he insists on "a small staff comprised of aggressive officers who [are] able to act with initiative, make rapid decisions and recommendations, and exercise good judgment." Because of the small staff, he makes it clear that everyone is expected to fill sandbags.[19]

In Washington, the creators of the emerging Bush Doctrine begin to grapple with the complexities of responding to an enemy without a state or even uniforms to identify them. Secretary of Defense Donald Rumsfeld starts sketching in the United States' response on September 12 in a note to President Bush, that will later be reported by David Martin of CBS News. Rumsfeld writes, "Best info fast. Judge whether good enough [to] hit SH [Saddam Hussein] at the same time. Not only UBL [Usama bin Laden]. Go massive, sweep it all up. Things related and not."[20]

By September 30, Rumsfeld expands on his recommendations in a memo titled "Strategic Thoughts."[21] The Bush Doctrine is now to include the Global War on Terrorism as official US policy:

The US strategic theme should be aiding local peoples to rid themselves of terrorists and to free themselves of regimes that support terrorism. US Special Operations Forces and intelligence personnel should make allies of Afghanis, Iraqis, Lebanese, Sudanese and others who would use US equipment, training, financial, military and humanitarian support to root out and attack the common enemies . . .

. . . It would instead be surprising and impressive if we built our forces up patiently, took some early action outside of Afghanistan, perhaps in multiple locations, and began not exclusively or primarily with military targets but with equip-and-train activities with local opposition forces coupled with humanitarian aid and intense information operations . . .

... A key war aim would be to persuade or compel states to stop supporting terrorism ...

... If the war does not significantly change the world's political map, the US will not achieve its aim. There is value in being clear on the order of magnitude of the necessary change. The USG [US government] should envision a goal along these lines:

New regimes in Afghanistan and another key State (or two) that supports terrorism (to strengthen political and military efforts to change policies elsewhere).

Syria out of Lebanon.

Dismantlement or destruction of WMD capabilities in [redacted].

End of [redacted] support for terrorism.

End of many other countries' support or tolerance of terrorism.

For reasons known only to the gods of war, Mattis is once again at the tip of the spear as a front-line commander leading America against a Middle Eastern enemy. Everything he has ever studied and worked for seems to have prepared him for this moment commanding America's powerful war machine. What he is unaware of at the time is the extent of Rumsfeld's intentions with the Global War on Terrorism, as revealed in Rumsfeld's first private note to President Bush the day after 9/11. Saddam Hussein was included at the top of the enemies list, along with Osama.

Saddam has earned his top spot on Rumsfeld's list. Since his defeat at the hands of Mattis and other "crusaders" in 1991, he has been supporting a wide variety of revolutionary, liberation, nationalist, and Islamic terrorist organizations and investing heavily in training camps for foreign "fighters," particularly Palestinians. Documents captured after the fall of Baghdad in 2003 reveal meticulous accounts written just after 1991 of development, construction, certification, and training for car bombs and suicide vests. Along with Osama, Saddam had been actively hunting Americans for over a decade when 9/11 happened.

Although Saddam and Osama do not agree on the ultimate goals of jihad, they have each promoted it for their own purposes. Both want Europeans out of Arab lands, but Osama wants an Islamic caliphate ruled by theocrats, and Saddam wants a pan-Arab state ruled, presumably, by himself. In America they've found a common enemy. For his part, Saddam has financed, equipped, and trained groups that are either associated directly with al-Qaeda, such as the Egyptian Islamic Jihad, led at one time by Osama's deputy Ayman al-Zawahiri, or generally share al-Qaeda's vision. The popular claim by Bush Administration opponents that Saddam had nothing to do with Osama and 9/11 is technically true but, in practical terms, naive. Rumsfeld, Wolfowitz, and Bush have not been fooled by Saddam's front groups or Osama's denials of responsibility. They expanded the Bush Doctrine to attack both enemies, and then went looking for a gunfighter like Mattis to track them down and kill them both.

9

Graveyard of Empires

When you're wounded and left on Afghanistan's plains,
And the women come out to cut up what remains,
Jest roll to your rifle and blow out your brains
An' go to your Gawd like a soldier.
  —Rudyard Kipling, "The Young British Soldier"

May God keep you away from the venom of the cobra, the
teeth of the tiger, and the revenge of the Afghans.
  —Alexander the Great

The Marines' invasion of Afghanistan is a task only one of a very few, like Mattis, could have managed. Extending that campaign into a second long war with Saddam Hussein is a task that almost none but Mattis, a bachelor with few commitments at home, could have completed. Even with Mattis's unique qualities of leadership, neither of these goals are good bets in 2001.

The distance from the sea that Marines can travel inland and still be effective, according to decades-old Marine doctrine, is 200 miles. Just to get to the border of landlocked Afghanistan from the Arabian Sea is 350. Mattis considers this first problem of existing Marine doctrine and eventually concludes, "Doctrine is the refuge of the unimaginative."[1]

He has to get access to critical seaports and airfields from America's unsteady ally Pakistan to transport his task force north into Afghanistan. He flies northwest 700 miles from the USS *Peleliu* to Islamabad, Pakistan, with Lieutenant Colonels Broadmeadow and Carl, paying a surprise visit to Wendy Chamberlin, the new US ambassador to Pakistan. Only a few weeks earlier, Chamberlin presented her credentials to Pakistani president Mussharaf. Now, surprised and annoyed to see Mattis and his Marines standing in front of her without an appointment, she asks sharply what they are doing in her office. In his gentlemanly and respectful way, Mattis introduces himself and his officers, then answers her question with a grin: "Me and about a thousand of my best friends are going to go up north to Afghanistan to kill some people."[2]

Chamberlin, apparently relieved or amused by Mattis's straight talk, a rarity in her line of work, invites him and his men to sit down. In what will become a fast friendship and close working partnership, the relatively new general and new ambassador talk for a long while about the general's concept of operations and limited military intelligence and basing resources, as well as the intent of the Bush Administration after 9/11. In spite of her relative inexperience in Pakistan, Mattis will later comment that Chamberlin was "magnificent," going on, "Frankly, we couldn't have done the job without her leadership and assistance and her guts in taking risks. I hid nothing from her, held nothing back on the details of our coordination with the Pakistanis and the Con-Ops [concept of operations] for our attack."[3]

A few weeks before the attacks, Chamberlin had a private dinner with President Pervez Musharraf at the Pakistani ambassador's house, where Musharraf said, "My vision of the country hinges on increasing foreign investment in Pakistan and economic growth, but the level of domestic terrorism is currently too high. Pakistan needs strategic depth in Afghanistan to ensure that there is a friendly regime on Pakistan's western border."[4]

Musharraf was speaking of the Taliban. This was the friendly regime on the Pakistani border ensuring the strategic depth he needed. His intelligence service, the ISI, had painstakingly developed and encouraged the Taliban's control of Afghanistan over the past decade. It was about to become Chamberlin's job to persuade Musharraf to betray the Taliban and risk not only his strategic depth in Afghanistan but his own survival at the hands of his notoriously bad-tempered intelligence service.

In Washington at that time, the negotiations were almost as difficult. President George W. Bush and his National Security Council were struggling with the strategy to topple the Taliban and seize northeastern Afghanistan. At this point Mattis and the Marine Corps were not even considered a possible option. As Historian Benjamin Lambeth notes, "The decision-making process for Enduring Freedom was very much the opposite of that of the Gulf War, in which General Norman Schwarzkopf led from his forward headquarters in Riyadh, Saudi Arabia, issuing broad guidance to his component commanders and expecting them to develop and execute specific operational-level plans. Instead, decision making for Afghanistan was closer in character to Operation Allied Force [in Yugoslavia], in which top civilians and the JCS [Joint Chiefs of Staff] chairman in Washington kept General Wesley Clark on a short leash."[5]

In short, it is a tug-of-war between the administration and the military for control of the coming war in Afghanistan. Even within the military, the Joint Chiefs of Staff seem at odds with each other and with General Tommy Franks, commander in chief at US Central Command. Franks is a flinty, mercurial dictator with a soft spot for his subordinates and a hard edge for his superiors. He met with Pakistani ISI chief General Mahmoud Ahmed the day before the 9/11 attacks, when Franks had already targeted al-Qaeda for punishment and wanted Pakistan's cooperation. He said of the meeting, "I had informed General Mahmoud that cooperation was a two-way street. Pakistan needed parts for its military aircraft and America needed targeting information on al-Qaeda. Mahmoud 'got the message' and promised to brief President Musharraf."[6]

But that meeting was too late. While Franks and Mahmoud were meeting, Osama's men, masquerading as journalists, assassinated Ahmad Shah Masood, the one real leader among Afghanistan's

Northern Alliance and America's only ally in the region. Two days later, Osama launched the attacks on 9/11. America reeled in disbelief, having ignored several unspecific warnings of a terrorist attack. It was a massive failure of military intelligence, and General Franks seemed to have been outplayed by a ragtag band of terrorists. It didn't help the tone of negotiations with the Joint Chiefs.

The day after the attacks, Franks is already deep into strategizing the killing of Osama and destruction of al-Qaeda. After reviewing maps of the region, he comes to the early conclusion that the Marines won't be playing a part in the operation. "We can't make use of the Marines' amphibious capabilities," he says. "Whatever the final shape of the operation, it'll depend on airlift."[7]

It appears that Franks, lacking Mattis's disregard for doctrine and reliance on creative problem-solving, is referring to the doctrinal limits of Marines to operate within two hundred miles of the seacoast. The arc of history bends back toward Mattis's leadership in the war with further high-level talks.

On September 11, just hours after the attacks, Pakistani General Ahmed receives America's demands from Deputy Secretary of State Richard Armitage, who explains to the general without diplomatic niceties, "No American will want to have anything to do with Pakistan in our moment of peril if you're not with us. It's black or white."

Ahmed begins to waver, pleading that Armitage has to understand history. Armitage cuts him off: "No. History begins today."

The next day, September 12, in Islamabad, Ambassador Chamberlin receives State Department instructions and goes to see President Musharraf to ask him a simple question: Are you with us or against us?

The meeting is tense. President Bush is demanding a quick, unequivocal answer from Musharraf. After an hour, there is little progress. Musharraf wavers in his commitment to the United States, so Chamberlin resorts to a dramatic bit of negotiation technique called "the takeaway." Sitting familiarly close to him like the friend she has become, she half turns away and looks down, seemingly troubled. Musharraf asks, "What's wrong, Wendy?"

She answers with a heavy heart, "Frankly, General Musharraf, you are not giving me the answer I need to give my president." Musharraf quickly weighs his options and makes his decision. He states firmly, "We'll support you unstintingly."

A few days later, on September 15, President Bush assembles his war cabinet at Camp David in Maryland. CIA director George Tenet presents a multidimensional plan, including soliciting support from a dozen tribal leaders in southern Afghanistan who oppose the Taliban, al-Qaeda's hosts in the region. He also proposes attacking their financial resources, tracking down their sympathizers in the United States, and conducting covert operations to detain al-Qaeda operatives.

But when the Joint Chiefs present options developed by Franks and the Central Command planners, Bush finds their suggestions insufficient. Secretary Rumsfeld agrees, even calling the options outdated. He argues for unconventional special operations forces. He scolds the Chiefs and Franks, "Get a group functioning fast. Lift out of the conventional mind-set. This is chess, not checkers. We must be thinking beyond the first move."

Bush, Rumsfeld, and Mattis all see the problem of this new asymmetrical warfare the same way. The old ways of fighting a war are not going to work in Afghanistan. Brute force, as the Soviets and all those who came before them learned, will not work in the Graveyard of Empires. This is going to be a thinking man's war. This "new" type of war at the crossroads of history plays to Mattis's particular strength, as a lifelong scholar of warfare. He already knows from his studies that there is nothing truly new about fighting in Afghanistan that hasn't already been learned by past invaders like Alexander the Great, Genghis Khan, various Persian empires, the British Empire, the Sikh Empire, and recently the Soviet Union. The challenge is getting the twentieth-century Marine Corps up to speed for this ancient challenge.

★ ★ ★ ★

On 9/11 the Marine Corps has only a tan double-wide trailer up on cinder blocks in the parking lot in back of General Tommy Franks's imposing Central Command headquarters in Tampa, Florida. Colonel John A. Tempone is the Marine commander in charge. He corresponds frequently with a similar skeletal Marine presence in Bahrain. These two men and a handful of junior officers are the total Marine Southern Command, covering twenty-five countries, including Afghanistan. The rationale behind this minimal force is the Marine Corps' reputation for improvising and getting the job done no matter what, whenever called upon. Since 1775 at Tun's Tavern in Philadelphia, when General Washington was in a hurry to recruit fighting sailors to attack the British at Fort Nassau in the Bahamas, the Marines have always been first in line when there was trouble but last in line at budget time. Apparently nothing much has changed since then.

The luck or the fate that has shone on Mattis during his career still seems to be lighting his way. He happens to be in Bahrain commanding the First Marine Expeditionary Brigade (I MEB) in a cooperative exercise with the Egyptians called Operation Bright Star when Osama attacks the Twin Towers for the second time, and the Pentagon and White House. Mattis is the most forward deployed (closest) Marine force to Afghanistan.

After General Franks's traditional land invasion strategy is shot down by Rumsfeld and Tenet and the new CIA, Special Forces and Marine strategy starts to be developed. Mattis is called into the office of US Navy vice admiral Charles W. Moore, commander of US Naval Forces Central Command in Bahrain. Moore offers Mattis the job of commander of a new naval expeditionary force to go after Osama. Normally this command would fall to a naval officer, but Moore favors the Marine Mattis as the best choice to lead the combination of ground combat operations, CIA, Army and Navy Special Forces, and the Northern Alliance that has been picked to get the job done.

Mattis is ready. He begins by taking his existing I MEB command staff, including Lethin, Broadmeadow, and Carl, and folding in Tempone and his junior officers as his liaison at Central Command. With this tiny group, he staffs a reaction force that changes Marine doctrine by achieving the deepest insertion of Marine seagoing forces in history. Officially they are called Naval Expeditionary Task Force 58. Their mission; find Osama bin Laden and his al-Qaeda organization and kill them all.

To ensure that his small staff is strong enough to manage such a complex mission, Mattis draws from the book *Good to Great* by Jim Collins. This is a key book in the Mattis library that he recommends pointedly for staff members. Essentially, Collins accelerates the process of natural selection. He advises that, once recognized, a weak staff member be immediately marginalized. His duties and responsibilities are then gradually fed to the wolves, the stronger members of the staff. If the weak staffer gets stronger because of this, he survives; if not, his entire job gets eaten by the pack. He is immediately sent back to his parent command. No explanation, no excuses, no second chances. Within weeks Mattis's small staff is honed into a powerful, cooperative wolf pack of leaders.

Beyond his immediate command staff, Mattis cuts out entire echelons of administrative staff, supporting them using a technique called "skip echelon" outlined by British field marshal Sir William Joseph Slim in his book *Defeat into Victory*.[8] He also learned of skip echelon from an Iraqi Army major captured in Desert Storm. Since Iraq was once a British colony, it is likely the Iraqi major also learned the technique from Field Marshal Slim's book. Staff reduction is necessary because of the limited space and resources allotted to Marine command in Bahrain. Mattis eventually settles on a general staff of approximately thirty-two by eliminating, among others, the brigade's surgeon, staff judge advocate, chaplain, and sergeant major.

America is in a big hurry to taste revenge while it is still hot. They want Osama's head on a stick and don't much care who or what the obstacles are. It comes down to Mattis's team to sort out the logistics of coordinating and moving a task force from eleven countries, including eight thousand US Marines and sailors, over four hundred miles inland, and capturing a forward operating base (FOB) they call Camp Rhino. Mattis's operations officer, Lieutenant Colonel Lethin describes some of that process:

> There were a couple of desert landing strips; Bastogne, An-zio, one other that they were using. So the idea was, maybe we go in there and we seize that for a 72-hour period and run a FOB, or an ISB [intermediate staging base], or a FARP [forward arming and refueling point] to go and do a limited raid and come back.
>
> . . . We'd already been looking at how we were going to do it, developing the plans to do that, so when we did get the orders, it didn't take much to speed up. In fact, we were ready to move before they were ready to unleash us.[9]

With US ambassador Wendy Chamberlin successfully paving the way across Pakistan by securing access to staging areas and supply routes, Mattis begins his assault. Marine Corps commandant James Jones sums up Mattis's approach and its effect on al-Qaeda's host, the Taliban: "[Task Force 58's] arrival hundreds of miles from their Navy base ships in the North Arabian Sea took the Taliban by surprise; they had not expected to face the traditional 'assault from the sea' Marines in the land-locked nation of deserts and mountains they had ruled for more than a decade."[10]

Mattis dives into the job of what many military analysts consider to be "the most difficult amphibious landing in 20 years."[11] He continues to draw heavily from his reading of military history in order to "practice informed boldness."[12] He credits the lessons of history, including British major general Orde Charles Wingate's operations in Burma, the firebase concept used during Vietnam, and Grierson's Raid during the Civil War. As Mattis says, these "broaden your operational reach, giving you mental models that you can apply imaginatively."[13]

Major Wingate fought in Burma under Field Marshal Slim. Between these two, Mattis has the models for his "skip echelon" command structure and innovative field tactics for mountainous terrain that he will update for Afghanistan. In 1944, Wingate developed the tactic of flying his forces behind Japanese lines to "operate in comparatively small, lightly equipped columns to harry communications and rear establishments."[14] Mattis affirms Wingate's tactic, saying, "Give me 1,000 men ashore for 30 days and we could make the enemy's life hell on earth for raids." At the supreme commander level, Field Marshall Slim's objectives for Wingate included inflicting "the greatest possible damage and confusion on the enemy in North Burma."[15]

This echoes the intent of Mattis's supreme commander, President George W. Bush. Mattis also seizes on Slim's directive of confusing his enemies. It is the polar opposite of the clarity and efficiency of Mattis's own operations. Feints and slashing, lightning-speed advances to throw the enemy off balance become the hallmarks of Mattis's way of war. Perhaps as a constant reminder, he adopts the radio call sign Chaos, which will stay with him for the rest of his career. With typical humor, he claims the call sign is an abbreviation for "commander has an outstanding suggestion."[16]

0800 Hours—13 September 2001— The White House

CIA director George Tenet, Secretary of State Colin Powell, and counterterrorism chief Cofer Black brief President Bush on the agency's fully developed plan to merge CIA paramilitary teams, US Special Operations Forces, and airpower to kill Osama and destroy al-Qaeda and the Taliban. But even with overwhelming US advantages, there will be a price. Black has been told that al-Qaeda does not surrender or negotiate. The great martyred Northern Alliance leader Massoud once told him, "We've been fighting these guys for years and I've never captured one of these bastards." The reason is that any time al-Qaeda is overrun, they bunch together and detonate a hand grenade, killing themselves.

Black explains to Bush, "Mr. President, we can do this. No doubt in my mind. We do this the way that we've outlined it, we'll set this thing up so it's an unfair fight for the US military. But you've got to understand people are going to die."[17]

Bush is tired of talking. He wants Osama and all of his friends dead. Black says, "When we're through with them they will have flies walking across their eyeballs."[18] Bush looks around at the faces of his advisers for any last objections. Finally he nods and agrees with Black. America's Global War on Terrorism begins. Moments later in Bahrain, Mattis receives orders from Central Command, including an operation with the CIA code name Operation Jawbreaker.[19]

2045 Hours—7 October 2001— Kandahar, Afghanistan

American and British Special Operations teams "paint the targets" with laser indicators on the ground as fifteen US bombers and twenty-five strike aircraft attack. US and British ships and submarines offshore of the Pakistani coastal city of Karachi, 470 miles south, fired about fifty Tomahawk missiles an hour earlier. Fireballs erupt from Taliban air defense installations, the defense ministry, airport-based command centers, airfields, electrical grids, and fuel depots. America is clearing its throat, preparing to deliver its answer to Osama for his attacks.

Mattis starts the ground campaign against the Taliban in the north, because opposition from neighboring Tajik and Uzbek tribes against the Pashtun Taliban is strongest there. Three hundred and forty miles north of Kandahar, in the Dar-ye Suf and Balkh River Valleys, CIA teams fight their way up the valleys with Northern Alliance allies toward the city of Mazar-e-Sharif. The smallest four-wheel vehicles are too big and too heavy for the narrow and fragile mountain trails, so men and equipment travel on horseback along the precarious paths, with thousand-foot drops on one side.

Several of the CIA's Jawbreaker team have never been on a horse before. They are told to ride with their downhill foot out of the stirrup in case the horse stumbles. They then have a chance to fall back onto the trail while the horse plummets a thousand feet down the cliff. The Jawbreakers take their weapons off safety and rest the muzzles aimed at the back of their horse's head, prepared to shoot the animal if it stumbles.

After a day or two of riding, the Jawbreakers are terribly saddle-sore, close to becoming combat ineffective. A hundred jars of Vaseline are delivered by airdrop. Unfortunately, the dirt in Afghanistan is a fine rock dust that lingers in the air and covers everything. This fine dust collects on the Vaseline, which, instead of helping, is turned into sandpaper. Two hundred pairs of pantyhose arrive by airdrop. In Mattis's operations shop, a thinking man has reasoned that if pantyhose worked to relieve skin irritation for quarterback Joe Namath in Super Bowl III in 1969, it would work for the CIA cowboys in Afghanistan. It does. Pantyhose saves Operation Jaw-breaker.

The Jawbreakers with their Northern Alliance allies sweep up the Dar-ye Suf Valley, taking the villages of Bishqab, Cobaki, Chapchal, and Oimetan. On November 5, they overrun the Taliban manning the Soviet-built defensive posts at Bai Beche. Fifty-eight miles to the east, in the narrow Balkh River Valley, Jawbreakers capture the key blocking city of Ac'capruk. A rapid advance to the objective, Mazar-e-Sharif, is now possible.

On November 10 Mazar-e-Sharif falls, collapsing the Taliban

position in northern Afghanistan. Taliban defenders near Bamiyan in central Afghanistan offer only light resistance before surrendering on November 11. Before the battle for Bamiyan, Taliban commander Mullah Mohammed Omar uses scarce ordnance to blow up the 150-foot-tall fourth-century Buddha statues carved into the side of a limestone cliff outside the city. Buddhist religious art is apparently a greater threat than the US Special Forces bearing down on him. Kabul surrenders without a fight on November 13. Also, apparently, the native Afghan Taliban fighters don't share their Arab al-Qaeda allies' preference for death before surrender and are captured en masse.

On November 20, Mattis flies with nineteen of his command staff from Bahrain to the USS *Peleliu* off the coast of Karachi. They cram into their floating forward command post, about the size of a Manhattan studio apartment. Within minutes, one bulkhead wall is covered with computer screens. A paper map of Pakistan and Afghanistan covers the other. Radio, telephone, and face-to-face chatter floods the room, bouncing off the metal floor and walls. The noise level inside rapidly escalates to uncomfortable.

Minutes later, Mattis and his staff assemble in a briefing room to hear their weeks of planning repeated back to them in detail in a three-and-a-half-hour confirmation briefing. D-Day is set for 1700 Zulu (Greenwich Mean Time), six hours behind local time, on November 23. Combining the humanitarian relief elements, the CIA, US Army and Navy Special Forces, and eleven allies, it is easily the most complex landing plan in anyone's memory.

Because Mattis trusts his staff's capabilities, he is able to focus on issues facing his front-line grunts. For example, Central Command (CENTCOM) has sent rules of engagement for taking FOB Rhino that require a hostile act or intent to be committed or demonstrated prior to the engagement of potential targets. It sounded like a load of diplomatic fertilizer to Mattis. He shoots back an official request that all personnel in the landing zone be declared hostile. Ground force commanders have to be able to engage targets at will. After some time wrestling with CENTCOM and engaging Admiral Moore in the fight, Mattis wins, and his rules of engagement are approved.

The initial three-and-a-half-hour confirmation briefing on the *Peleliu* also isn't enough time to cover the flow of Marines from the landing areas like FOB Rhino to the intermediate staging bases in Pakistan and coordination with Marine liaison elements already on the ground. It also isn't enough time to review much detail of Mattis's overall concept of command, which integrates the Fifteenth and Twenty-Sixth Marine Expeditionary Units (MEUs) with his Headquarters unit.

The thrown-together Task Force 58 contains three separate command structures—Mattis's headquarters and the two subordinated commands of the Fifteenth and Twenty-Sixth MEUs, totaling seven ships containing dozens of ground and aviation elements, and over eight thousand individuals who have never before trained together as one unit. Mattis decides that keeping the MEUs separate and using "supporting / supported" relationships, depending on the mission, is the most logical choice under the time constraints. They will soon find out if Mattis's call sign, Chaos, better describes Task Force 58 or the enemy.

2300 Hours—25 November 2001— Operation Swift Freedom

Mattis's first objective inside Afghanistan is a former hunting camp with a 6,400-foot dirt runway and a few buildings surrounded by a white cinder-block wall. Sometime in the distant past it was the retreat of an Afghan prince, used for hunting with falcons. Now it is a cement and dirt compound in the middle of a frigid, barren landscape 3,285 feet above sea level and ninety miles south of Kandahar.

Guard towers stand at the four corners of the block wall, protecting a warehouse, a water tower, half a dozen smaller buildings, and a mosque. Each of the towers has a single hole from a cannon round in its roof. Many of the buildings were shot up during Operation Sword, which kicked out the Taliban on its way north a few weeks earlier. Now the place looks lifeless and empty under the freezing night sky.

Battalion Landing Team 1/1, that includes Alpha, Bravo, Charlie, and a weapons company, steps out of transport helicopters just outside the walls, weapons ready. The mission tonight is to secure the compound. It will be the command post for the coming attack against Kandahar. A reconnaissance team moves inside the walls as the others set a watch. In minutes, recon reports buried enemy dead inside, possibly booby-trapped, and ordnance left behind from the Operation Sword raid. Otherwise, it's clear.

That first night Lieutenant Nathaniel Fick and Bravo Company sleep on the icy cement floor of the warehouse. At daybreak they move outside the walls and dig in. Bravo takes the southeastern corner. Charlie Company is on their left flank, and Alpha on the right. The landing team's weapons company digs in their mortar positions behind Bravo's position. Explosive ordnance disposal (EOD) teams comb the grounds inside the compound for mines, booby traps, and unexploded munitions. So far, the operation is textbook seize and hold. No sign of chaos on the ground, no word from Chaos on the radio. The perimeter is secure, and word goes back to the *Peleliu.* Forward Operating Base Rhino is captured without a shot. Task Force 58 is operating smoothly—no confusion, no accidents—except for one diplomatic complication. Operation Swift Freedom is a success.

Support personnel, flown in from the staging base at the Pasni airfield in Pakistan, partition buildings and select spaces for the command post, hospital, maintenance areas, supply warehouse, antenna array, and latrines. Samples from the water well are flown back to the *Peleliu* for testing.

On the hangar deck of the *Peleliu,* more Marines prepare to ferry ashore to Pasni on hovercraft for an evening helicopter flight to FOB Rhino to reinforce Operation Swift Freedom. Reporters watch as the Marines load gear and ammunition into multiple rucksacks. Marine doctrine specifies 50 pounds as the correct combat load for a rifle or weapons company Marine; these Marines routinely carry up to 175, in multiple packs. Finished packing, they paint their faces with tan-and-black camouflage war paint. Mattis enters the deck and visits with his fighters. Embedded news reporters move to Mattis. They want to know how the operation is going so far. Feeling optimistic and probably relieved at the smooth function of the operation, he lets his guard down and makes a political blunder. He tells the reporters that the Marines are "going to support the Afghan people's effort to free themselves of the terrorists and the people who support terrorists. . . . The Marines have landed and we now own a piece of Afghanistan."[20] Colonel Thomas D. Waldhauser, commanding officer of the Fifteenth MEU, will later recall, "It was really . . . awesome . . . one of those days where things go well and you just have to savor it."[21]

Similar relief and pride swells throughout the ranks of the Marines. At FOB Rhino, Lieutenant Fick wants to check out a small hill next to the base runway as a possible observation position, since the corner guard towers would be the first targets in an attack. He takes his sergeant with him and keeps one eye on the ground, since a landmine might have been missed by the EOD teams. Fick writes in his book *One Bullet Away*:

> While looking down at the ground, I spotted a piece of paper plastered against the dried husk of a bush by the incessant desert wind. I peeled it off. It was notepaper, the size of a thank-you card, bearing a photocopy of the famous picture of three firefighters raising the American flag over the rubble of the World Trade Center. Above them, in block letters, were the words FREEDOM ENDURES.[22]

Nearby, an American flag waves on an improvised flagpole in the freezing winter wind. Sergeant Joseph R. Chenelly, a combat photographer assigned to Fifteenth MEU, writes in his journal, "One of the first platoons on the ground raised an American flag high into the new dawn sky on a makeshift pole proudly marking the Marines' successful landing."[23]

That first platoon is Charlie Company. Charlie's staff sergeant Norris, a native of Brooklyn, stands under the flag and speaks to the handful of grunts who gather around it. He speaks emotionally, the images of 9/11 still raw in his memory: "This is for our great country, the United States, and the great city of New York. Marines take pride in raising the flag, and pride doesn't begin to describe the feelings today. I hope these colors can be seen all the way across Afghanistan."[24]

Unfortunately for Sergeant Norris and General Mattis, they are. They are seen all the way to Washington, DC. The State Department gets wind of the flag raising and hears Mattis's comments on the evening news reports. Mattis gets a call the next day: the Marines are to stow their pride and take down the flag. In a Washington press briefing later that day, Secretary Rumsfeld walks back Mattis's comments, saying that the Marines are

> not an occupying force. Their purpose is to establish a forward base of operations to help pressure the Taliban forces in Afghanistan to prevent Taliban and al-Qaeda terrorists from moving freely about the country. We think of them as a— establishing a forward operating base. And we don't discuss future plans or developments, so there's really nothing one would say beyond that, except that that's what the—these are hundreds, not thousands, of Marines.[25]

Although he does not mention him by name, Rumsfeld covers for Mattis saying he is a, ". . . very fine officer . . . clearly exuberant . . . speaking figuratively, not literally."[26]

On Mattis's end, every Marine he sees peppers him about the flag coming down and the diplomatic backtracking. Mattis toes the political line, saying no one wants the Afghans to think they are being conquered. They are being liberated. The final slap comes from General Franks at Central Command. He bans use of the name Operation Swift Freedom.[27] The Marines' first act of retaliation for 9/11 is uncelebrated and will remain unnamed.

Slightly more than two months after 9/11, the most strategically important city in Afghanistan, Kabul, surrenders to Afghan forces advised by Americans. After a twelve-day siege, five thousand Taliban and al-Qaeda fighters are trapped in the city of Kunduz, ninety-seven miles east of Kabul. They surrender on November 26. The Taliban's capital city of Kandahar in the south is next in Mattis's playbook.

On the *Peleliu*, Mattis gives the order to begin moving his command post up to FOB Rhino. On November 27, a Marine KC-130 transport flies Mattis, Colonels Lethin and Broadmeadow, other key command staff, a communications team, and a Seabee liaison officer to FOB Rhino. Task Force 58 staff is now stretched between Rhino, the *Peleliu*, and Bahrain. Mattis delegates naval operations to the shipboard commander of the *Peleliu* and focuses his attention on the ground operations of taking Kandahar.

Mattis strides down the loading ramp of the plane, carrying his own gear, and crosses Camp Rhino toward his new forward command post. Fick and his sergeant are scouting resources for Bravo Company among the bustle of activity on the base when they see the general coming toward them. "Good afternoon, sir," they greet Mattis without saluting—Marines in the field don't salute officers, to avoid identifying them to enemy observers and snipers. Mattis is genuinely happy to see the men. He grabs Fick's whole arm and works it like a water pump. "Good afternoon, young warriors."[28]

Fick goes on to describe his first encounter with Mattis: "Of slender build and wearing glasses, he carried his pistol in a leather shoulder holster. Without preamble or small talk, he praised our mission in Afghanistan. 'You need to know how much you've already accomplished by being here. You prove that the United States has the balls to put troops on the ground in Afghanistan. You've emboldened the Northern Alliance to renew its pressure on the Taliban and al Qaeda in Kandahar. You've reassured Americans at a time when they sorely need it.'"[29]

Mattis chats with the men for a moment longer, and he's on his way. He finds the small, windowless building that is in the process of becoming his forward command post, climbs the stairs, and pushes through the plastic sheet doorway into another overcrowded room. Computer stations fill the far corner; overhead lighting shines on the laminated maps taped together across the longest wall. Rifles are stacked by the door like brooms. Chatter and activity from the dozens of infantry officers, helicopter pilots, SEALs, Australian Special Air Service men, and CIA operators in parkas and wool caps crowded around the monitors and maps is already jacked up like the bar at a Saturday-afternoon ski lodge.

Mattis gets down to work. His military plans are complicated by the simultaneous humanitarian assistance campaign. Decades of war and several recent years of drought have brought Afghanistan to the brink of starvation just as international aid organizations are fleeing the country, fearing the US military campaign. Now, with winter closing in, hundreds of thousands of Afghans depend on supplies that the United States and her allies deliver.

Airdrops started weeks before from C-17s flying out of Ramstein Air Base in Germany, delivering food rations, blankets, and other supplies. Over the course of Operation Enduring Freedom, 2.5 million meals, along with raw wheat, 55,000 blankets, and other humanitarian supplies, are delivered.

Future Afghan president Hamid Karzai commands Afghan recruits advised by US Special Operations Forces in an advance on Kandahar from the north. Karzai's father, Abdul Ahad Karzai, was the chief of the powerful southern Popalzai tribe until he was assassinated in

1999 by agents of the Taliban. Now Hamid, as the new chief of the Popalzai, whose home territory is Kandahar Province, joins forces with
Gul Agha Shirzai—nicknamed Bulldozer for his coercive tactics—
who advances from the south, also advised by US Special Forces.

Troops and munitions continue to arrive at Camp Rhino in the
buildup toward offensive operations against Kandahar. Fick's Bravo
Company, with 168 troops and nine Humvees, is stretched with
Alpha and Charlie Companies over a J-shaped defensive perimeter
enclosing the airfield, ammunition supply point, fuel dump, helicopter park, and headquarters. The front line covers almost two
miles, and it takes about two hours to walk the line, checking on the
Marines in their fighting positions.

1120 Hours—27 November 2001—FOB Rhino

An armored convoy is detected fifty miles northwest of the base,
near Lashkar Gah. There are fifteen vehicles, including two Soviet-
era armored personnel carriers. Central Command observes
the convoy for three and a half hours to make sure it is not a
humanitarian group. Eventually two patrolling Grumman F-14B
Tomcats from the USS *Carl Vinson* attack the two personnel carriers at the head of the convoy. Two AH-1W Super Cobra helicopters hear the F-14 pilots over their radios and join in the attack
on the rest of the column, destroying it.

Captain Barranco, piloting one of the Cobra helicopters, describes the attack: "At least some of the Taliban were out of the
vehicles. I'm guessing they thought they hit a mine since the F-14s
were so high. They heard us and some of them started firing wildly
in the air toward the sound of the Cobras—the rest started running.
We made several passes destroying the vehicles and killing the
squad."[30] Passing back over the convoy, the pilots use their night-
vision goggles and infrared sensors to make sure that nothing and
no one survives.

Back at FOB Rhino, Mattis seems concerned that this early encounter with armored vehicles could mean enemy tanks aren't far behind. He calls his light armored vehicles forward to reinforce the dozens of Humvees now at Rhino. A section of C-17 transports fire up onboard the USS *Peleliu* and prepare to deliver the vehicles to Rhino.

At Fick's front line, the grunts dig deeper to improve their fighting positions, but discover limestone bedrock under twelve to eighteen inches of sand and rock dust. Standard-issue entrenching tools pry up chunks of rock. Improvised picks and crowbars are scrounged from the supply depot to break the hard rock. Mortars are test-fired in earthshaking blasts that send plumes of dust high into the desert sky. Several times a day Fick and his Marines clean the talcum-fine rock dust from their weapons. They adopt an operations cycle starting at 0500 hours, about an hour before sunrise. The Marines "stand to" in the bone-chilling predawn wind, manning their fighting positions, raising their security posture to 100 percent alert. An hour after sunrise they "stand down," dropping to 25 percent alert, where one man in four is armed and ready for action. Charlie Company's Captain Putman recalls, "The Marines were not suffering from boredom; we kept them focused."[31]

One night, well after midnight, when the temperature is again far below freezing, Fick walks the defensive perimeter, checking on his men. He finishes inspecting about half the fighting holes in his sector and is in the middle of a gravelly flat near the runway's end when he approaches another fighting hole, careful to come from the rear and listen for the verbal challenge. It is a combined anti-armor team made of one anti-tank Javelin rocketeer and a rifleman. There should be two Marines in the hole, but in the bright moonlight, he sees three heads silhouetted against the sky. He slides down into the hole and finds Mattis leaning against a wall of sandbags, chatting with the sergeant and lance corporal like they are waiting in the chow line.

Fick writes about this encounter,

> This was real leadership. No one would have questioned
> Mattis if he'd slept eight hours each night in a private room,
> to be woken each morning by an aide who ironed his uni-
> forms and heated his MREs. But there he was, in the middle
> of a freezing night, out on the lines with his Marines.
>
> General Mattis asked the men if they had any complaints.
> "Just one, sir. We haven't been north to kill anything yet."
> Mattis patted him on the shoulder. I had heard that he was
> old school, that he valued raw aggression more than any other
> quality in his troops. "You will, young man. You will. The first
> time these bastards run into United States Marines, I want it
> to be the most traumatic experience of their miserable lives."[32]

Mattis is about to keep his word to the young lance corporal. He
has already drawn up orders to send his men to cut off the southern
escape route from Kandahar. Reports that nineteen thousand Taliban
currently hold the city mean that they will certainly be outnumbered by escaping fighters as Afghan forces under Karzai from the
north and "The Bulldozer" Gul Agha Shirzai from the south close
in. Their saving grace will be air power overhead, the force multi-
plier that allows Mattis to maintain a fast, light assault force against
much larger numbers.

The strategy and tactics of Mattis's plan are derived in part from
the Vietnam era "firebase" concept of using airpower instead of artillery for fire support. Only his critical personal trust in Combined
Forces Air Component commander General T. Michael Moseley allows Mattis the confidence to leave behind his artillery for the first
time in thirty years and entrust Moseley with the lives of his Marines.

Mattis also consciously draws from his study of the Civil War,
particularly Grierson's Raid in Mississippi. This was a demonstration of how a relatively small unit can create chaos in the enemy's

rear by attacking lines of communication. With continuing pressure in the north, Mattis's Marines and Afghan partners will simultaneously attack Kandahar in the south, forcing the Taliban into a dilemma and sowing the enemy chaos Mattis covets. In his commander's intent document that every Marine is ordered to commit to memory, he describes his intended outcome, ". . . Taliban/Al Qaida leaders in disarray, facing an operational dilemma on how to allocate their forces [northern front or southern Afghanistan]." He goes on to describe his intent for the enemy's state of mind: ". . . destroy the enemy's sense of security and shatter his will."[33]

In the fighting holes on this cold night, Mattis checks the one fundamental element he can't find in his study of the history or theories of war: he checks the actual understanding of his commander's intent and the level of motivation of the young men he will soon send to face overwhelming numbers of the enemy.

Kandahar is the spiritual home of the Taliban movement and appears to be their Alamo as well, as resistance in the north continues to collapse. Fifty miles east of Rhino a force of four hundred fighters is detected, and sixty miles to the north a SAM missile is launched at a Navy fighter jet. The Taliban consul general announces that "the fireworks would begin . . . in the United States during the last week of Ramadan in mid-December and that Americans would . . . die like flies."[34]

Australians fight in the Helmand River valley to the west, while SEALs and Special Forces take down Taliban units along the Pakistani border to the east. Karzai's fighters capture a bridge four miles north of Kandahar International Airport.

In Washington, Air Force general Richard B. Myers, chairman of the Joint Chiefs of Staff, summarizes the situation for reporters: "Omar [Taliban commander Mullah Omar] seems to be trying to organize the fighting of the Taliban, and bin Laden, on the other hand, seems to be concentrating on hiding. . . . Again, in Kandahar it's sort of the last bastion, we think, of Taliban resistance. You get mixed reports on whether they're about ready to leave and give up or not. I will go with the secretary on this, in that, from Omar's standpoint, we think . . . they'll dig in and fight, and perhaps to the end."[35]

Just as the pace of men and equipment into Rhino for the assault on Kandahar is stepping up, Mattis runs into a bit of chaos from Central Command. They notify Mattis that they are limiting the number of Marines and sailors allowed at FOB Rhino to 1,000. This throws Mattis a curve in the middle of his meticulously planned operation. Responding coolly that there are already 1,078 personnel on deck, and more on the way, he effectively ignores the order, while over the next few days, Central Command gradually raises the allowable number to 1,400.

In spite of Mattis ignoring Central Command, he confides to other commanders that Command ". . . knew thoroughly that I wasn't asking for 4,500 Marines with the idea of using only 1,000 of them," and that the decision to scale back the number of troops was ". . . managerially incompetent."[36]

Mattis's supply chain rattles to a halt as subcommanders chose which personnel to keep and which to send back to the ships. Lieutenant General Gregory S. Newbold, former director of operations for the Joint Chiefs of Staff and a friend of Mattis, learns of the force cap through e-mail exchanges and gets involved. He later explains,

> The only way that [Task Force] 58 or any other operation in the south could have had an effect is if it threatened the Taliban materially—if it were able to strike and distract or defeat. And ultimately, it had to encircle al-Qaeda and the Taliban in a way that could result in their destruction. . . . That was not possible because of the constraints that General Franks personally put on the introduction of forces there, and it was only much, much later that we moved other ground forces in there, as you know, the 10th Mountain Division.[37]

Newbold queries General Myers if he is aware of the cap. Myers knows nothing about it and contacts General Franks at Central Command, who denies the existence of the order. Myers brings the issue to the attention of Secretary Rumsfeld, who not only denies that his office placed the restriction but also indicates that he never wanted one. Rumsfeld calls Franks and reminds him that Central Command can have whatever resources it needs.

Moving past this command level snafu, Mattis runs into constant demands for more information that drains time and energy from his small staff. He refers to these demands as the ". . . insatiable need for information from higher headquarters."[38]

Commander Frick of the Twenty-Sixth MEU, Mattis's backup force, describes the issue: "That is always going to be a headache, and until somebody can look over my shoulder inside the Pentagon to see what I'm doing, they want to see real time video. . . . Our mindset is like, 'Let me do my job and let me go.' . . . There is a dichotomy between the mindset of the warrior and the information age we live in."[39]

On top of this constant information drain, the slower-reacting US Army takes over tactical control of Task Force 58 from the Navy on November 30, as planned. Previously Admiral Moore, Mattis's strong supporter, and his Navy staff tended to issue over-all mission-type orders, allowing Mattis tactical control on the ground. Incoming Army lieutenant general Paul T. Mikolashek, the Combined Forces Land Component commander, has a differ-ent idea. Mikolashek begins to request more detailed information on a widening range of topics. As the Army staff grows into the hundreds, Mattis's little band of thirty-two begins to strain under the burden of keeping them informed.

One of Mattis's key staff members, Lieutenant Colonel Broad-meadow, explains, "The same guy that yesterday used to do a range of things for you was now doing one thing and one thing only. So, all of a sudden, that one phone call that you could make to get things to happen now became three or four and you had to talk to different guys."[40]

At one point, Mikolashek's crew requires Mattis to submit a concept of operations brief in advance of even small-scale operations, and then he questions the general when he fails to clear a small operation. Mattis will later recall, "I explained I didn't generally ask permission to wipe my nose and that my intentions messages laid out clearly what operations I had coming up."[41]

Colonel Lethin is less diplomatic when he gets hold of one of the Army staff: "Look, Sir, there is one of me and there are 800 of you. I'll talk to you, your deputy, and your current ops, but you guys really need to choose your questions wisely, because I'm [working] 22, 23 hours a day, and I can't answer all of your action officer's, all of your watch officer's questions. I can answer your questions, but I can't answer everyone else on your staff."[42]

By mid-December, as the pace of operations is increasing, Mattis's Task Force 58 is spread across eight different operations centers, including Bahrain, the *Peleliu*, the Ramstein, Pasni, and Jacobabad airfields, the American Embassy in Kabul, and FOB Rhino. Mattis's crew of thirty-two has managed to wrestle control back from the Army and is managing the logistics of the war. Colonel Broadmeadow explains, "It wasn't like your normal logistics system, where you drop a requisition and things start to flow to you magically because of some supply system. It was guys on the phone, people on e-mail, working with their counterparts [in] the other agencies and making things happen on a personal level, as opposed to a systems perspective. So that became a big work-around right there—very, very dependent on personal relations as opposed to systems."[43]

On the ground, Mattis's lightened logistics for fast maneuverability means that the Marines have to make up in determination what they lack in supplies. Snow covers the mountain peaks, and an occasional dusting reaches the rock-strewn Afghan plains where

Lieutenant Fick's Bravo Company is airlifted in to join light armored reconnaissance (LAR) and recon teams already in place. The command post tent is on a rocky rise overlooking a small river. Like the Spartans at Thermopylae, this band of three hundred men will be the anvil to the war hammers that are pounding Kandahar and driving Taliban into their sector.

In freezing temperatures, with the constant Afghan wind robbing whatever heat it finds, the Marines are dressed for the Egyptian desert where they were a few weeks ago on Operation Bright Star. They wear well-ventilated desert boots, light gloves, and thin jackets. Fick is warned by his second lieutenant, Jim Beal, not to touch his rifle in the morning without gloves on. Beal removes his glove and shows him a quarter-sized piece of missing skin where the cold stuck his palm to his rifle barrel.

They are to move into position to stop any traffic on Highway 4, the pitted two-lane road snaking along the side of the river below. The rock pile they are on descends into a scree field of ankle-turning skull-sized rocks that stretches out over several miles toward the highway. The LAR and recon teams fire up their trucks for the move. Fick requests that his men offload some of the 175 pounds off their backs into the trucks. Request denied. The trucks are already fully loaded and will snap an axle with more weight. Fick requests that some of the recon Marines walk on foot with Bravo Company, so the trucks can instead hold some of the Bravo gear. Request denied. The battalion commander doesn't want the companies to get mixed together.

The battalion pulls out, and Bravo Company Marines earn the honored title of grunts as they pick their way across the teetering rocks like overburdened pack mules, faces sweating with strain even in the freezing wind. Fick writes, "I carried six mortar rounds in my pack, plus the radios and all their batteries. But most of the Marines carried even more."[44]

All of Fick's men carry at least their own body weight. This is where the cost of lightened logistics is paid on the battlefield. But

Fick explains why Mattis's system works for Marines: "Strong men hauled heavy loads over rough ground. There was nothing relative about it—no second chances and no excuses. It was elemental and dangerous. It was exactly why I'd joined the Marines."[45]

2–6 December 2001—Highway 4, Thirty Miles South of Kandahar

Fierce skirmishes flare up along Highway 4 south of Kandahar as the Taliban flee the pounding from allied airpower and Hamid Karzai's Afghan national forces breaching the city defenses from the north and Gul Agha Shirzai, capturing Kandahar International Airport to the east. On the night of December 6, Mullah Omar and senior Taliban leadership flee the city and go into hiding. Taliban rule ends in Afghanistan. Mattis's attention turns toward Osama.

The *New York Times*, the *Washington Post*, and the major television news programs in America make no mention of Mattis's achievements. There is no mention of the deepest insertion of assault forces in Marine Corps history, the nearly flawless execution of one of the most difficult and complex operations in recent memory, done with a small staff of thirty-two Marines, and the toppling of a battle-hardened, numerically superior enemy force without one American casualty from enemy fire. Nor has anyone mentioned the historical precedent of a foreign power conquering Afghanistan and then having the good sense to leave the country in the hands of the Afghans.

Like the capture of FOB Rhino in Operation Swift Freedom, Mattis's achievements in Afghanistan are publicly nameless and will remain uncelebrated. But among those who served in Operation Enduring Freedom, Mattis's performance is well noted. Over 2,200 servicemen and women will eventually die in Afghanistan over the coming years of war, but on Mattis's watch nearly everyone comes home.

Osama is tracked to the caves of Tora Bora ("Black Dust," in Pashtun). A twelve-week assault takes the lives of nine Marines and injures dozens of others. Osama escapes to Pakistan, and suspicion falls on the ISI security forces of President Musharraf as the supporting culprits in the escape. Five months after 9/11, Mattis's work is done. For a time, he owned a piece of Afghanistan; now he's giving it back to the Afghans.

As he packs up FOB Rhino for the return flight to the *Peleliu,* Mattis gets a call from his friend and champion Admiral Moore, who tells him to enjoy his return trip and time back at Camp Pendleton, but warns him not to get too comfortable. He will have just enough time to get his Marines reloaded and recocked before they head back to Iraq for a second fight with Saddam Hussein. Mattis hasn't been keeping up on policy developments in recent weeks, and is shocked. It is believed that he replies, "You're shittin' me."

10

City of Mosques

Fallujah's the most morally bruising place in Iraq. It's going
to rock you when an IED goes off and there's blood and shit
all over you. Hold the line. Show the people respect. We're
here to win.

—*Mattis's address to Marines arriving in Fallujah*

Mattis and his Marines take a victory-lap cruise to Australia on their
way home from Afghanistan for well-earned rest and recreation. Unlike Desert Storm, there are no blazing headlines of triumph and no
ticker-tape parades waiting for them at home. Osama has gotten away,
and America's thirst for vengeance is now more urgent than ever.

Probably the last place in the world Mattis and his men want to be
is in a parade of any kind or in their dress blues in front of a droning
politician basking in the reflected honor of their achievements. Their
sense of accomplishment and pride in their performance is more
than enough to keep their spirits high. The admiration of pogs (the
disdainful abbreviation for "people other than grunts," pronounced
with a long *o*) doesn't mean a lot. Being a veteran of Afghanistan is
like being a member of a small, private adventurer's club.

Like many, Mattis's thoughts on the long voyage may have turned
to relationships at home. In recent years he has been keeping company with Barbara, a striking blond photographer with a particular
interest in Marine subjects. She comes from a family who operates
hotels in the San Diego area near Camp Pendleton. She is a quiet,
restful presence who complements Jim Mattis's studious side. They

are often seen together at private dinners, and occasionally at Marine events.[1]

The heads-up from Admiral Moore that Mattis will be shipping out again, very soon, for a second match with Saddam Hussein catches the fifty-two-year-old general off guard. Since returning to a field command for Operation Bright Star, he's missed the final touches added to the Bush Doctrine, which now include CIA director George Tenet's "Threat Matrix"[2] of eighty separate operations. The global war against Osama and Saddam is in high gear. Osama is checked for the moment, and Saddam is next on the list. But this time, unlike Operation Desert Storm ten years earlier, Mattis is not a sheriff delivering an eviction notice from Kuwait; he is an executioner fulfilling a death warrant.

0848 Hours—1 May 2003—USS *Abraham Lincoln*, Off the Coast of San Diego, California

Speaking from the flight deck of the USS *Abraham Lincoln,* one of the United States' most advanced aircraft carriers, President Bush declares that major combat operations are over in Iraq. Two months earlier, Mattis planned and led the march up to capture Baghdad and extended that march to Saddam's hometown of Tikrit. After the longest insertion of forces in Marine Corps history in Afghanistan, the march in Iraq set another record for the longest sustained overland march in Corps history. President Bush explains:

> We have difficult work to do in Iraq. We are bringing order
> to parts of that country that remain dangerous.
> Our mission continues. . . . The War on Terror continues,
> yet it is not endless. We do not know the day of final victory,
> but we have seen the turning of the tide.
> Major combat operations in Iraq have ended. In the battle
> of Iraq, the United States and our allies have prevailed.[3]

The difficult work left to do in Iraq is about to get much more difficult in the backwater industrial city of Fallujah. Once a thriving center of Sunni Ba'athist dominance under Saddam, it is now an impoverished ghetto, seething with resentment against the conquering Americans and their allies. Deposing their leader Saddam as if he were a petulant, nearly defenseless child is one level of insult; to then summarily disband their army of professionals with the stroke of a pen, without thought of how they will then make a living in Iraq's destroyed economy, is an entirely new and intolerable slap in the face.

The five million Sunnis favored under Saddam's reign are used to ruling over their twenty million Shiite and Kurd countrymen. They are used to prestige, power, and deference. They are used to giving orders and having them obeyed. But now they are little more than lowly tribesmen again, pariahs and often targets in the hundreds of revenge killings that happen every day.

As President Bush speaks of the work left to do in Iraq, Saddam's men are seeking a new leader. In Fallujah, Abdullah al-Janabi, a businessman and fundamentalist cleric, is emerging among the Sunnis.[4] Janabi begins to bring together the fractured tribes to negotiate with US Army commanders in the Sunni Triangle north of Baghdad during their transition from power.

But the monster of jihad, instead of having a stake driven through its heart in Afghanistan and then Iraq, pursues Mattis into the Sunni Triangle.[5] An enthusiastic young Jordanian murderer who ran a training camp in Afghanistan, Abu Musab al-Zarqawi, follows Mattis to Iraq and forms Tanzim Qaidat al-Jihad fi Bilad al-Rafidayn, or al-Qaeda in Iraq (AQI).[6] Osama has been grooming Zarqawi for years to advance their dream of a caliphate empire by terrorizing Western and Arab civilians with gruesome soft-target attacks, public hostage beheadings, and improvised suicide weapons. Zarkawi is given the title Emir of al-Qaeda in the Country of Two Rivers[7] and uses his skills to escalate the nascent insurgency against US troops into a Shia-Sunni civil war. He quickly earns the celebratory title Sheik of the Slaughterers.[8]

★ ★ ★ ★

In Camp Pendleton, California, Brigadier General Mattis rests and rearms the twenty-two thousand Marines of his First Division after their historic five-hundred-mile march from Kuwait City to Tikrit, Iraq, in seventeen days of sustained combat. It is never far from his mind that the grunts, the front-line lance corporals and sergeants, are the ones who do the hardest and most dangerous work. To honor them and assign proper credit, Mattis uses some of his time between deployments to elevate the small and visually unimpressive Combat Action Ribbon (CAR) to honor the warriors who truly did the fighting. Under Mattis's new rules, a Marine or sailor must "receive and return fire" or participate directly in ground combat to earn a CAR.

Instead of handing out the ribbons as participation trophies for all support and rear echelon personnel as before, field commanders must now identify the specific combat action when fire was exchanged. The process can take months and now includes close scrutiny by fighters who were "in the shit." Possession of this small decoration, largely unrecognized by civilians, becomes extremely meaningful to Marines.

28 September 2003—Camp Pendleton, California

The last elements of the First Marine Division, Mattis's original combat battalion, the 1/7, finally return to Camp Pendleton from Operation Iraqi Freedom. On the last plane with the 1/7 is their current commander, Colonel Joe Dunford. Dunford and the 1/7 have been home for just over a week, enough time to unpack and visit with some of their family members, when Dunford "[gets] the word" from Mattis. He assembles the 1/7 and tells them, "Okay gang, we're going back for OIF II."[9]

The verbal response from the gathered Marines was not recorded, but some suggest it was a muffled, collective "Fuck." Orders were orders, and Dunford's 1/7 now has theirs. While Dunford offers a colorless summing-up of his unit's response to a local reporter— "So, we immediately went into preparation for it"[10]—the men save their more colorful comments for the One More That's It bar in nearby Oceanside.

They will not be preparing for the type of campaign they have just fought, a lightning-fast, overland rout that propelled them with tanks, artillery, and air cover through the open terrain of the relatively friendly southern provinces. The battlefield that awaits them now in the Sunni Triangle is very different.

Mattis makes certain that every Marine knows the critical differences in the situation they are stepping into. Colonel Clarke Lethin, Mattis's chief of operations since Afghanistan, explains, "The general talked to every Marine in the division at least three times, usually in battalion size. He wanted to talk them through, and image them through, the issues they would face. He wanted to talk about morality on the battlefield, how to go through an ambush one day and have your buddy blown up, and then face Iraqis the next day."[11]

Over the course of the meetings, Mattis circulates more than one thousand pages of reading material, much of it pulled from his own personal library, in three separate emails. The selections range from ancient texts to recent news articles and contain the general's personal commentary on many of the items. It is perhaps the most extensive briefing in the five-thousand-year history of armed conflict. It may have also been the most concise graduate course in insurgency warfare ever created. Thomas Ricks in his book, *Fiasco: The American Military Adventure in Iraq 2003–2005*, writes, "Battalion commanders were required to certify in writing that their subordinates had read and understood the material."[12] No one who followed Mattis into the battlefields of Anbar Province could say they hadn't been told what to expect or what was expected of them.

Ricks continues, quoting Mattis's email:

> "While learning from experience is good, learning from others' experiences is even better,"[13] Mattis wrote in his introductory comment. Again and again the theme of the readings was that Iraq could be frustrating, difficult, and complex, and that leaders needed to prepare their troops for that environment. The articles called for maintaining discipline, honing skills, and having faith in each other—and warned of what can go wrong when soldiers lose hold of those fundamentals.[14]

Ricks writes that among the news articles in Mattis's first batch of material, the general commented on a recent article about the charges against Lieutenant Colonel Allen West, a US Army battalion commander who fired his .45 sidearm next to a detainee's ear during an interrogation:

> Mattis wrote, "[T]his shows a commander who has lost his moral balance or has watched too many Hollywood movies. By our every act and statement, Marine leaders must set a legal, moral and ethical model that maintains traditional Marine Corps levels of discipline."[15]

But privately to a friend, Mattis had a personal concern about his Marines' mental readiness in spite of all he had done to prepare them. Ricks quotes this email:

> Ultimately, a real understanding of history means that we face nothing new under the sun. For all the "Fourth Generation of War" intellectuals running around saying that the nature of war has fundamentally changed, the tactics are wholly new etc., I must respectfully say, "Not really." Alexander the Great would not be in the least bit perplexed by the

enemy that we face right now in Iraq, and our leaders going into this fight do their troops a disservice by not studying— studying, not just reading—the men who have gone before us. We have been fighting on the planet for 5,000 years and we should take advantage of their experience. "Winging it" and filling body bags as we sort out what works reminds us of the moral dictates and the cost of incompetence in our profession.[16]

Perhaps with the example of Lieutenant Colonel West on his mind, Mattis again stresses moral discipline regarding the enemy and the innocent:

Recall Beirut, my fine young men, and the absolute need for Iraqis to see the American military as impartial. We will be compassionate to all the innocent and deadly only to those who insist on violence, taking no "sides" other than to de- stroy the enemy. We must act as a windbreak, behind which a struggling Iraq can get its act together.[17]

On professional humility and respect for the capabilities of the enemy, Mattis sends, very likely from his personal library, T. E. Lawrence's *27 Articles*, in which Lawrence of Arabia warns his fellow Englishmen about fighting an Arab war: "Do not try to do too much with your own hands. Better the Arabs do it tolerably than you do it perfectly. It is their war, and you are to help them, not to win it for them." Lawrence goes on, "Unnumbered generations of tribal raids have taught them more about some parts of the business than we will ever know."[18]

Mattis reviews and emphasizes the importance of the reading material in numerous follow-up meetings. His commander's intent is loud and clear: the coming fight will be confusing, difficult, and bloody, and their first command is "Be ready at all times to win the ten-second gunfight."[19] The second is to avoid harming Iraqi civilians. In Mattis's words, "If someone needs shooting, shoot him. If someone does not need shooting, protect him."[20] The third and final is to to win hearts and minds by respecting and helping the Iraqis.

The First Division prepares for the coming bloodshed comforted with a deeper understanding. This comfort is tempered by the alarming fact that, on Mattis's orders, they are leaving behind the watchful Marine artillery that shielded and saved them so often during OIF 1.

In contrast to the success of Mattis's Marines in the southern provinces, four separate US Army units operating in the Sunni Triangle, ending with the Eighty-Second Airborne, tried and failed to win the hearts and minds of the suddenly powerless Sunni tribes. The Army failed mainly because US envoy Paul Bremer, head of the Coalition Provisional Authority (CPA), was in the process of destroying all remnants of Saddam's army, along with his Ba'ath political party. Part of this process was to cut off all payments, in spite of the billions of dinars sitting in the captured Iraqi treasury, to any Ba'ath party member or Iraqi Army officer of the rank of colonel or above. More than any other action, this inflamed the once privileged army commanders and intelligence officers and guaranteed their violent insurgency.

Ba'athists were then purged from the Iraqi parliament, and the remaining Shia leaders showed no sympathy for the plight of their recent tormentors. Into this political vacuum stepped former enemy Iran, al-Qaeda leaders like Zarkawi, and local clerics like Muqtada al-Sadr, who wanted to add the now furious Sunnis to their own ranks. Saddam's disbanded army gathered by platoons and companies and whole battalions, complete with weapons, ammunition, and Iranian support, in northern cities like Ramadi and Fallujah. The Army's Eighty-Second Airborne didn't stand a chance of mollifying them.

As insurgent attacks increased, the Eighty-Second responded with overwhelming firepower, killing local civilians in the exchanges.

Suddenly America was in a blood feud with an entrenched, well-equipped, well-led urban enemy that was being protected by local civilians. Once liberators, the Americans were now seen as occupiers, exactly what Mattis had warned against and successfully avoided in the south.

Saddam and Osama were now both in hiding, but by the capricious gods of war had the Americans exactly where they wanted them. It would be bloody house-to-house and hand-to-hand combat. It would be a havoc of medieval savagery, including beheadings, dismemberments, and impalings. It would kill thousands, including women, children, Iraqis, and Americans indiscriminately. It would generate horrible headlines and many body bags returning to America. It would not be quick.

As Mattis would tell new Marines coming into Fallujah to prepare them emotionally, "Fallujah's the most morally bruising place in Iraq. It's going to rock you when an IED goes off and there's blood and shit all over you. Hold the line. Show the people respect. We're here to win."[21]

January 2004—Sunni Triangle, Iraq

Major General Mattis and aides conduct a recon of Anbar Province, examining the enemy, terrain, and recent after-action reports. Mattis orders First Division headquarters to remain in Ramadi, where the Eighty-Second Airborne is headquartered in a captured palace on the banks of the Euphrates, halfway between Baghdad and the Syrian border. Ramadi is the political capital of Anbar Province, with strategic access to the Euphrates River valley. The new headquarters is called Camp Blue Diamond, after the First Division's insignia.

The former palace, located on a spit of land cooled by the breezes off the winding Euphrates, was a favorite retreat of Saddam's government ministers. It is in the better part of Ramadi, among the expensive riverfront homes of many of Saddam's former senior intelligence officers. In other words, it is surrounded on three sides by nests of very sophisticated spies. Some neighboring houses and many street corners, shops, and markets along Route 10, a main east-west boulevard leading to and from the front gate of Mattis's headquarters, are often listening posts, feeding information to the insurgent network.

Within the Camp Blue Diamond compound itself, the Kellogg, Brown, and Root company employs dozens of Indians, Pakistanis, Turks, and Bangladeshis to provide meals, clean laundry, distribute newspapers and magazines, and dispose of trash. The workers, hired through Jordanian and Turkish subcontractors, are everywhere. They see who comes into the base, they see when patrols go out and how long they stay out. They may hear snatches of unguarded conversation in the chow line. They see deference paid to a certain slight, bespectacled, and energetic general with two stars embroidered on his flak vest, who sometimes appears in the American newspapers. They likely provide discarded newspapers to the surrounding spy houses where Saddam's officers read that the new American commander's name is Jim Mattis.

Major General Charles Swannack, the Eighty-Second Airborne's commander, welcomes Mattis. He tells him he has three problems with Mattis's approach.[22] First, he says the Marines are going to need their artillery. Swannack will comment later, "After seeing how we got mortared and rocketed in the evenings, they decided to bring it." Second, he advises Mattis against the US Marines' Combined Action Program (CAP) for law enforcement and infrastructure rebuilding, which Mattis had applied successfully to win hearts and minds in southern Iraq. "I told them that the CAP program wouldn't work," Swannack will say, "that Anbar Province wasn't ready for it then, and maybe never, because they didn't want us downtown." Third and most pointedly, he disparages Mattis's plan for Marines to distinguish themselves from the Army troops, with their sand-colored desert camouflage, by issuing green jungle camouflage and black boots to the Marines. Swannack let Mattis have it: "I told him that was a personal affront to me, and that a relief should be seamless." Mattis agrees with Swannack about the artillery and the uniforms, saying, "What I was trying to do was break the cycle of violence. He took it personally. I appreciated his candor."[23]

But Mattis doesn't budge on his version of CAP. Each Marine battalion will have one platoon that is briefed in depth on Arab customs and language. That platoon will teach its parent company, and then all the companies will inform the battalion at all levels.[24]

Swannack feels the Eighty-Second Airborne is doing a good job in Ramadi and the restive nearby city of Fallujah: "I think Fallujah was being managed appropriately, with surgical operations based on precise intelligence."[25] But up the chain of command the assessment, especially concerning Fallujah, is not good. General John Abizaid, commander of all US forces at Central Command, is pressuring Swannack to do more about Fallujah. Mattis has heard the scuttlebutt but had high confidence in his own plan for the city: "I knew Fallujah would be tough. We were going to use the softer forms, focus on lights and water, and go in with small teams to kill the bad guys at night."[26]

But the vagaries of war dash Mattis's plan almost immediately. Fallujah spins out of control soon after the First Division arrives, and quickly descends into tragedy. Lieutenant General James Conway, Mattis's superior officer and commander of all Marine forces in Iraq, says today about the situation they inherited back then, "The first week we were in Ramadi we had four Marines and one corpsman dead."[27]

Pacification of Anbar and the northern provinces also suffers from the Washington, DC, mythology that the Marines can always be counted on to adapt, overcome, and get the job done with less, particularly with the lucky and gifted Jim Mattis running things on the ground. But with the northern provinces covering an area about the size of North Carolina and with a few of its major cities already in flames, limited support from the withdrawing US Army, and wavering support from Bremer's CPA in Baghdad, the First Division is simply stretched too thin.

Mattis saw the problem the previous April, even as Rumsfeld and the Pentagon officials continued to insist that there were enough troops. He noted in an internal message, "The lack of Army dismounts [regular infantry] is creating a void in personal contact and public perception of our civil-military ops."[28]

Colonel John Toolan, a key commander on the march up to Baghdad and now in charge of Regimental Combat Team 1 in Fallujah, recalls the four basic missions for field commanders in Anbar: control major supply routes (MSRs), develop Iraqi security forces (ISF), destroy insurgent sanctuaries, and create jobs. He described the Marines' problem this way: "The challenge was, when we controlled the MSR and developed the ISF, there was no one left to eliminate sanctuaries or create jobs. So it was like whack-a-mole."[29]

Instead of quietly pacifying the people, the Marines quickly end up engaging in some of the most savage fighting America has ever known. Mattis's lucky streak appears to be running out.

0920 Hours—12 February 2004—Ramadi

As the transition from Eighty-Second Airborne to the First Marine Division is under way, the outgoing Swannack and his boss, Lieutenant General John Abizaid of Central Command, ride through Ramadi in convoy to meet with Sunni leaders for top-level discussions. They are under the highest level of protection from Iraqi security forces, as well as US armored units in the convoy.

The streets are crowded with vehicles and pedestrians. The convoy slows to a crawl along Route 10 as beggars in dark dishdashas and checkered kaffiyeh scarves line the roadsides, hands outstretched for a coin or bottle of water. Children jostle for position yelling at the convoy for candy and the highly prized Oreo cookies. They are all smiles and thumbs-up, but behind them on the sidewalks, loitering in the shadows of the open-air clothing and vegetable stalls, are a thousand eyes of the insurgency. Cell phones text the location of the convoy down the route to young men on motorbikes, who join the flow of traffic ahead of the American generals. On rooftops above the convoy, Iraqi security melts away and is replaced by faces hidden behind wrapped kaffiyehs. RPGs come up to their shoulders, sighted in on the center of the roadway. As the convoy rolls slowly into the kill zone, fire pours down on it from all directions.

The convoy returns fire, and the generals' armored vehicles plow headlong between the vehicles ahead of them, pushing small cars, bicycles, and motorbikes aside or rolling over them, crushing innocent motorists beneath their wheels. Motorbikes zoom up, flanking the convoy, spray it with fire from AK-47s, and then disappear down narrow alleys where the American vehicles can't follow. Prepositioned artillery shells camouflaged in piles of trash along the route explode on signal from nearby cell phones. The generals are slammed against the sides of their rocking vehicles as the ambush zeroes in on them. Fire erupts from RPGs, slamming into unlucky civilian vehicles. Shrapnel sprays across the sidewalks into the crowds of children and shoppers.

The battered convoy races out of the kill zone, with two of America's top military commanders bruised but alive. The scheduled discussions with Sunni leaders and Iraqi security commanders is an unhappy and brief encounter, and a source of deep shame for the Iraqis. They have failed spectacularly in their duty to protect the Americans. Talk of further cooperation is curt and inconclusive. The generals return to Camp Blue Diamond by a different route.

6 March 2004—Fallujah

The First Marine Division is nearly up to strength as troops and equipment pour into Camp Blue Diamond. Mattis, as commander on the ground in Anbar Province, and General Conway, commander of Marine forces in Iraq, coordinate to apply Mattis's successful strategy in the south to the northern provinces. Mattis will handle the interface of Marines with local Iraqis; Conway will run interference with Washington and Baghdad to get the Marines what they need, including a free hand to operate differently than the Army.

General Conway recalls one of the first pacification missions for a CAP unit in Iraq: "Somewhere down south, the date palms needed to be sprayed. The bugs would eat the dates and the region would lose the whole crop. We didn't know what kind of spray or whatever they needed like equipment, but we got on the phone and we got those trees sprayed."[30]

As expected, in spite of the Marines' good works, the war rages on. On the outskirts of Fallujah, insurgents set a fuel tanker ablaze and create a staged multicar accident to divert Iraqi police away from the center of the city. As police arrive at the blazing tanker, they are immediately surrounded with a snarl of screaming, honking motorists. In the city, insurgents launch a massive attack against three police stations, the mayor's office, and a civil defense base. At least seventeen police officers are killed, and as many as eighty-seven imprisoned insurgents are sprung out of jail cells.

In spite of the fact that the Eighty-Second Airborne has largely withdrawn and no longer regularly patrols the streets of Fallujah, not even retaliating for the earlier attack on Swannack and Abizaid, Swannack decides that the police murders demand a response. He retaliates by conducting lightning raids of homes, businesses, and schools, which damage property and sometimes lead to shootouts with the locals. The Eighty-Second also blows up city property that they think might be used to hide IEDs, such as curbs and road barriers. The Army's retaliation provokes angry demonstrations in the city, during which the Eighty-Second claims that shots are fired at them. They return fire into the crowd, and seventeen local Fallujans are killed. It is now a full-blown blood vendetta between besieged Fallujans seeking retribution and the American occupiers.

1100 Hours—20 March 2004—Camp Blue Diamond, Ramadi

Exactly one year to the day after Mattis and the First Division crossed the berms from Kuwait and successfully marched on Baghdad, Lieutenant General Swannack transfers authority over Anbar Province to the I Marine Expeditionary Force, commanded by Lieutenant General Conway and Major General Mattis.[31] In what might be a critical oversight in the transfer of authority, unlike the Shia in the south, Saddam's loyal Sunnis in Anbar and the north were never actually defeated during Mattis's spring blitzkrieg. Many in Anbar have not yet begun to fight. Lighting the fuse of this powder keg is accomplished by Paul Bremer's de-Ba'athification program that has impoverished and insulted seventy thousand proud Fallujah men. These seventy thousand now nurse their grudges against the Americans and plot revenge. Conway and Mattis are not really inheriting a pacification mission; more accurately, they are continuing the march from Kuwait but against a different and highly motivated enemy.

Making matters on the ground even worse, the insurgents have access to what is estimated to be more than a million metric tons of ordnance and weapons in ten thousand bunkers spread across Iraq—mortar shells, RPGs, rifle ammunition, and high explosives. US commanders rolling through Iraq in the spring invasion avoided detonating the bunkers for fear they contained poison gas or radioactive stockpiles, Saddam's infamous WMDs, that might be blown into the air, killing US soldiers and Iraqi civilians. So the bunkers have remained fully stocked and available to the insurgents.

But that isn't all. In his paper *U.S. Marine Corps Operations in Iraq, 2003–2006*, Marine Lieutenant Colonel Ken W. Estes describes an Anbar Province crisscrossed by "terrorist infiltration routes, termed 'rat lines,' extending from Syria to Ramadi and Fallujah," where "age-old smuggling routes, tribal cross-border associations and active Syrian support provided the insurgencies with a steady supply of money and sanctuaries . . . radical elements could infiltrate through a system of safe houses, counterfeit document providers, training areas, and routes."[32]

The final opportunity to avoid the bloodbath that Conway and Mattis now face is squandered by Washington's attempt to justify its main reason for the war—WMD. Thousands of weapons experts, translators, and other specialists, along with all their support personnel, divert attention and resources from addressing the mushrooming insurgency to finding any scrap of evidence of nuclear or biological weapons.

One senior military intelligence officer argues for a simple, effective, and inexpensive project to identify the emerging opposition in Fallujah by simply translating the list already in the Army's possession of Fallujans who have volunteered for suicide missions against Israel. From this document it would then be just basic police work to map each of these men's houses and visit them. But, the officer will later recall, he couldn't even get the list translated; all the Army's assets were focused on WMD.

Saddam's air force second in command, General Georges Sada, who knew of commercial airliners ferrying Saddam's WMD to Damascus, Syria, just before the 2003 invasion, later gave an American television interview on Fox News, stating, "Well, I want to make it clear, very clear to everybody in the world that we *had* the weapon[s] of mass destruction in Iraq, and the regime used them against our Iraqi people. . . . I know it because I have got the captains of the Iraqi airway [air force] that were my friends, and they told me these weapons of mass destruction had been moved to Syria. Iraq had some projects for nuclear weapons but it was destroyed in 1981."[33]

So while Washington's inspectors scour the country looking for nonconventional weapons that don't exist, they are increasingly attacked with conventional weapons that do. This fact is ignored, until Fallujah.

In spite of what some see as a mishandling of the northern provinces by the US Army, Mattis still seems to believe that the Marines will be able to restore order. He relies largely on the *Small Wars Manual*, a critical item in the reading he demands of every Marine before returning to Iraq. In its fifteen chapters is a blueprint for tactical operations based on four decades of Marines fighting insurgencies and small wars throughout South and Central America, the "Banana Wars." He tells his men, as they prepare to fight again in Iraq, "This [Anbar] is the right place for Marines in this fight, where we can carry on the legacy of Chesty Puller in the Banana Wars in the same sort of complex environment."[34]

In Iraq, as the time to execute Mattis's plan approaches, he issues a fragmentary order, officially titled "Fallujah Opening Gambit," though it is known throughout the division as the "First 15 Plays."[35] It outlines a carefully integrated approach of using combat operations with focused, informed civil improvements like repairing schools and farm irrigation systems, providing fresh municipal water, and removing trash. He reminds his men over and over again, "Remember, Iraqis aren't your enemy, don't let the insurgents make you think that. The people are the prize."[36] And, regarding the insurgents, "There is only one retirement plan for terrorists."[37]

0930 Hours—31 March 2004—Fallujah

Morning traffic jostles along the divided four lanes of Route 10 in typical Iraqi fashion, with drivers laying on the horn as they weave in and out of traffic at speed. A five-vehicle convoy, three empty Mercedes-Benz flatbed trucks and two Mitsubishi Pajero sport utility vehicles, are on the way to service the KBR concessions at Camp Fallujah and then on to Camp Blue Diamond in Ramadi. At a checkpoint at the Fallujah city line, the procession stops. A weary Iraqi police officer glances in at the driver of the lead SUV,

Wes Batalona, ex-military, now private security for Blackwater USA, and waves him on. Blackwater USA is the security firm subcontracted by KBR to escort its vehicles as they pick up trash and deliver supplies to American bases. With Batalona is Scott Helvenston, former SEAL. In the following SUV is Jerry Zovko, retired from the Eighty-Second Airborne, and Michael Teague, a Bronze Star recipient for his bravery in Afghanistan.[38]

Beyond the checkpoint, the contractors creep along as four lanes become two lanes through the center of town. They pass the main police station and compound of the city council, formerly the impressive Ba'ath Party headquarters, now graffiti-strewn and in need of repair. The inhospitable reputation of Fallujah is immediately apparent in the flinty stares and curses directed at the convoy. There are no smiling children yelling for cookies, as the Americans might have found in Ramadi. If they had checked with Blue Diamond beforehand, they might have avoided taking Route 10 into the scarred heart of the Sunni insurgency. Messages fly from cell phone to cell phone down Route 10 in front of the men.

Traffic comes to a complete stop among the small shops on either side of the street. Suddenly, young men run from the shadows inside the shops. Batalona and the others have no time to reach for their automatic weapons before the insurgents are upon them, spraying both unarmored SUVs with AK-47 automatic fire. Three of the four men are riddled with bullets and die instantly. One of the Americans staggers out and falls to the ground, to be beaten, stabbed, and then dismembered in the street.[39] A crowd of about three hundred men, women, and children gathers around the gory celebration, chanting "Allahu Akbar! Allahu Akbar!" as a young boy runs up with a can of gasoline, douses the SUVs, and joins in the dancing while flames engulf the Americans' bodies. The charred remains are then dragged through the streets and strung up from the trestle bridge over the Euphrates that the Americans call the Brooklyn Bridge.

At Blue Diamond Division headquarters, Mattis's chief of staff, Joe Dunford, gets a call from General Conway's I MEF headquarters, according to Bing West in his book *No True Glory: A Frontline Account of the Battle for Fallujah.* The MEF officer tells Dunford, "Baghdad has reports of Americans killed in Fallujah. What are you getting?"[40]

Dunford walks from his office into the operations center, where video from a surveillance drone tracks a mob swarming around two smoking vehicles, red flames leaping from the burning tires. On another screen, live satellite TV, either Al Jazeera or Al Arabiya, shows Iraqi men and boys stomping on a charred and shriveled body.

Dunford reaches Mattis in the field by radio: "A mob in Fallujah has killed some American contractors. It looks like a scene from Somalia. Baghdad [US Army Lieutenant General Ricardo Sanchez, the Joint Task Force commander in charge of all coalition forces] wants us to go in."

Mattis and Dunford discuss the situation. "What's your take?" asks Mattis.

"The contractors are dead. If we go in to get their bodies, we'll have to kill hundreds, including kids. Captain Sullivan says the police chief promises to return the bodies. I recommend we stay out."

"Where does the MEF stand?"

"General Conway thinks we should let the mob exhaust itself."

"That's it, then. Rushing in makes no sense."[41]

In Fallujah, the celebrations continue, and the crowds grow. The crowds shout in unison as women ululate in glee, "Viva mujahideen!"—Long live the resistance![42]

A news crew from Al Jazeera, reporter Ahmed Mansur and cameraman Laith Mushtaq, film the uproar as Mansur comments on the great victory of the mujahideen over the invaders. Bing West reports on the scene:

> Crowds in the souk and along the highway were swept up
> in the murderous atmosphere. No police tried to restore
> order; no fire truck put out the flames smoldering around

the SUVs; no ambulance came for the bodies. When two Iraqi nurses tried to take the bodies to a hospital, they were told to leave or be shot. At dusk the remains of three bodies were dumped in a cart pulled by a gray donkey for a final triumphal haul down Highway 10. Men and boys followed the cart yelling. "Shwaretek!" (Americans, you've lost your nerve!).[43]

The horrific images are broadcast that evening in America on all major networks. Floods of calls and emails pour through communication lines in Washington.

In Ramadi, the Marines are saddened but not fazed by the senseless killings. They are, after all, at war, and they know full well that senseless killing is a part of it. Nothing has changed. They will execute their plan to win over the people of Fallujah and Anbar with strength, service, and resolve. Dunford writes an email to the media, intended to calm and reassure all Americans that justice will be done in regard to the contractors and that Iraq is not coming apart, in spite of what they've just seen on the evening news. "We're not going to overreact to today's violence," he writes. "We have a methodology of patient, persistent presence. We will identify who was responsible, and in cooperation with Iraqi security forces, we will kill them."[44]

But in Baghdad, Joint Task Force commander Sanchez wants immediate, highly visible retaliation. And so does Washington. Democrats in Congress take advantage of the situation and attack Bush's war policy; it's only seven months to election time. Secretary Rumsfeld demands action in a video teleconference with Sanchez: "We've got to pound these guys. This is also a good opportunity for us to push the Sunnis on the Governing Council [the future government of Iraq] to step forward and condemn this attack, and we'll remember those who do not. It's time for them to choose. They are either with us or against us." Sanchez goes at I MEF commander Conway, suggesting that they bomb the Brooklyn Bridge.[45]

Conway rejects that option—they need the bridge to run convoys. Sanchez comes back, "All right then, bomb the computer shop."[46]

The Marines decline because of the presence of children at the email café.[47] Plus, they don't want to burn the records; they want to read them.

Sanchez tries again: "Well, bomb the compound on the Euphrates."

Conway explains that families live there, and the ringleaders might not be home when the bombs fall. He suggests that Sanchez "go sit down and think about it."

Sanchez is furious. He gets off the phone. Bing West reports on Sanchez's reaction, "'Write an order for the Marines to attack,' General Sanchez told his staff, 'and I don't mean any fucking knock-before-search, touchy-feely stuff.'"[48]

Of course, this is the exact opposite of Mattis's approach.[49] Once again thinking outside the box—or, more exactly, thinking inside and outside the box of military doctrine simultaneously—Mattis prepared a civilian kid-glove response to Iraqi civilian attacks within an active war zone even before leaving Camp Pendleton. After his lightning-fast sweep across southern Iraq earlier in the year, a friend asked him how he was able to conceive of the First Marine Division's multiple maneuvers against Baghdad. He replied, "I visualized the battlefield."[50] He made everyone else visualize the battlefield as well by creating a topographical map to scale and having commanders walk through the campaign with him as he narrated each maneuver.

Then, as he prepared his division to return to Iraq a second time, he was able to understand cities like Fallujah both as a battlefield and as home to hundreds of thousands of Iraqi civilians. He relied on decades-old doctrine in the *Small Wars Manual*, but also sought out nonmilitary resources, including academics and experts in counterinsurgency, retired Vietnam-era CAP platoons, Marines, and even Los Angeles Police Department detectives. Mattis wants his CAP units to know how to be effective police detectives in a war zone. LAPD detective instructor Ralph Morten, a twenty-seven-year police veteran, said, "When you get down and look at the daily incidents in Iraq, you see so many things that we see as police officers. Investigation, tying cars and bad guys together, forensics, collecting evidence from bombings, shooting, testing people for explosive residue, tracking the electronics . . . all the things we do every day."[51]

So Mattis's Marines learn how to match cars with bad guys, conduct forensics at a crime scene and isolate gang leaders for swift, bloodless captures. Given time, the Marines might have captured or killed all of the Fallujah attackers without further enflaming tensions in the region, saving hundreds of Iraqi and American lives. But time, along with sufficient troops, were things Mattis was not given.

In a video teleconference with Secretary Rumsfeld and CPA head Bremer, General Abizaid presents the plan for Fallujah and states frankly that Central Command agrees with the Marines. "The timing is not right," he says, "and they haven't had time to implement their engagement program. We should wait."[52]

Rumsfeld shoots back, "No, we've got to attack. And we must do more than just get the perpetrators of this Blackwater incident. We need to make sure that Iraqis in other cities receive our message."

Abizaid realizes the decision has already been made at the White House. He turns over the meeting to General Sanchez to present his non-touchy-feely plan, Operation Vigilant Resolve. The plan's four objectives are to eliminate Fallujah as a safe haven for Sunni insurgents, eliminate all weapons caches from the city, establish law and order for long-term stability and security, and capture or kill the perpetrators of the Blackwater ambush. The I MEF will lead the effort, joined by elements of the Iraqi Civil Defense Corps, which is intended to become the new Iraqi Army. Sanchez estimates three to four weeks of intense fighting.[53]

Abizaid makes one more attempt to buy the Marines time by appealing directly to President Bush. Bush says he appreciates the caution, but then orders the attack. Abizaid and Sanchez acknowledge the order and reaffirm that there will be a lot of collateral damage—in both infrastructure and civilian casualties. They also mention that Al Jazeera is certain to broadcast live reports on the battle that will create major problems in the Arab world. "If we're going to proceed," Abizaid advises, "we must be prepared to counter Al Jazeera with a coordinated strategic communications plan."

Bush replies, "Yes, we understand. We know it's going to be ugly, but we are committed."[54]

"Very well, Mr. President," says Abizaid. "Then Operation Vigilant Resolve is a go."[55]

After the teleconference, Abizaid calls General Conway. "Jim, the decision has been made to execute Vigilant Resolve. We communicated your concerns to the President, but we are launching the offensive anyway."[56]

Conway replies, "Okay, General. I don't like it, but we're prepared to execute."[57]

When Conway tells Mattis, Mattis says, "This is what the enemy wants."[58] Then, likely realizing that once this kind of primitive, brutish gunfight starts, the worst thing you can do in this part of the world is to show weakness by quitting in the middle of it, he adds, "Don't stop us."

Mattis makes his final preparations without the normal time needed to insert human intelligence assets or sensors, conduct formal reconnaissance, position sufficient reinforcements, or shape the battle space. This is going to be a down-and-dirty, blood-and-guts shootout between two well-armed, well-led, and highly motivated armies—with the civilians of Fallujah in the middle.

0500 Hours—3 April 2004—Fallujah

Colonel Toolan, commanding Regimental Combat Team 1, begins to surround the city in a cordon of concertina wire and concrete barriers. The cordon will prevent any reinforcements or additional weapons from reaching the insurgents. RCT-1 captures a local radio station and calls in a psyops team to broadcast instructions to residents to remain inside their homes and call American forces at command headquarters to identify foreign fighters and any Fallujans who were involved in the Blackwater deaths. They drop leaflets over the city from helicopters, again reminding residents to stay indoors and call Blue Diamond with information.

General Conway explains that it is part of the overall plan to "drive a wedge between the insurgents and the good people of Iraq."[59]

After dark, on Mattis's signal, Toolan will attack from the northwest and the southeast to quickly cut the heart out of the insurgency by taking the mayor's complex and military compound in the center of Fallujah. Toolan will then launch a series of raids to capture twenty key individuals that CIA intelligence has linked to the contractor's ambush. This will bloody the nose of the insurgents and bait the trap.

Toolan will withdraw to the compound in the center of the city, holding as many insurgent leaders as he can catch. These leaders will be the irresistible bait. When the insurgents move out of their fortified positions to take back their city center and free their comrades, Mattis will spring the trap. He will launch a full-scale assault by 2,500 Marines, supported by AC-130 gunships and attack helicopters overhead, and artillery at close range.

The plan is a complex assault with multiple coordinated maneuvers that relies on understanding the pride and fervor that will drive the enemy out of their fighting holes and into a trap. And it is only the first few of the fifteen moves Mattis has planned. Major General Robert H. Scales, former commander of the Army War College, comments on Mattis and his methods, "He is the product of three decades of schooling and practice in the art of war. No one on active duty knows more about the subject. He is an infantryman, a close-combat Marine. He is one of those few who willingly practices the art of what social scientists term 'intimate killing.'"[60]

There is quite a bit of intimate killing expected in Mattis's plan. And most of ancient, central Fallujah, known as the City of Mosques, is also not expected to survive.

0630 Hours—3 April 2004—Fallujah

As Toolan's tanks and armored bulldozers clank and groan, building traffic checkpoints and fighting positions around Fallujah, Mattis and the twenty-nine men of the jump platoon that protects him seem to be everywhere, checking every route, alleyway, and fighting position in the city. His rolling LAV command post has been crackling with communications twenty-four hours a day for the past few days as the general personally reviews every detail of the coming offensive. Unfortunately, the command post's high-powered multi-channel communications gear requires a cluster of antennae that sprout from the roof, clearly marking it as a command vehicle to any observer.

The only countermeasure available to obscure the antennae is speed. Mattis's driver, Lance Corporal Andrew Wike, among other evasive maneuvers, often executes ninety-degree turns at full speed, more than once throwing Mattis against the side of the vehicle. Like all Marines, Mattis's jump Marines thrive on being in the action. They get plenty of it as they race between the most forward fighting positions and down dangerous streets. As the pace of operations picks up, they frequently roll into active firefights and on several occasions are hit by IEDs. It quickly becomes obvious that riding with the general is exceptionally hazardous duty.

But hazardous duty seems to be the proving ground of a grunt's supreme virtue, contempt for death. In his book *Blood Stripes: The Grunt's View of the War in Iraq,* Captain David Danelo describes how suspected IEDs were dealt with in Fallujah at that time: "When the unit noticed an object that appeared to be hiding an IED, a Marine would walk up and kick it. If his foot hit metal, the unit would cordon the area and call in an explosive ordnance disposal team."

To "pogs"—people other than grunts—this seems like an insane technique. But according to Captain Danelo, the reason behind the technique was his fellow Marines' devotion to the Spartan way. He recounts in his book, "The Spartan king Leonidas, who died with his men at Thermopylae, sacrificing himself for the sake of his country's independence and way of life, was once asked to name the supreme warrior virtue, from which all other virtues derived. 'Contempt for death,' he replied."[61] For Mattis, some contempt for death is obvious in his personal choice to stay on the front lines. But he doesn't presume the same for members of his jump platoon.

The jump platoon's mission is to protect Mattis and maintain his fully functioning command post as he runs from one end of the battlefield to the other. The platoon is called a jump because it jumps into action on a moment's notice to take the general wherever he wants to go. With Mattis, this could be at any hour, and generally to the most dangerous places by way of very dangerous routes. General Conway feels he has to say something: "Jim, you keep running around like this and you're gonna get hit."[62]

Mattis shrugs off the warning. It's simply part of his job. He can't be effective unless he knows exactly what his men are facing, what their plan is, and how they're feeling. In April, after the first time Mattis's jump is hit by an IED and small-arms fire, he calls his hand-picked chaplain, Father Bill Devine, from his command vehicle and asks the priest to be present when the men return to Blue Diamond. At the base, Devine remembers, "He said to them if anyone wanted to transfer out of the jump, there would be no loss of respect for them. He told them, just to see me, the chaplain, and there would be no questions asked. No questions asked at all. Not one of them ever came to me. None."[63]

Mattis later commented on this phenomenon of selfless commitment, even to the risking of one's life, that warriors have to each other and the mission, "The combination and focused direction of social energy and spiritual power makes a military organization so tight, all the commander has to do is point his unit in the right direction and tell them what they already know. Social energy is the framework through which spiritual power flows. Social energy is the pipes and hoses. Spiritual power is the fuel."[64]

As the battle for Fallujah descends into a bloody siege and the jump is decimated by one casualty after another, ending up with one of the highest casualty rates of any unit in the fight, these men in Mattis's small band never waver in their commitment. They demonstrate the spiritual power that Mattis cultivates with such care and depends on for success. This particular jump platoon, because of its commitment and spiritual power, makes a deep and lasting impression on the general.

1830 Hours—5 April 2004—
Jolan District, Fallujah

Dusk settles over Fallujah. A full moon peeks over the horizon drawing nervous howls from alley dogs on the hunt for a rat among the strewn garbage. Light breezes off the Euphrates rattle through the date palms as the temperature drops quickly. Down the wide streets from the northwest and up from the southeast, Toolan's clanking, groaning steel giants roll forward like medieval nightmares. Marines on foot follow the tanks, watching rooftops for moving silhouettes.

Overhead, the gunship Slayer One, an Air Force C-130 loaded with infrared targeting scopes, Gatling guns, and a 105-millimeter howitzer, contacts Echo Company on the ground. Bing West reports on the conversation:

> "Oprah, this is Slayer One. About one hundred meters south of your strobe I see a group of about twenty in a courtyard. Want me to take them out?" The Air Force officers in the AC-130 were informal and low-key. "Slayer One, this is Oprah," Captain Michael Martino, a forward air controller with Echo, replied. "We'd appreciate it." The ensuing burst of 20mm fire had a low, ripping sound, like a chain saw cutting through hard wood. "This is Slayer One. Scratch that group. We'll make another pass over your sector. If we don't see anyone else, we'll swing over to War Hammer."[65]

The bodies of about twenty young men of Fallujah are now torn to pieces and scattered across the courtyard. These young, naive Fallujans begin to die by the dozens. They charge into the open and at the Marines as if they believe the Americans will run when gunfire starts. They are trained enough to know not to bunch together where one round might kill or wound several, but their training obviously hasn't covered how to fight Marines. In these early hours of the battle, these youngest jihadis die first.

The evening calm is breached by sporadic gunfire and RPG explosions as Toolan presses forward, diagonally bisecting the city on his mission to take its center. Loudspeakers mounted on roving Humvees begin to blast young Fallujan fighters with the filthiest insults that Marines can imagine, which are then interpreted and screamed at the insurgents by Iraqi interpreters. This is followed by heavy metal music from AC/DC and Metallica to further infuriate the fighters and drown out the evening call to prayers. This psyops assault has some success in coaxing infuriated fighters to leave their positions or betray their location by firing at the noise. In both cases, these infuriated young fighters are next to die in the assault.

These local psyops are outmatched by international psyops conducted by the Al Jazeera live broadcasts. Reporter Mansur with cameraman Mushtaq show fearless local citizens firing machine guns and strolling nonchalantly through the open Jolan market carrying loaded RPG launchers.[66] Mansur breathlessly narrates the wanton murder of Fallujan women and children at the hands of the Marines. Of course, no such murders are taking place. Seeing these reports in real time, residents grab their children and a few baskets of food and belongings and flee the city. Checkpoints are soon flooded with tens of thousands of refugees, who are directed to holding areas of concertina wire.

Emboldened by the live coverage of their heroic fight and believing Al Jazeera's reports, the estimated twelve or so "hardcore" groups of insurgents pour on their attacks from several fortified positions along both lines of Toolan's advance. Almost immediately the operation is behind schedule. The most intense close-combat fighting since Hue City in Vietnam spatters blood across the streets. Local fighters are well supplied with RPGs, machine guns, mortars, and anti-aircraft weapons, some of it supplied by the Iraqi police.

Mattis's carefully calibrated assault to separate the insurgents and spare the civilian population quickly devolves into a brawl as Fallujah civilians pour out of the city and stop feeding information to Blue Diamond about the leaders of the revolt. Fallujah's two main hospitals close, in spite of the hundreds of injured being laid at their doorsteps. To make matters even more miserable, the weather turns freezing cold, and it begins to rain.

The Marines and the insurgents fight on through the night, the Marines gaining ground slowly, taking regular casualties while the insurgents now die by the hundreds. Panicked civilians are caught in crossfires or are deliberately used as shields by many of the foreign fighters who make up a large part of the insurgency. Given the time for proper intelligence preparation before the assault, the fact of large numbers of foreigners would almost certainly have been uncovered. Intense and consistent local resident outreach could have provided the wedge between bad guys and local citizens that Mattis and Conway have used before to avoid the kind of bloody mayhem they are in now. Now it is up to the grunts to win most of the ten-second gunfights happening throughout the city.

Bing West describes the common infantry technique used in Falluja:

> The basic tactic was called the stack. A dozen marines in a squad lined up outside the courtyard wall and shouted and stomped, hoping any insurgents inside would fire prematurely. Usually they didn't. The marines then breached the outer iron gate, ran across the tiny patch of grass, and flattened themselves along the wall next to the front door. On signal, the door would be smashed in and four marines would rush into the front room, each pointing his rifle toward a different corner, each betting his life that none of the others would freeze or not shoot quickly enough.[67]

This last step in the stack is duplicated in every room of the house and is exactly what Mattis hoped to avoid. In his cultural sensitivity meetings in Camp Pendleton, this was the intended method of searching an Iraqi house: "If you knock at the door for a 'cordon and knock,' try not to look directly into the house when the door opens. If searching, be careful. Do not destroy possessions and furniture and ask the leader of the household to open rooms and cupboards. Nor should that man be dishonored before his family. If something is found, do not throw the leader of the house to the ground in front of his family. Give him some honor. Tell them he needs to explain to his wife and children that he is coming with you."[68]

But Bing West, in his *The Strongest Tribe: War, Politics, and the Endgame in Iraq*, records what actually does happen in Fallujah, with some units encountering stiff resistance and others more sporadic fighting: "Lima Company of Battalion 3–1 had twenty-five fights inside houses, killing sixty insurgents while losing five Marines. In three days, the thirty-eight Marines in 1st Platoon of Lima Company engaged in sixteen firefights, losing three killed and twelve wounded and evacuated, while killing thirty-eight of the enemy."[69]

West doesn't mention civilian casualties in this instance, but there are many. Civilians' bodies and their wounds are broadcast live around the world by Al Jazeera, along with outraged claims of an American crusade against Islam taking place in the revered City of Mosques. As well as a general nightmare of close urban combat, it is an epic international public relations disaster. There are no American or European media crews to give the other side of the story, as was promised in Washington when they ordered the hasty attack. The news reporting and the fighting feed on each other, quickly spiraling down to basic savagery, some of it staged for the cameras.

The siege of Fallujah grinds on through the next two days and nights as fighting also erupts throughout Central Iraq and along the Lower Euphrates. The Mahdi Army, the local militia of media savvy Shiite cleric Muqtada al-Sadr, begins attacks in Baghdad. Foreign fighters do the same in Ramadi. Civilian foreign workers are taken hostage in the British-controlled southern city of Basra; some are killed immediately, the others held to barter for political and military concessions. Elements of the Iraqi police, and even the future American-equipped and trained Iraqi Civil Defense Corps, turn on the coalition or simply abandon their posts.

Predictably, leaders around the world begin to condemn American aggression. The Iraqi Governing Council, the future government of Iraq, threatens to disband. Leading council member Pachachi pounds his desk: "These operations by the Americans are unacceptable and illegal!"[70] Rumors fly that British prime minister Tony Blair has informed President Bush that he will withdraw from the coalition if the offensive is not stopped.

On April 8, General Abizaid finally gives an interview to an American reporter, saying, "We'll get Fallujah under control."[71]

But the very next day the order comes down to stop the offensive. Again, this is exactly what Mattis warned against. He is furious, lashing out at General Abizaid, his superior officer. Marines and US soldiers have just been killed, and for what? "If you're going to take Vienna, take fucking Vienna!" he yells at Abizaid, paraphrasing Napoleon. Abizaid stays quiet and takes it, letting Mattis blow off steam.

Ricks reports on the situation in Fallujah: "Mattis believed he had the enemy on the ropes and was within a few days of finishing them off. The insurgents lacked bunkers and ammunition. They weren't able to get additional supplies through the cordon the Marines had thrown up around the city."[72]

Mattis rounds up his jump, and once again they run the gauntlet out to Toolan's command post. "He was very frustrated," Toolan will recall. "It was hard for him to tell me. He didn't understand why we were told to stop."[73] Mattis has lost thirty-seven Marines killed, and dozens wounded.

7 April 2004—Fallujah

After three days of fighting, Marines control a third of the city, including the city center and most of the insurgents' key defensive positions. The Marines tighten the cordon around the outskirts and hold their part of center city but, under orders, leave the rest to the insurgents. It's a standoff for Mattis, but a victory for al-Qaeda and Iran. Like a western sheriff who came to clean up Fallujah, Mattis stands defiantly in the center of town, facing down the villains every day.

Mattis loses no time turning his attention to the rest of Anbar. He is true to his often-quoted reply to a sour, doubtful reporter: "Failure? I can't even spell the word."[74]

Out in the far northwest desert is an obscure and powerless group of tribes called the Desert Wolves. Several Marine commanders

have established outposts and have actively been cutting cooperative deals with local sheikhs. The commanders follow the plan used
in the Shia south; they put pockets of coalition forces in and among
the population and then grow Iraqi security forces, including police,
from inside the population. It is the same basic law of counterinsurgency that Mattis has drummed into every grunt's head—the
people are the prize.

Lieutenant Colonel Nick Merano, commander of Mattis's old outfit, the 1/7, is having great success creating platoon-sized combat
outposts with the Desert Wolves. While Fallujah is still simmering
with hatred, everything is cool with the Desert Wolves and the coalition. Neighboring commander Lieutenant Colonel Scott Shuster
describes what a successful CAP effort looks like in northwestern
Anbar: "I've got three municipal mayors and three municipal coun-
cils. And then I have a regional mayor and a regional council. So I've
got four governments I'm interacting with. Also there is the dynamic
here between the tribes and the local government . . . [in which] the
tribes decide what's going to happen. They're the executive agent.
The municipal or civil government acts on the desires of the tribes."[75]

Conway and Mattis jump on the success happening at the far
ends of Anbar in al-Qa'im. They start building out this success to
neighboring tribes and reporting on it directly to Washington. Pacification is going to spread like a growing ink spot across the map,
they decide, all the way back to Fallujah and on to Baghdad—an
outside-in strategy. They are going to clear, hold, and build between
al-Qa'im and Fallujah isolating the city and cutting off access to the
rat-lines of outside support.

A meeting is set in late June with key tribal leaders near al-Hit.
Word is out that the Americans are making deals, and al-Qaeda
is making only misery for the Sunnis. The sheiks know that Conway and Mattis have been flying other Anbar leaders to Kuwait and
Jordan to show them what is possible when they cooperate with
America. On the other side of the coin, Mattis remembers clearly
the duplicity and sabotage he encountered when negotiating with

certain civic leaders in and around Fallujah, and he is wary of Iraqi promises.

Mattis's jump is driving east from Ramadi to the meeting. A convoy of US Army MPs is traveling in the opposite direction. As the two convoys pass, they are both hit by a massive IED car bomb planted in a pickup truck parked on the median, killing and wounding men from both convoys. While the general and a few others tend to the wounded and dying, someone spots a group of likely attackers speeding away. A perfectly timed explosion like this one could only be triggered by someone close by, with a clear view of the flow of traffic. Speedy driver Wike jumps behind the steering wheel of the closest Humvee, and Mattis's men who are able jump in with him. They tear off after the attackers. A group of MPs follow close behind in their own vehicle. A few miles down the road, Mattis's posse catches up to the muj (mujahideen fighters). It is over in seconds. The posse opens fire and kills them all, leaving their perforated bodies leaking across the middle of the road.

When he walks into the meeting with the local sheiks, a half hour late and with his mens' blood on the pants of his uniform, Mattis is in no mood for games. Conway is already well through the customary niceties of tea drinking and small talk when Mattis's turn comes around in the long-winded greetings and acknowledgments. Everyone knows what they are there for. The Marines offer security, working electricity, and running water; the sheiks offer peaceful cooperation and support. Mattis cuts out the small talk, looks each sheik in the eye, and with barely restrained emotion says some version of his now famous threat, "I come in peace. I didn't bring artillery. But I'm pleading with you, with tears in my eyes: If you fuck with me, I'll kill you all."[76]

Today Conway doesn't recall Mattis's exact words at the meeting but remembers clearly it was a threat. He remembers Mattis's growing mistrust of the sheiks at this point, his emotional distress from seeing his beloved jump platoon wounded and bleeding on the road, including Staff Sergeant Jorge Molina Bautista, who died in the attack just moments earlier, and the blood on Mattis's uniform. Yet he remembers the commander was disciplined and businesslike in the negotiations.

At the meeting, Conway checks the reaction around the room, and everyone seems to be okay with the general's opening threat. They all know of Mattis and what he is capable of, if provoked. Conway breaks the tension and continues to lay out the rewards and responsibilities being offered to the sheiks. It won't be the last time Conway covers for Mattis's plain speech.

In their long history as friends since Desert Storm, Conway has learned that, as he says, "If you ask Jim Mattis a question you're going to get the answer. If you're not ready for tough answers, don't ask him. Because he'll tell you."[77]

Conway and Mattis are cut from the same cloth. He knew what Mattis meant when his friend, an avid historical scholar, spoke like a semiliterate Wild West sheriff defending the American way and a lady's honor in another widely publicized quote: "You go into Afghanistan, you got guys who slap women around for five years because they didn't wear a veil. You know, guys like that ain't got no manhood left anyway. So it's a hell of a lot of fun to shoot them. Actually it's quite fun to fight them, you know. It's a hell of a hoot. It's fun to shoot some people. I'll be right up there with you. I like brawling."[78]

For that one, it went all the way up to the commandant of the Marine Corps to get Mattis off the media hot seat. Commandant General Michael Hagee delicately shared with the press that Mattis "often speaks with a great deal of candor."[79]

As happened in Afghanistan, Mattis is unguarded speaking to his troops, and in his enthusiasm forgets that there are eager reporters present. Once, welcoming two hundred Marines arriving at the al-Asad airbase in Iraq, Mattis said, "The first time you blow someone away is not an insignificant event. That said, there are some assholes in the world that just need to be shot. There are hunters and there are victims. By your discipline, cunning, obedience and alertness, you will decide if you are a hunter or a victim. It's really a hell of a lot of fun. You're gonna have a blast out here. I feel sorry for every son of a bitch that doesn't get to serve with you."[80]

Once again Conway has to help tamp down the media brushfire that Mattis lights. The White House bends Conway's ear for a long while on that particular occasion, and afterward he catches up with his friend and subordinate officer to tell him, "Jim, goddamn it. If you don't shut up, I'll wear your ass out!"[81]

And again, a commandant of the Marine Corps also has to come to Mattis's defense. Commandant Jim Jones gets Mattis on the phone and chews him out, particularly regarding the reaction of their European coalition partners to Mattis's western sheriff routine. "Europeans don't really like cowboys,"[82] Jones tells his outspoken general.

So it is no surprise to Conway that Mattis threatens the Anbar sheiks with the first thing out of his mouth. It's exactly what any frontier town sheriff might do. He just moves the conversation forward quickly and hopes (in vain) that he won't be reading about Mattis's threat later.

CAP continues to stabilize and pacify the north and eastern parts of Iraq by providing reliable basic services, self-generated security, and elected local government. But widely, throughout much of the rest of Iraq, the insurgency is still going strong. IEDs have been supplied by Iran's Revolutionary Guard and upgraded to armor-piercing explosively shaped charges that can puncture LAVs and up-armored Humvees. Zarkawi and Muqtada al-Sadr are actively attacking coalition forces in Baghdad and Anbar.

On Mattis's frequent trips to the front lines in Fallujah and throughout Anbar to meet with sheiks and provincial leaders, the jump platoon is repeatedly attacked. Through the initial assault in Fallujah and then weeks of siege, the jump suffers three ambushes and three extended firefights. Mattis's aide, Lieutenant Steven Thompson, is the first seriously injured member of the jump in late April. Then, Staff Sergeant Jorge Molina Bautista is killed by a roadside IED outside Fallujah in May on the way to Mattis's blood-soaked meeting with local sheiks, and in June Lance Corporal Jeremy L. Bohlman is killed in Ramadi. In all, seventeen out of twenty-nine of Mattis's jump platoon are killed or wounded. Yet, during the entire Fallujah campaign, in spite of their 59 percent casualty rate and standing offer to transfer them out at any time without shame, not one of the jump asks for a transfer out of the unit. Mattis says about Molina Bautista and Bohlman, "Staff Sergeant Molina Bautista was devoted to his family and kind towards the young men in the Jump—I trusted him totally. Bohlman was keenly attentive on patrol and high-spirited off duty. He was a lot of fun for the rest of the team to have around."[83]

In Washington, after months of increasing attacks, President Bush is desperate to stop the rebellion. He offers General Conway twenty thousand additional troops and new US Army leadership under Major General David Petraeus. Petraeus is like-minded with Conway and Mattis on winning the hearts and minds of the people. He has been very successful at it in Mosul, north of Anbar in Nineveh Province. Bush appeals to Conway and Petraeus to shut down the insurgency elsewhere in the country. Conway reassures the president that things aren't as bleak as he may be hearing: "Sir, I support the surge but we're winning in the west."[84]

Indeed, Conway and Mattis are winning. Their success is summed up in the cheery-sounding name the Great Sunni Awakening. For a war-weary America, this sounds hopeful, even positive—an awakening! The media jumps at the chance to bring a positive angle into the dreary procession of gruesome death they have been serving for months. President Bush and General Petraeus jump on the bandwagon by announcing the surge: they will be sending more troops to help turn the tide in Iraq. Soon they are being credited with snatching victory in Iraq from the jaws of defeat. They are heralded around the world as the great strategists and peacemakers of Anbar. Along with the troops, pallets of US cash are flown into Anbar to grease the wheels of the awakening.

Eventually, even Fallujah itself is pacified, so much so that it becomes a safe haven for frightened refugees from other parts of Iraq. President Bush is once again seen as a hero and liberator by many Iraqis. On the idea that the surge pacified Anbar, General Conway comments, "The surge had nothing to do with it. We were winning those people over for months beforehand."[85]

But even as the awakening blossoms, and Saddam's sadistic sons Uday and Qusay are hunted down and killed, former high-ranking Iraqi leaders are captured, and finally Saddam himself is captured in a rat hole outside Tikrit, the price of long-term occupation comes due for Mattis. In Haditha, a family of fourteen Iraqis, including young children, is wiped out in one Marine raid. Charges are brought against the Marines, and certain American media outlets promote the idea that the Marines may be guilty of war crimes. Some call it a new My Lai massacre.[86]

In the small village of Mukaradeeb near the Syrian border, a wedding party of forty-two people is killed in a Marine air strike. Brigadier General Mark Kimmitt, deputy operations director for the Joint Task Force in Iraq, says, "There was no evidence of a wedding: no decorations, no musical instruments found, no large quantities of food or leftover servings one would expect from a wedding celebration. There may have been some kind of celebration. Bad people have celebrations, too."[87]

Video footage obtained by the Associated Press from an unknown source seems to contradict Kimmitt. The video shows a series of scenes of a wedding celebration and footage from the following day, showing fragments of musical instruments, pots and pans, and brightly colored bedding used for celebrations scattered around a destroyed tent. The images can't be verified as authentic but are broadcast widely. Mattis is again in the spotlight, this time for the atrocities committed on his watch. He backhands the accusations against his Marines: "How many people go to the middle of the desert to hold a wedding 80 miles from the nearest civilization? These were more than two dozen military-age males. Let's not be naive."[88]

He later commented that it had taken him thirty seconds to deliberate on bombing the location. In both cases, Mattis was instrumental in testifying for the Marines at trial, winning acquittals or convictions on lesser charges for all of the Marines involved. With their honor tarnished by the accusations of murder, the Marines continue to cultivate the Sunni Awakening even as they suffer continuous ambushes by insurgents.

Under orders from Washington and Baghdad, Mattis surrenders the hard-won center of Fallujah to a collection of local officials and tribal leaders who call themselves the Fallujah Brigade. Within weeks the Fallujah Brigade transforms into an insurgent front group and begin stockpiling weapons and making fortifications throughout the city, guaranteeing a second battle for Fallujah.

The Second Battle of Fallujah will explode in November under the command of Lieutenant General Rich Natonski. This conflict will escalate death tolls from dozens and hundreds during Mattis's siege into the thousands. It will be the bloodiest fighting since the Pacific islands of Guadalcanal, Iwo Jima, and Tarawa during World War II.

In spite of serious continued attacks on coalition forces, on June 28, 2004, Ghazi Mashal Ajil al-Yawer is elected president of the Iraqi interim government. The first phases of pacification have finally reached the capital of Baghdad. Mattis has beaten the enemy to a standoff in Fallujah but been stopped from driving a stake through its heart. More importantly, he has won the prize—the Desert Wolves and surrounding tribes of Anbar. On his watch, they have grown into the living proof of a possible peaceful future for all Iraqis.

August 2004—al-Asad Airbase,
Western Anbar Province, Iraq

As the summer heat roasts the Iraqi desert, Mattis prepares notes for his farewell address in a stifling, unadorned airplane hangar. He has spent most of his career leading Marines to war on battlefields a few hundred miles from where he now sits, and now it is time to say farewell for the last time. He has been nominated for a third star and will spend the rest of his career in Quantico, Virginia, and Washington, DC, leading the charge on behalf of his beloved Marines. He will take time off to be with his mother and his lifelong friends who live almost as far from Washington, DC, as one can get—"safely west of the Rockies," as he likes to say.

In his off time, he'll volunteer at the local food bank, fish in the mighty Yakima River, and catch up on his reading of history. He will ascend to one of the highest military positions in the United States, commander of US Central Command. After his military career, he will accept a fellowship and lecture at the Hoover Institution in California and become involved briefly with a private company called Theranos that will collapse into lawsuits, ending his one and only venture into the private business sector. In mid-2016 a long-shot presidential candidate named Donald Trump will call him to talk about a possible future as secretary of defense.

But for now, as he reviews his notes, they bring to mind the people, the men and women of the Marine Corps, who had kept him returning to the barren deserts of the Middle East. It was his Marines, especially the dirty, exhausted, and unbreakable grunts, filled with their special type of spiritual power, who inspired him and kept him coming back. It was the grunts who overcame discomfort, who faced death with utter contempt, and who often suffered most deeply the heartbreak of warfare. To them, the front-line warriors, he now says goodbye:

Today, I haven't the words to capture what is in my heart
as I look out at these beautiful grunts who represent thou-

sands of cocky, selfless, macho young troops of our infantry division. Infantry—infant soldiers, young soldiers, young soldiers of the sea, who have given so much, and who have taught me courage as they smiled, heading out to risk their lives again, to destroy the enemy. So lacking the words, I will close with a warrior's prayer from a man who understands:

> Give me God, what you still have.
> Give me what no one else asks for.
> I do not ask for wealth, success, or even health.
> People ask you so often, God, for all these things that you cannot have any left.
> Give me what people refuse to accept from you.
> I want insecurity and disquietude.
> I want turmoil and brawl.
> And if you should give them to me, my God, once and for all, let me be sure to have them always.
> For I will not always have the courage to ask for them.

May God be with you, my fine young Marines, as you head out once again into the heat of the Iraqi sun, into the still of the dark night to close with the enemy. Beside you, I'd do it all again. *Semper Fidelis.*[89]

For the last time as a Marine, he leaves the deserts of the Middle East as an invincible warrior and visionary peacemaker. Without fanfare or further ceremony, Mattis shakes a few hands and carries his own bags onto a waiting military transport plane. In his briefcase, among his important papers, he carries his most precious, personal possession. It will stay with him, always in sight, in whatever billet, hotel room, or easy chair he happens to find himself. It is a photograph of all twenty-nine fearless young grunts of his jump platoon.

Epilogue:
No Better Friend,
No Worse Enemy

On March 22, 2013, after forty-one years of service in the Marine Corps, Jim Mattis retires from active duty.[1] He has shown that a small, focused, and ethical force can prevail against a larger, modern enemy. He has shown that this same small force can then transform a temporary military conquest into a durable peace. He has expanded decades-old, restrictive Marine Corps doctrine to create sea-based combat divisions that can meet any threat at any point on the globe. By insisting that his Marines engage their minds before they engage their weapons, he leads the Marine Corps to master the complexities of terrorism, insurgency, and asymmetrical warfare into the twenty-first century. At his retirement ceremony, Secretary of Defense Chuck Hagel says, "General Mattis has demonstrated to the world that truly there is no worse enemy, and no better friend, than a United States Marine. He has devoted his life, his energy, his intellect, and his force of courage and personality to the US Marine Corps, our military, and our country. And our nation is forever grateful for his service."[2]

As with other indispensable, visionary men and women in the history of the United States, Mattis's retirement doesn't last long. America's enemies continue to grow in strength and influence during his absence. Soon, he will be called upon to lead the fight again, against not only the nation's but Western civilization's bloodthirsty foes. Less than a month after his retirement, the Islamic State of Iraq and the Levant (ISIL) expands its range to include eastern Syria, and changes its name to the Islamic State of Iraq and Syria (ISIS).[3]

In July 2013, Mattis is invited to join the high-powered board of directors of a biomedical device company called Theranos.[4] On the board are ex-Marine and Secretary of State George Schultz, former secretary of defense William Perry, former secretary of state Henry Kissinger, former US senator Sam Nunn, former US senator and heart-transplant surgeon Bill Frist, retired US Navy admiral Gary Roughead, former Wells Fargo CEO Richard Kovacevich, and Riley Bechtel, chairman of the board and former CEO at Bechtel Group.[5]

Theranos founder Elizabeth Holmes dazzles the all-male board and earns Mattis's support. "She really does want to make a dent in the universe—one that is positive,"[6] he claims. Holmes does make a dent—but unfortunately, it is in everyone's reputation. She has used a shell company she owns to apparently conduct sham tests and falsely validate the effectiveness of her blood-testing device.[7] It is an allegedly elaborate and outright fraud. To make matters worse, George Schulz's son is the whistleblower who brings worldwide shame and suspicion down on all their heads. Mattis's introduction to the private sector is an eye-opening display of apparent deceit even beyond the imagination of the shiftiest tribal sheik in Iraq.

Mattis seizes the opportunity to retreat behind the citadel walls of Stanford University[8] and the Hoover Institution.[9] He lectures on the subjects of war, revolution, and peace. He joins the American Public Policy Think Tank and Research Institution and participates in research on Iran, the Middle East, military history and strategy, and national security. He becomes an Annenberg Distinguished Visiting Fellow and speaks to international policy makers. He gathers directorships, fellowships, and awards by the bushel. He adds General Dynamics to his portfolio as a member of the board of directors. He becomes a Davies Family Distinguished Visiting Fellow.[10]

But the enemy doesn't sleep while Mattis rests on his laurels. In May 2014 the city of Raqqa, Syria, is overtaken by ISIS and becomes the de facto capital of the caliphate.[11] The dream of caliphate is now carried by a new generation of leaders, a global jihadist gang of sadistic mass murderers. Fallujah[12] and Ramadi are retaken by the jihadis, and strict Sharia law is instituted.[13] This includes roving

virtue police who beat women with canes in the street for insufficient Islamic modesty.[14] Doubtless, Mattis is upset by seeing the
cities won with so much bloodshed returned to the same soulless
men, beasts who beat women.

Mattis is invited on to the board of the US Naval Institute
and accepts. He receives an honorary doctor of laws degree from
George Washington College.[15] The Marine Corps University Foundation awards him the 2014 Semper Fidelis award. In his acceptance
speech, Mattis says, "On evenings like this most of us will remember the tragedy of losing comrades. Beautiful Marines whose rambunctious spirits gave us what F. Scott Fitzgerald called 'Riotous
excursions with privileged glimpses into the human heart.' And we
remember them, everyone, who gave their lives so our experiment
called America, could live. And for us who live today. . . . We do so
with a sense that each day is a bonus and a blessing."[16]

Back in his small hometown near the Yakima River, he volun-
teers at the Tri-Cities Food Bank that provides emergency food to
the needy residents of the area. He agrees to sit on their board of
directors. He joins the board of the Center for a New American
Security and is called to testify before the Senate Armed Services
Committee about global challenges and US national security. He
warns against the growing threat in Iraq: "The international order, so
painstakingly put together by the greatest generation coming home
from mankind's bloodiest conflict, is under increasing stress. . . .
Like it or not, today we are part of this larger world and must carry
out our part. We cannot wait for problems to arrive here or it will be
too late; rather we must remain strongly engaged in this complex."[17]

Mattis coauthors *Blueprints for America,* a book of policy solu-
tions for economic and political issues, with other leading Hoover
Institute fellows. It is edited by former Secretary of State George
Schultz. At the Marines' Memorial Club in San Francisco, he is the
guest speaker on the topic "You Built Your Own Monument." His
speech soars, reaching out to the spiritual core of his audience of
fellow veterans: "No granite monuments, regardless of how grandly

built, can take the place of your raw example of courage, when in your youth you answered your country's call. When you looked past the hot political rhetoric. When you voluntarily left behind life's well-lit avenues. When you signed that blank check to the American people payable with your lives. And, most important, when you made a full personal commitment even while, for over a dozen years, the country's political leadership had difficulty defining our national level of commitment."[18]

In December 2015 he joins the advisory board of the nonprofit Spirit of America, which supports the safety and success of American troops and the local people they seek to help. He coauthors *Warriors and Citizens: American Views of Our Military* with Kori Schake, a fellow researcher at the Hoover Institute. Mattis writes, "We undertook this project to better understand attitudes of the American public about their military forty years into having an all-volunteer force and after fifteen years of being continuously at war. One of the most important gaps evident in the survey data collected for this project is public disaffection with their elected leaders on issues of war strategy."[19]

Late in the presidential campaign season of 2016, as it begins to look possible that Donald Trump might win, he receives a call from the Trump campaign. Weeks later, he is confirmed as secretary of defense with a rare, nearly unanimous waiver of restrictions that prevent a recently active member of the military from serving as secretary of defense.[20] He resigns from General Dynamics' board of directors and withdraws from his remaining organizations forfeiting several generous and relatively trouble-free streams of income for a government salary and intense public scrutiny and criticism.[21]

At his swearing in on January 20, 2017, Mattis says, "Together with the Intelligence Community we are the sentinels and guardians of our nation. We need only look to you, the uniformed and civilian members of the Department and your families, to see the fundamental unity of our country. You represent an America committed to the common good; an America that is never complacent about defending its freedoms; and an America that remains a steady beacon of hope for all mankind. . . . I am confident you will do your part. I pledge to you I'll do my best as your Secretary."[22]

Soon after the inauguration, President Trump says that he has full confidence in Mattis to make the necessary defense policy adjustments. Within days, Mattis announces that the policy of the United States toward ISIS is changing from "attrition" to "annihilation."[23] Mattis is going to actively hunt down and wipe out ISIS permanently, all of them and any known associates. He will take back Ramadi and Fallujah and again rescue the Desert Wolves of Anbar from foreign jihadis.

In May, he speaks to the graduating class of West Point:

> By the time this class was in first grade classrooms in every state across our union, our country had been thrust into a war by maniacs who thought that by hurting us they could scare us. Well, we don't scare, and nothing better represents America's awesome determination to defend herself than this graduating class.
>
> Every one of you—every one of you could have opted out. You'd grown up seeing the war on 'round-the-clock news. There was no draft. Colleges across this land would have moved heaven and earth to recruit you for schools that would never make such demands on you as West Point . . .
>
> You graduate the same week that saw the murder of 22 innocent young lives. Manchester's tragic loss underscores the purpose for your years of study and training at this elite school. For today, as General Caslen said, you join the ranks of those whose mission is to guard freedom and to protect the innocent from such terror, the innocent noted in your class motto, "so others may dream."
>
> . . . In terms of serving something larger than yourself,

yours is the same oath that was taken by the young men of ancient Athens. They pledged to fight for the ideals and sacred things of the city, to revere and obey the city's laws.

We in the Department of Defense recognize that there are a lot of passions running about in our country, as there ought to be in a vibrant Republic. But for those privileged to wear the cloth of our nation, to serve in the United States Army, you stand the ramparts—unapologetic, apolitical, defending our experiment in self-governance. And you hold the line.

You hold the line, faithful to duty, confronting our nation's foes with implacable will, knowing that if there's a hill to climb, waiting will not make it any smaller.

You hold the line, true to honor, living by a moral code regardless of who is watching, knowing that honor is what we give ourselves for a life of meaning.

You hold the line, loyal to country and defending the constitution, and defending our fundamental freedoms, knowing from your challenging years here on the Hudson that loyalty only counts where there are a hundred reasons not to be.

So fight—So fight for our ideals and our sacred things; incite in others respect and love for our country and our fellow Americans; and leave this country greater and more beautiful than you inherited it, for that is the duty of every generation.[24]

Back at work in the Trump administration, Mattis and the president agree that, unlike previous administrations, there will be no public discussion of American military plans or timetables. Instead, Mattis quietly drops out of sight. By September 2017, 80 percent of the caliphate capitol of Raqqa is retaken.[25] Mattis meets with commanders in nearby Kubal, Iraq. A few moments later, after his plane lifts off the Kubal airport runway, ISIS attacks the airport. It is believed the attack was intended to kill Mattis. But instead the lucky Marine flies on to have a front-row view of the final fall of Raqqa.[26]

A coalition of Kurds, the Syrian Democratic Forces, and American advisers finally drive a stake through the heart of the enemy on October 17, 2017, in the central square of the city of Raqqa.[27] Celebrations erupt from some surviving Raqqa citizens. Globally, praise and condemnation explode in volcanoes of heated rhetoric.

On a nondescript desert airfield not too far from Raqqa, Mattis again quietly takes a seat in an indistinguishable military transport plane. He carries his well-worn copy of *Meditations* by Marcus Aurelius to distract him and help him rest. In moments he is airborne, in the immaculate clouds, free of the heavy yoke of duty for just a few moments. He finds some peace in the Spartan solitude of the big, empty plane. Alone and quiet in his thoughts, he flies on toward his next front line.

ACKNOWLEDGMENTS

Thank you, Dr. Bill Proser, my older brother, guiding light, protector, and lifelong supporter. I would not be here without you. To my cousin, contributor, and sage Daniel Zoller, a reliable friend in darkest times and one hell of a shortstop. To my beloved wife, Adoley, thanks are not nearly enough. You are my morning sun. To my stalwart pals John Paxson and David Fallon, who kept faith and never faltered when our world was collapsing.

To the Marines Colonel Ken Jordan USMC (ret.), who saw what was in my heart and let me know I could speak about it plainly and reach many Marines. I have never had or will ever have a better teacher. To General James T. Conway USMC (ret.), who recommended my first book to all Marines and shared his recollections freely of the Desert Wolves and his close friend Jim Mattis. To Colonel N. R. Hoskot USMC (ret.), who helped me understand front-line command during Operation Iraqi Freedom, and to Major General Chris Cortez USMC (ret.), who guarded Mattis's right flank as a commander in Operation Desert Storm. To Marine Generals Mike Myatt, O.K. Steele, Daniel Yoo, and Lawrence Snowden, who welcomed me at the Marine Memorial many years ago and encouraged me to examine the warrior's path. To Gunnery Sergeant Nathan Osowski USMC, who guided me through OIF 1 with the general; to Sergeant Ryan Woolworth USMC, who shared his memories of traveling in the command LAV; to Captain Joe Plenzler USMC (ret.), who encountered the general's skepticism but received his warmth as just another gun-hand around the ranch; to Lieutenant David Pittelkow USMC (ret.), for your abiding love and respect for the general; to Chaplain Bill Devine USMC (ret.), whose generous love and faith has strengthened so many, including my own family, during terrible challenges; and to the many Marines who choose to remain anonymous. Finally, to the twenty-nine Marines of the general's jump platoon in Fallujah, for your courage, commitment, and spiritual fire. Although I have never met or spoken with you, please know that this citizen of a grateful nation stands in awe and humble appreciation of your service. Thank you all and *Semper Fi.*

I stand on the shoulders of magnificent warriors who were there, who risked all for freedom and lived to tell the tale, including Nathaniel Fick, Bing West, David Danelo, Richard S. Lowry, Michael Scot Smith, Patrick K. O'Donnell, Dick Camp, Peter Mansoor, and Andy Bufalo. And to the many war correspondents like Evan Wright, Thomas Ricks, Sebastian Junger, and Peter L. Bergen, who risked all for the truth, I hope I have helped to promote your work and sacrifices in some small way. To committed analysts and scholars, including Seth G. Jones, Garrett M. Graff, Charles River Editors, and Emma Sky, thank you for your commitment, efforts, and insight. Special thanks to Dr. Fred Allison and Captain Joshua Pena USMC of the Marine Corps Oral History Division.

Special thanks to Eric Nelson of HarperCollins for taking a chance on this relative newcomer, to Eric Meyers for patiently guiding my hand in this work, and to Bob Diforio for beating the drum. To my intrepid crew of researchers; Cieja Montgomery, tireless and selfless enthusiast; Lieutenant Colonel Curt Bruce USMC (ret.), for adapting and overcoming; Howard Berkowitz, for your insight; Pete Fallon, LCDR, DC, USN (ret.), for always being there and ready to help; Penelope Huala, for meticulous and invaluable cross-referencing; Gary Dixon, for your early work and constancy; and Shammai Siskind, for your insight on military matters and inspiring work ethic.

To the great friends and family of me and my wife, Adoley, who know what extraordinary challenges we faced during the writing of this book. Your love and acts of kindness were the hand of God on us. And to my great friend and the greatest warrior poet of our age, Sergeant Bill Lansford USMC and First Lieutenant US Army, one of Carlson's Raiders, a grunt on The Long Patrol, author of the biography of Pancho Villa and the poetry of *The Masks of Quet-zalcoatl*: you are always with me, buddy, in every word, standing watch. *Semper Fidelis.*

Jim Proser
Sarasota, Florida

NOTES

Distances in military operations are generally calibrated in kilometers. Kilometers in this book have been converted to miles for easier comprehension by most American readers.

Introduction

1. Josh Feldman, "Senate Near-Unanimously Votes to Confirm Gen. James Mattis for DefSec," *Mediaite*, January 20, 2017, https://www.mediaite.com/online/breaking-senate-near-unanimously-votes-to-confirm-gen-james-mattis-for-defsec/.
2. Kathleen Elkins, "11 Powerful Quotes on Leadership and Success from Gen. James 'Mad Dog' Mattis," CNBC.com, December 2, 2016, https://www.cnbc.com/2016/12/02/11-powerful-quotes-on-leadership-and-success-from-general-james-mad-dog-mattis.html.
3. James T. Conway, interview by author, November 30, 2017.

Chapter 1: No Better Friend

1. Stanton S. Coerr, "I Served with James Mattis. Here's What I Learned from Him," *Federalist*, December 2, 2016, http://thefederalist.com/2016/12/02/served-james-mattis-heres-learned/.
2. Ibid.
3. Joe Plenzler, "15 Things Mattis Taught Me about Real Leadership," *We'll All Die as Marines*, December 20, 2016, http://wellalldieasmarines.net/2016/12/mattis-2/.
4. Will Durant, *Heroes of History: A Brief History of Civilization from Ancient Times to the Dawn of the Modern Age* (New York: Simon & Schuster, 2002), 131.
5. Seth Moulton, "No Better Friend, No Worse Enemy: America's Foreign Policy for the Next President," *Real Clear Defense*, February 7, 2016, https://www.realcleardefense.com/articles/2016/02/08/no_better_friend_no_worse_enemy_108991.html.
6. Ellis Group, "21st Century Maneuver Warfare," *Marine Corps Gazette: Professional Journal of U.S. Marines* 100, no. 11 (November 2016), https://www.mca-marines.org/gazette/2016/11/21st-century-maneuver-warfare.

7. Coerr, "I Served with James Mattis."

8. Nathaniel Fick, *One Bullet Away: The Making of a Marine Officer* (Boston: Houghton Mifflin Harcourt, 2006), 191.

9. Nathan Osowski, interview by author, May 27, 2017.

10. Evan Wright, *Generation Kill: Devil Dogs, Ice Man, Captain America, and the New Face of American War* (New York: G. P. Putnam's Sons, 2008), 72–73.

11. Ibid., 74.

12. Osowski, interview (quote paraphrased).

13. Evan Wright, *Generation Kill* (Penguin Publishing Group, Kindle Edition), 56.

14. Wright, *Generation Kill*, 83.

15. Ibid.

16. Osowski, interview.

17. "Death Highway, Revisited," *Time*, March 18, 1991.

18. Wright, *Generation Kill*, 415.

19. Ibid.

20. Ruth Sherlock, "Profile: General James 'Mad Dog' Mattis, Donald Trump's Pick for Secretary of Defence," *Telegraph*, December 2, 2016.

21. Wright, *Generation Kill*, 26.

22. Fick, *One Bullet Away*, 163.

23. Elkins, "11 Powerful Quotes."

24. Fick, *One Bullet Away*. 163

25. Ibid.

26. Ibid.

27. Ibid.

28. Ibid.,164.

29. Ibid.

30. Ibid.

31. Ibid.

32. Wright, *Generation Kill*, 27.

33. Ibid.

Chapter 2: No Worse Enemy

1. Marcus Aurelius, *Meditations* (Ariston Publishing, Kindle Edition, loc. 2581).

2. Ashley Fantz, "For Years, former POW Jessica Lynch Kept the Hurt Inside," July 20, 2015, CNN.com, https://edition.cnn.com /2015/07/20/us/jessica-lynch-where-is-she-now/index.html.

3. Thomas E. Ricks, *The Generals: American Military Command from World War II to Today* (New York: Penguin, 2013).

4. Ibid.

5. Bing West and Ray L. Smith. *The March Up: Taking Baghdad with the United States Marines* (Random House Publishing Group, Kindle Edition, loc. 730–732).

6. Ibid., loc. 776.

7. Christopher Cooper, "How a Marine Lost His Command in Race to Baghdad: Col. Joe Dowdy's 'Tempo' Displeased Superiors; Balance of Mission, Men," *Wall Street Journal*, April 5, 2004.

8. Thomas E. Ricks, *The Generals: American Military Command from World War II to Today* (Penguin Publishing Group, Kindle Edition, loc. 5427).

9. Cooper, "How a Marine Lost His Command."

10. Ibid.

11. Hal Bernton and David Gutman, "James 'Mad Dog' Mattis, Trump's Defense Secretary Pick, Always Comes Home to Richland," *Seattle Times*, January 7, 2017. Background information that follows about Richland and Mattis's upbringing there is also drawn from this source.

12. Ibid.

13. Ibid.

14. Ibid.

15. Ibid.

16. Ibid.

17. West and Smith, *The March Up*.

18. Ibid., loc. 1986.

19. Ibid.

20. Ibid.

21. Ibid.

22. Ibid., loc. 2275.

23. Ibid.

24. Ibid., 148.

25. Ibid., 149.

Chapter 3: Liberation

1. West and Smith, *The March Up,* loc. 2416.
2. Ibid., loc. 2416.
3. Ibid., loc. 2418.
4. "Honor the Fallen: Marine 1st Lt. Brian M. McPhillips," *Military Times*, https://thefallen.militarytimes.com/marine-1st-lt-brian-m-mcphillips/256544.
5. Christopher M. Kennedy, Wanda J. Renfrow, Evelyn A. Englander, and Nathan S. Lowrey, *U.S. Marines in Iraq, 2003: Anthology and Annotated Bibliography*, U.S. Marines in the Global War on Terrorism (Washington, D.C.: History Division, US Marine Corps, 2006), 2.
6. West and Smith, *The March Up,* loc. 3085.
7. Ibid.
8. Thomas E. Ricks, *Fiasco: The American Military Adventure in Iraq, 2003 to 2005* (Penguin Publishing Group, Kindle Edition), 72.
9. Ibid., 73.
10. Ibid., 78.
11. Ibid., 313.
12. Captain Joseph Plenzler, phone interview with Jim Proser, June 22, 2017.
13. Captain Brian B. Smalley, interview, May 3, 2003, MCHC, Quantico, VA. Original source in Reynolds, "Baghdad, Basrah."
14. Colonel Nicholas E. Reynolds USMCR, *U.S. Marines In Iraq, 2003: Basrah, Baghdad and Beyond: U.S. Marines in the Global War on Terrorism* [Illustrated Edition] (Tannenberg Publishing, Kindle Edition, loc. 2820).
15. "Marine: Flag a Symbol of Liberation, not Occupation," CNN.com, April 10, 2003, http://edition.cnn.com/2003/WORLD/meast/04/10/sprj.irq.chin/index.html.
16. West and Smith, *The March Up.*
17. Margaret Warner, "A Marine's View," Public Broadcasting System Online News Hour, Sept, 26, 2003.

Chapter 4: Beyond Baghdad

1. Fick, *One Bullet Away.*
2. "Gen. James Mattis Q&A," *Small Wars Journal*, May 24, 2010.

3. Andrew Anthony Bufalo, *Not as Lean, Not as Mean, Still a Marine! Even More Marine Corps Sea Stories and Politically Incorrect Common Sense* (Riverview, FL: S&B Publishing, 2004), 7.

4. Donald Rumsfeld, interview by Tim Russert, *Meet the Press*, NBC, April 13, 2003.

5. James Aylmer Lowthorpe Haldane, *The Insurrection in Mesopotamia, 1920* (Edinburgh: W. Blackwood and Sons, 1922).

6. Ricks, *Fiasco.*

7. Dick Camp, *Operation Phantom Fury: The Assault and Capture of Fallujah, Iraq* (Minneapolis: Zenith, 2009), 33.

8. Reynolds, *Basrah, Baghdad, and Beyond*, 155.

9. Ibid.

10. Madeline Conway, "9 Unforgettable Quotes by James Mattis," *Politico*, December 12, 2016, https://www.politico.com/blogs/donald-trump-administration/2016/12/james-mattis-quotes-232097.

Chapter 5: A Girl Named Alice

1. David Danelo, *Blood Stripes: The Grunt's View of the War in Iraq* (Mechanicsburg, PA: Stackpole Books, 2006).

2. Ibid.

3. John Dickerson, "Gen. James Mattis, USMC: The General Who Is Fighting a Constant Battle to Keep the Military Innovating," *Slate*, August 9, 2011.

4. Blago Kirov, *Napoleon Bonaparte: Quotes and Facts* (BookRix, 2014).

5. Danelo, *Blood Stripes.*

6. Harry Kreisler, "Reflections: A Conversation with General James Mattis," *Conversations with History*, University of California Television, June 5, 2014, https://www.youtube.com/watch?v=HOc38ZwEO8s, at 3:19.

7. H. R. Haldeman, *The Ends of Power* (New York: Times Books, 1978), 122.

8. Henry A. Kissinger, news conference on the status of Vietnam peace negotiations, October 27, 1972, transcript. https://www.mtholyoke.edu/acad/intrel/paris.htm

9. Sun Tzu, *The Art of War: Complete Texts and Commentaries* (Shambhala, Kindle Edition, loc. 3559).

10. Ruth Sherlock, "Profile: General James 'Mad Dog' Mattis, Donald Trump's Pick for Secretary of Defence," *Telegraph*, December 2, 2016.

11. Geoffrey Ingersoll and Paul Szoldra, "19 Unforgettable Quotes from Retiring General James 'Mad Dog' Mattis," *Business Insider*, January 23, 2013, http://www.businessinsider.com/general-mad-dog-mattiss-best-quotes-2013-1.

12. "Captain Mattis," Task Force Trinity, April 20, 2013, http://www.taskforcetrinity.com/archives/2759.

13. "Iranians Overthrow the Shah 1977–1979," https://nvdatabase.swarthmore.edu/content/iranians-overthrow-shah-1977-79.

14. Ken Jordan, interview by author, April 10, 2017.

15. Ibid.

16. David Pittlekow, interview by author, June 28, 2017.

17. Ibid.

18. Ken Jordan, "Command Fitness Report—Captain James Mattis," November 30, 1980, private collection of Ken Jordan.

19. Ibid.

Chapter 6: The Enemy of My Enemy

1. "Shlomo Argov," obituary, *Telegraph*, February 24, 2003.

2. "Beirut Marine Barracks Bombing Fast Facts," CNN.com, June 13, 2013, updated October 18, 2017, https://edition.cnn.com/2013/06/13/world/meast/beirut-marine-barracks-bombing-fast-facts/index.html.

3. James Mattis, "Amphibious Raids: An Historical Imperative for Today's Marines," student paper, Marine Corps Command and Staff College, Quantico, VA, 1985.

4. "Talking with the P.L.O.: From Birth through Terrorism to Dialogue with the U.S.," *New York Times*, December 16, 1988.

5. Jim Proser, *I'm Staying with My Boys: The Heroic Life of Sgt. John Basilone, USMC* (New York: St. Martin's Press, 2004).

6. Elaine Sciolino and Michael R. Gordon, "Confrontation in the Gulf; U.S. Gave Iraq Little Reason Not to Mount Kuwait Assault," *New York Times*, September 23, 1990.

7. "This Aggression Will Not Stand," *New York Times*, March 1, 1991.

8. West and Smith, *The March Up*.

9. Operations Desert Shield and Desert Storm, August 1990–March 1991, *War in the Persian Gulf Operations: Desert Shield and Desert Storm, August 1990–March 1991* (Washington, DC: Center of Military History, United States Army, 2010).

10. Charles H. Cureton, *U.S. Marines in the Persian Gulf, 1990–1991 with the 1st Marine Division in Desert Shield and Desert Storm* (Washington, DC: History and Museums Division Headquarters, US Marine Corps, 1991).

11. James Clarke, "This Retro Interview Reveals A Young Jim Mattis Before He Was 'Mad Dog,'" *Task & Purpose*, September 1, 2017.

12. Richard W. Stewart, *American Military History: The United States Army in a Global Era, 1917–2003* (Washington, DC: Center of Military History, US Army, 2009).

13. Paul Westermeyer, *The Battle of al-Khafji* (Washington, DC: US Marine Corps, History Division, 2008), sec. 2, http://www.marines.mil/Portals/59/Publications/U.S.%20Marines%20in%20Battle%20Al-Khafji%20%20PCN%20106000400_2.pdf.

14. Cureton, *U.S. Marines in the Persian Gulf.*

15. Ibid.

16. Ken Jordan, interview by author, September 26, 2017.

Chapter 7: Task Force Ripper

1. Cureton, *U.S. Marines in the Persian Gulf*, 57.

2. Anonymous friend of Mattis family, interview by author, May 19, 2017.

3. Otto Kreisher, "Marines' Desert Victory," *U.S. Naval Magazine* 30, no. 1 (February 2016).

4. Ellis Group, "21st Century Maneuver Warfare."

5. Frank Colucci, "Heavy Duty: Overhaul Under Way for Abrams Tank Engine," *National Defense*, 1 September 2006, https://www.the-freelibrary.com/Heavy+duty%3a+overhaul+under+way+for+Abrams+tank+engine.-a0151394635.

6. Richard P. Hunnicutt, *Patton: A History of the American Main Battle Tank* (Novato, CA: Presidio, 1984).

7. Cureton, *U.S. Marines in the Persian Gulf*, 83.

8. Ibid., 70.

9. Ibid., 71–73.

10. Ibid., 73.

11. Ibid., 83.

12. Ibid., 79.

13. Ibid., 80.

14. Ibid., 82.

15. Ibid.

16. Ibid., 92.

17. Ibid., 103.

18. Ibid.

19. "The Badass of the Week: Chesty Puller," Badassoftheweek.com, http://www.badassoftheweek.com/puller.html.

20. Claude W. Curtis, "The Tip of the Spear," *Leatherneck* 74, no. 8 (August 1991).

21. Ibid.

22. "Death Highway, Revisited," *Time*, March 18, 1991.

Chapter 8: The Sleeping Enemy

1. Bobby Ghosh, "How I Got Saddam's Flag," *Time*, January 22, 2008.

2. James N. Mattis, *Concept of Command—Recruiting Duty* (Quantico, VA: Archives Branch, USMC History Division, Marine Headquarters, 1983).

3. Lawrence R. Adair, *The Macedonian Conundrum: Focal Point of the Balkans* (Washington, DC: National War College, 1993).

4. Ibid.

5. Ashton B. Carter, John D. Steinbruner, and William J. Perry, *A New Concept of Cooperative Security* (Washington, DC: Brookings Institution, 1992).

6. Ibid.

7. Phillip Shenon, "Officials Say Size of Bomb Caught Military by Surprise," *New York Times*, June 27, 1996.

8. Abdel Bari Atwan, *The Secret History of al Qaeda* (Berkeley: University of California Press, 2008).

9. Michael Ray, "James Mattis," *Encyclopedia Britannica*, https://www.britannica.com/biography/James-Mattis.

10. "Paul Wolfowitz: 1943–," Jewish Virtual Library, http://www.jewish-virtuallibrary.org/paul-wolfowitz.

11. *U.S. Options in Confronting Iraq: Hearing before the Committee on International Relations*, 105th Cong. 17 (1998).

12. Ibid.

13. Alan Sipress and Ellen Nakashima, "Jakarta Tenure Offers Glimpse of Wolfowitz: Indonesians Cite Stance on Rights, Reform," *Washington Post*, March 28, 2005.

14. *Rebuilding America's Defenses: Strategy, Forces and Resources for a New Century* (Washington, DC: Project for the New American Century, 2000).

15. Mark Walker, "Mattis to Assume Command of I-MEF," *San Diego Union Tribune*, June 2, 2006.

16. Nathan S. Lowrey, *U.S. Marines in Afghanistan, 2001–2002: From the Sea* (Washington, DC: US Marine Corps, 2011).

17. Gretel C. Kovach, "Just Don't Call Him Mad Dog," *San Diego Union Tribune*, January 19, 2013.

18. Michael L. Valenti, *The Mattis Way of War: An Examination of Operational Art in Task Force 58 and 1st Marine Division* (Fort Leavenworth, KS: US Army Command and General Staff College Press, 2014).

19. "Forming: 27 October to 5 November 2001," *Strategy Page*, https://www.strategypage.com/articles/tf58/forming.asp.

20. Joel Roberts, "Plans For Iraq Attack Began On 9/11," *CBS News*, September 4, 2002.

21. The Office of the Secretary of Defense, "Strategic Thoughts," memorandum, September 30, 2001, Top Secret/Close Hold Document 13, National Security Archive.

Chapter 9: Graveyard of Empires

1. Mark Moyar, *A Question of Command: Counterinsurgency from the Civil War to Iraq* (New Haven, CT: Yale University Press, 2009).

2. Colonel Nathan S. Lowrey, *U.S. Marines in Afghanistan, 2001–2002: From the Sea* (Tannenberg Publishing, Kindle Edition, loc. 2928).

3. Ibid.

4. Seth G. Jones, *In the Graveyard of Empires: America's War in Afghanistan* (New York: W. W. Norton, 2010).

5. Lowrey, *U.S. Marines in Afghanistan*.

6. Ibid.

7. Ibid.

8. Valenti, *Mattis Way of War.*

9. Clarke Lethin, oral history interview by Chris Warnke, January 17, 2002, US Marine Corps Oral History Division.

10. J. R. Wilson, "Enduring Freedom: The First 49 Days," Defense Media Network, pt. 8, https://www.defensemedianetwork.com/stories/operation-enduring-freedom-the-first-49-days-8/.

11. Valenti, *Mattis Way of War.*

12. Ibid.

13. Ibid.

14. William Slim, *Defeat into Victory: Battling Japan in Burma and India, 1942–1945* (New York: Cooper Square Press, 2000).

15. Lowrey, *U.S. Marines in Afghanistan.*

16. Dickerson, "Gen. James Mattis, USMC."

17. Bob Woodward, *Bush at War* (New York: Simon & Schuster, 2003).

18. Ibid.

19. Ibid.

20. Lowrey, *U.S. Marines in Afghanistan.*

21. Ibid.

22. Nathaniel C. Fick, *One Bullet Away: The Making of a Marine Officer* (Houghton Mifflin Harcourt, Kindle Edition, loc. 112).

23. Ibid.

24. Joseph R. Chenelly, "Marines Land, Seize Desert Strip," November 25, 2001, Marines: The Official Website of the United States Marine Corps, http://www.15thmeu.marines.mil/News/News-Article-Display/Article/545226/marines-land-seize-desert-strip/.

25. Lowrey, *U.S. Marines in Afghanistan.*

26. Ibid.

27. Ibid.

28. Fick, *One Bullet Away.*

29. Ibid., 114.

30. Lowrey, *U.S. Marines in Afghanistan.*

31. Ibid.

32. Fick, *One Bullet Away*, 118.

33. Valenti, *Mattis Way of War.*

34. Fick, *One Bullet Away*, 107.

35. "Text: Pentagon Briefing with Rumsfeld and Myers," *Washington Post*, November 26, 2001.
36. Lowrey, *U.S. Marines in Afghanistan*.
37. Ibid.
38. Ibid.
39. Ibid.
40. Ibid.
41. Ibid.
42. Ibid.
43. Ibid.
44. Fick, *One Bullet Away*.
45. Ibid.

Chapter 10: City of Mosques

1. Conway, interview.
2. Garrett M. Graff, *The Threat Matrix: Inside Robert Mueller's FBI and the War on Global Terror* (Boston: Little, Brown, 2011).
3. "Bush Speech: Full Text," *BBC News*, May 2, 2003, http://news.bbc .co.uk/2/hi/americas/2994345.stm.
4. Anthony Shadid, "Iraqi Fighters Keep Up Attacks," *Washington Post*, December 12, 2004.
5. Tony Perry, "Marines' 'Mad Dog Mattis' Battles for Iraqis' Support," *Los Angeles Times*, April 16, 2004.
6. "The Islamic State," Mapping Militant Organizations, Stanford University, October 23, 2017, http://web.stanford.edu/group/mappingmilitants/ cgi-bin/groups/view/1.
7. Zaki Chehab, *Iraq Ablaze: Inside the Insurgency* (London: I. B. Tauris, 2006), 8.
8. Michael Weiss and Hassan Hassan, "Sheikh of the Slaughterers," *ISIS: Inside the Army of Terror* (New York: Simon and Schuster, 2015).
9. Robert H. Shultz, *The Marines Take Anbar: The Four Year Fight against al Qaeda* (Annapolis, MD: Naval Institute Press, 2013).
10. Ibid.
11. Ricks, *Fiasco*.
12. Ibid.

13. Ibid.

14. Ibid.

15. Ibid.

16. Geoffrey Ingersoll, "General James 'Mad Dog' Mattis Email about Being 'Too Busy To Read' Is A Must-Read," *Business Insider*, May 9, 2013, http://www.businessinsider.com/viral-james-mattis-email-reading-marines-2013-5.

17. Ricks, *Fiasco*.

18. Ibid.

19. Reynolds, *Basrah, Baghdad, and Beyond*, 149.

20. Nicholas J. Schlosser, *U.S. Marines and Irregular Warfare: Training and Education, 2000–2010* (Quantico, VA: History Division, US Marine Corps, 2015).

21. Bing West, *The Strongest Tribe: War, Politics, and the Endgame in Iraq* (New York: Random House, 2008).

22. Ricks, *Fiasco*, 319.

23. Ibid.

24. Ibid.

25. Ibid.

26. Ibid.

27. Conway, interview.

28. Ricks, *Fiasco*, 144.

29. Ibid., 320

30. Conway, interview.

31. Colin Wyers, "I MEF Takes Command in Western Iraq," March 25, 2004, Marines: The Official Website of the United States Marine Corps., http://www.imef.marines.mil/News/News-Article-Display/Article/534440/i-mef-takes-command-in-western-iraq/.

32. Kenneth W. Estes, *U.S. Marine Corps Operations in Iraq, 2003–2006*, occasional paper (Quantico, VA: Marine Corps University, 2009), 14–15.

33. Georges Sada, interview by Sean Hannity, partial transcript from *Hannity & Colmes*, Fox News, January 26, 2006, http://www.foxnews.com/story/2006/01/26/exclusive-former-top-military-aide-to-saddam-reveals-dictator-secret-plans.html.

34. Camp, *Operation Phantom Fury*.

35. Ibid.

36. Ricks, *Fiasco*, 318.

37. Ibid., 315.

38. Bing West, *No True Glory: A Frontline Account of the Battle for Fallujah* (Random House, Kindle Edition, loc. 204).

39. Ibid.

40. Ibid., loc. 193.

41. West and West, *No True Glory.*

42. Tony Parkinson, "The Ugliness of Iraq's Regime Continues to Be Revealed," *The Age*, April 3, 2004, http://fddp.theage.com.au/articles/2004/04/02/1080544690423.html.

43. West and West, *No True Glory.*

44. Ibid.

45. Ibid.

46. Ibid.

47. Ibid., 6.

48. Bing West and Ray L. Smith, *The March Up: Taking Baghdad with the United States Marines* (Random House, Kindle Edition, loc. 4622–4623).

49. Jean Edward Smith, *Bush* (New York: Simon & Schuster, 2016).

50. Camp, *Operation Phantom Fury.*

51. Ibid., 35.

52. Ibid., 56.

53. Ricardo S. Sanchez and Donald T. Phillips, *Wiser in Battle: A Soldier's Story* (New York: HarperCollins, 2008).

54. Terry H. Anderson, *Bush's Wars* (New York: Oxford University Press, 2013).

55. Sanchez and Phillips, *Wiser in Battle: A Soldier's Story.*

56. Ibid.

57. Ibid.

58. Ricks, *Fiasco,* 332.

59. David M. Blum and J. Edward Conway, *Counterterrorism and Threat Finance Analysis During Wartime* (Lanham, MD: Lexington Books, 2015).

60. Camp, *Operation Phantom Fury*, 34.

61. Danelo, *Blood Stripes.*

62. Conway, interview.

63. Bill Devine, interview by author, December 22, 2017.

64. Danelo, *Blood Stripes*.

65. West and West, *No True Glory*, 66.

66. "Al Jazeera Reporters Give Bloody First Hand Account of April '04 U.S. Siege of Fallujah," February 22, 2006, Democracy Now!, https://www.democracynow.org/2006/2/22/exclusive_al_jazeera_ reporters_give_bloody.

67. Bing West, *The Strongest Tribe: War, Politics, and the Endgame in Iraq* (Random House, Kindle Edition, loc. 1178–1182).

68. Ricks, *Fiasco*, 315.

69. West, *The Strongest Tribe*.

70. *World Heritage Encyclopedia*, s.v. "Operation Vigilant Resolve."

71. Ricks, *Fiasco*, 342.

72. Ibid.

73. Ibid.

74. Chris Enloe, "James 'Mad Dog' Mattis Is Asked What Keeps Him Awake at Night—His Response Screams 'Merica," *The Blaze*, May 2017, https://www.theblaze.com/news/2017/05/28/james-mad -dog-mattis-is-asked-what-keeps-him-awake-at-night-his-response -screams-merica.

75. Shultz, *The Marines Take Anbar*.

76. Ricks, *Fiasco*, 314.

77. Conway, interview.

78. "General: It's 'Fun To Shoot Some People,'" CNN.com, February 4, 2005, http://edition.cnn.com/2005/US/02/03/general.shoot/.

79. Ibid.

80. Conway, "9 Unforgettable Quotes."

81. Conway, interview.

82. Ibid.

83. West and West, *No True Glory*.

84. Conway, interview.

85. Ibid.

86. Daniel Sauerwein, "How Does My Lai Compare to the Incident at Haditha?" July 2006, History News Network, https://historynews network.org/article/27334.

87. "Iraq Wedding-Party Video Backs Survivors' Claims," *Fox News*, May 24, 2004, http://www.foxnews.com/story/2004/05/24/iraq- wedding-party-video-backs-survivors-claims.html.

88. Travis J. Tritten, "Trump Confirms Mattis as His Pick for Defense Secretary," *Stars and Stripes*, December 1, 2016.

89. West and West, *No True Glory*.

Epilogue: No Better Friend, No Worse Enemy

1. Hope Hodge Seck, "Battle Rattle," *Marine Times*, March 3, 2014.

2. Chuck Hagel, remarks given at U.S. Central Command change of command ceremony, MacDill Air Force Base, Tampa, Florida, Friday, March 22, 2013, US Department of Defense Archives, http://archive.defense.gov/speeches/speech.aspx?speechid=1762.

3. Ray Sanchez, "ISIL, ISIS or the Islamic State?" CNN.com, September 9, 2014, updated October 25, 2017, https://edition.cnn.com/2014/09/09/world/meast/isis-isil-islamic-state/index.html.

4. "Theranos Announces New Members of Its Board of Directors," press release, Palo Alto, California, July 29, 2013, https://news.theranos.com/2013/07/29/theranos-announces-new-members-of-its-board-of-directors/.

5. Lydia Ramsey, "Theranos Is Getting Rid of High-Profile Board Members Including Henry Kissinger and George Shultz," *Business Insider*, December 1, 2016, http://www.businessinsider.com/theranos-retires-board-of-counselors-and-adds-to-board-of-directors-2016-12.

6. Roger Parloff, "This CEO Is Out for Blood," *Fortune*, June 12, 2014.

7. Christopher Weaver, "Theranos Secretly Bought Outside Lab Gear and Ran Fake Tests, Court Filings Allege," *Wall Street Journal*, April 21, 2017, https://www.wsj.com/articles/theranos-secretly-bought-outside-lab-gear-ran-fake-tests-court-filings-1492794470.

8. "James N. Mattis: Secretary of Defense," US Department of Defense, https://www.defense.gov/About/Biographies/Biography-View/article/1055835/james-mattis/.

9. "General Jim Mattis," Hoover Institution, https://www.hoover.org/profiles/james-mattis.

10. "James N. Mattis: Secretary of Defense."

11. Ben Hubbard, "Life in a Jihadist Capital: Order with a Darker Side," *New York Times*, July 23, 2014.

12. Liz Sly, "Al-Qaeda Force Captures Fallujah amid Rise in Violence in Iraq," *Washington Post*, January 3, 2014.

13. Samia Nakhoul, "Islamic State Expands Its 'State,'" Reuters, May 22, 2015, https://www.reuters.com/article/us-mideast-crisis-islamic-state-insight/islamic-state-expands-its-state-idUSKB N0O713M20150522.
14. "Islamic State Settles into Ramadi, but the Lull Unlikely to Last," Reuters, May 29, 2015, https://www.reuters.com/article/us-mid-east-crisis-ramadi/islamic-state-settles-into-ramadi-but-the-lull-unlikely-to-last-idUSKBN0OD2OS20150528.
15. "About James Mattis," FWA Consultants, http://fwaconsultants. homestead.com/MattisBio.html.
16. Camp Pendleton, "Gen. James Mattis (retired) gave a truly motivating speech recently," Facebook, March 6, 2014, https://www.facebook.com/MCIWPendletonCA/photos /a.308325997876.151385.244860127876/10152004686002877.
17. Kevin Knodell, "It Might Take a General to Convince Trump to Support the United Nations," *War is Boring*, January 4, 2017, https:// warisboring.com/it-might-take-a-general-to-convince-trump-to-support-the-united-nations/.
18. James N. Mattis, "The Meaning of Their Service," *Wall Street Journal*, April 17, 2015.
19. Jim Mattis and Kori Schake, eds., *Warriors and Citizens: American Views of Our Military* (Stanford, CA: Hoover Institution Press, 2016).
20. Tal Kopan, "Defense Nominee Mattis Emerges with Strong Support," January 12, 2017, CNN.com, https://edition.cnn.com/2017/01/12 /politics/james-mattis-defense-confirmation/index.html.
21. Nikita Vladimirov, "Mattis Agrees to Divest Stock, Resign from Board of General Dynamics," *The Hill*, January 7, 2017, http:// thehill.com/homenews/administration/313196-mattis-to-divest-stock-resign-from-board-of-general-dynamics-under.
22. "Defense Secretary Issues Message to Nation's 'Sentinels and Guardians,'" January 20, 2017, US Department of Defense, https:// www.defense.gov/News/Article/Article/1055908/defense-secretary-issues-message-to-nations-sentinels-and-guardians/.
23. Martin Pengelly, "Defense Secretary Mattis Says US policy against Isis Is Now 'Annihilation,'" *Guardian*, May 2017.
24. "Secretary of Defense Speech: U.S. Military Academy Graduation

and Commissioning," West Point, New York, May 27, 2017, US Department of Defense, https://www.defense.gov/News/Speeches/ Speech-View/Article/1196942/us-military-academy-graduation- and-commissioning/.

25. Anne Barnard and Hwaida Saad, "Raqqa, ISIS 'Capital,' Is Captured, U.S.-Backed Forces Say," *New York Times*, October 17, 2017.

26. Sayed Salahuddin, "Insurgents Attack Kabul Airport during Visit by Mattis; U.S. Airstrike Hits Civilians," *Washington Post*, September 27, 2017.

27. John Davison and Rodi Said, "Islamic State Defeated in its Syrian Capital Raqqa," Reuters, October 17, 2017, https://www.reuters .com/article/us-mideast-crisis-syria-raqqa/islamic-state- defeated-in-its-syrian-capital-raqqa-idUSKBN1CM0VC.

ABOUT THE AUTHOR

JIM PROSER is an award-winning author and filmmaker. His previous book, *I'm Staying with My Boys*, has remained on the Marine Corps Commandant's Professional Reading List since 2011. He lives in Sarasota, Florida.